NEXT LEVEL

To

From

I wish for you a life of wealth, health, and happiness; a life in which you give to yourself the gift of patience, the virtue of reason, the value of knowledge, and the influence of faith in your own ability to dream about and to achieve worthy rewards.

– Jim Rohn

NEXT LEVEL YOUR LIFE

Receive Special Bonuses When Buying
the *Next Level Your Life* Book

To access bonus gifts and to send us your testimonials and comments, please send an email to

gifts@NextLevelYourLifeBook.com

Published by
Kyle Wilson International
KyleWilson.com

Distributed by
Kyle Wilson International
P.O. Box 2683
Keller, TX 76244
info@kylewilson.com

Printed in the United States of America

EXCERPTS FROM *NEXT LEVEL YOUR LIFE*

The power of the whole is greater than the sum of the parts. And that's exactly what the SEAL Teams live. We are completely synergistic, which is how we are able to do outrageous things with so few assets and so little resources.

– TC Cummings, Former Navy SEAL, Leadership Training

There's an old saying, it's not what happens to you in this world that counts, what counts is what you do with what happens to you. And circumstances that appear to be "bad" or "horrible" on the surface can instantly transform themselves into amazing gifts-of-gratitude the moment you realize these circumstances are in fact opportunities for you to learn, grow, and evolve.

– Chris Chickering, Psychotherapist, Author, Recording Artist

Not many people would know where to start when training a wild horse. The prospect is daunting. Many of the horses stand in those pens for years, unadopted. In response to this issue, a competition was brainstormed, a showcase of how trainable and versatile these horses can be. Trainers have one hundred days to take a horse from, as they say, "wild to mild."

– Jennifer Kunrath, Solution Engineer, Author, Voiceover Actor

You can have a big impact while also solving a business problem. That impact then multiplies when you give away some of your profits in philanthropy. It's not that greed is good, but greed is not as evil as I thought it to be when I found it in my heart to become a teacher. It was a game-changer for me to understand that if you can make money, you're creating value.

– Gabriel Craft, Real Estate Expert, Apartment Investor

It wasn't until I committed to giving of myself at all costs that I really began to see results. A mental commitment to give first, to immerse myself, truly unlocked the conversations that became connections and then building blocks. Putting myself out there first finally produced the results I was looking for.

– Shannon Robnett, Developer, Syndicator

Then, tragically, my husband lost a good friend in a car accident. His friend was in a coma for about two weeks and then passed away. He had children, and that woke my husband up. Kevin said to me, "Angela, we must get private life insurance." This was a turning point, and little did we know, our ENTIRE financial future would soon be going in a very different direction.

– Angela Street, Financial Coach, Developer of Leaders

Growing up in a world of crisis, I learned to observe subtle clues. My very life depended on it. As an adult, I am attracted to crisis situations, because a crisis contains both a threat and an opportunity.

– Dr. Gurpreet Singh Padda, Physician Entrepreneur, Crisis Investor

Did people really want me to be like Zig Ziglar on stage? The answer was no. They wanted me to have the same principles and values but to be the best version of myself. When I am not myself, it comes across as fake, as wearing a mask. That understanding put the pressure in the right place, developing myself and understanding what people needed.

– Tom Ziglar, Speaker, Author, CEO Ziglar.com

I have the heart of a patriot, and I believe our flag is a sacred symbol of freedom. Immense sacrifice is sewn into every fiber of our flag and cannot be repaid. Patriots gifted us the United States of America and the best way of life the world has ever known. Our children deserve it, and patriots of the past demand a return on their investment.

– Jay Johnson, Entrepreneur, Investor, Veteran, Police, SWAT

Another moment of truth. Should I believe the data—or my gut? In the end, the team decided together to fly in the face of all the negatives and "head west" anyway. Like explorers Lewis and Clark, we were energized by the idea of discovering what was over the next hill. We didn't have all the answers, but we figured we were smart enough to figure them out on the way.

– Steve Nabity, Ironman Champion, CEO, Speaker, Investor

I had finally come to a place where I was tired of chasing something that was destroying me. I'd had enough of living without purpose. Something inside of me was ready for more.

– Becky Bouhsine, Entrepreneur, Investor, Coach

Scaling up was challenging. A lot of it was psychological though. I needed to level up my mindset and change my belief system. Part of it was overcoming my self-doubts and all the ANTS (automatic negative thoughts). It seemed overwhelming to think about a $9 million deal. I was thinking things like, "It's too big. Why me? How could I?"

– Baskal Korkis, Financial Expert, Tax Smart Investments

I've been bucked off plenty in business. Like how learning to move my feet finally just clicked in bronc riding, in business, you have to get bucked off and keep getting back on and nodding your head before things click.

– Jeremy Melancon, Builder, Developer, Real Estate Investor

I have felt the pain of wanting to grow and not knowing how, so now I feel compelled to help those who want to take their business and life to the next level. We all have persevered through challenges, and my obstacles have truly fueled my passion to help others.

– Wendy Griffis, Awarded Realtor®, Industry Leader, Trainer

I discovered that a paycheck is given to people who show up, but opportunities are given to people who think and work beyond what they're paid to do. So, we are willing to do what others won't do.
— Simon T. Bailey, Top Global Speaker, 10x Author

Years earlier, when some coworkers were complaining about our jobs, I remember saying, "We shouldn't complain; after all, this is just a job, not a career." At that moment, I realized I wanted a career. Years later, I had a career, but I realized that wasn't enough. What I really wanted was a calling. A God-given, God-sized, God-inspired, God-energized purpose. In 2011 I found that calling.
— Dale Young, Teamwork & Identity Coach, Author

Inspiration and reassurance are things we can give. It costs no money and only a little of our time. Someone around you requires what we can give. It might be a simple smile.
— Tammy Hane, Mentor, Optimist, Real Estate Investor

The same spirit of optimism of dreaming about a life with no limits that I had felt as a 10-year-old staring up at the night sky was alive again! I would read until the early morning hours, go to work with only a couple hours of sleep, and have more energy than ever before. I remember on one occasion being so inspired I got out scissors and cut the word "impossible" out of my dictionary.
— Marlin Yoder, Realtor, Entrepreneur, Real Estate Investor

Watching my mother act without thought of compensation, without thought of ROI, and without thought of gaining favor in the eyes of the community, I was challenged to leap forward in acts of service far beyond what I could have imagined.
— Dan Armstrong, Author, Entertainer, Speaker, Storyteller

When I left my marriage, I felt like I had lost everything. I had to find myself. I had to reawaken that little girl inside me with all those big dreams. I had a strong desire to start living for myself and my son. Over the years, I began to surround myself with like-minded people who were investing in themselves and their dreams. Find others who will encourage you and hold you accountable for the goals you want to achieve. Your relationships can help you reach your destination.
— Christina Alva, Author, Coach, Speaker, Elite Level Minds

I dropped some pounds, but more importantly, I was studying and learning habits, systems, and the importance of raising my standards. Once I saw and felt the results of my clothes fitting better, I wanted to continue and increase my efforts. Systems and processes drive results. Standards set the level of quality of your habits and your results.
— Greg Junge, Investor, Entrepreneur, Health Enthusiast

Ask yourself the very fundamental question, "Is my business changing the status quo?" If the answer is yes, proceed with every fiber of your being and be relentless in your pursuits. If the answer is no, go back to the drawing board.

— Moe Rock, Businessman, Producer, CEO of The LA Tribune

Ripping off my P100 respirator and taking off my white coat, I knew I had worn them both for the last time. That last night shift in the ER was horrendous. I was one physician taking care of an endless sea of patients, nonstop ambulances, and by the way, everyone had COVID. I was on the other end of the shift, and this time it was for good.

— Ronnie Shalev, MD, Physician, Entrepreneur, Real Estate Investor

The quality of life is exceptionally high in Belize! I've always maintained that you must keep a place in the country and a place at the Caye and have the ways and means to get to both. Anything else should be considered an investment.

— J. Trevor Miles, Developer, Strategist, Investor, Adventurer

Many of us are built for more than we're tapping into. The path to take life to the next level truly begins with a decision for what you want your life to BE. With clarity, you must take action. Leap and build your wings on the way! Remember, recalibrating is not failure, but growth. Cast vision, create a plan and surround yourself with others who raise you up. Rising tides raise all ships.

— April Marlewski-Hudzinski, Investor, Speaker, Transformational Coach

Everything improved as I began my journey to lose weight. Most importantly, my relationships with my wife, kids, employees, and friends. I was five times more productive. My business revenue increased by $2.3 million over the next few years. Endorphin release from daily exercise is so important in daily life. I almost remember what it was like to be a kid again.

— Craig Moody, Serial Entrepreneur, Biz Coach, Speaker

Young and naive, we were unaware that existing home sales were on the decline in the rest of the country. Our market was still booming but by fall, the crash caught up to us and we witnessed several people we looked up to as mentors get completely crushed. It was a lesson that helped us formulate our future investment philosophy.

— Randy Hubbs, Real Estate Broker, Investor, Master Educator

Nobody was going to hand me my dreams—I had to create them for myself. More than that, I started to realize I truly could design my life.

— Chris Schwagerl, Mental Health Expert, Investor, Educator

Be of service. Realize it's never about you, but the people you serve. The more you serve, the better you'll do. Want to have more in your life? Serve more people.

— Robert Helms, Top Real Estate Podcast, Developer, Speaker

After a few months working for Alaska Airlines, we took the first vacation of our lives. I was 32 years old, with $10,000 in the bank. Sitting by a swimming pool, I read Think and Grow Rich. *The most important lesson: "Whatever the mind can see, it can achieve."*

— Alan Neely, Real Estate Developer, Investor, Syndicator, Pilot

I realized I had been given a chance to reset. I had been given the gift of time with an unspecified end date. Time: the most precious commodity. There are only so many hours, in a day, month, a year. You cannot recreate the past, and you cannot foretell the future, but I do control my now.

— Robin Binkley, Investor, Entrepreneur, Podcast Host

None of this would have been possible if we had quit trying and not finished what we started. There is not a day that goes by that I do not thank GOD for everything I have been blessed with because of what we lost. As my father instilled in me, always finish what you start, be true to your word, and never quit.

— Derek Dombeck, Real Estate Investor, Speaker, Private Lender

The best part about my apartment investing business is that we provide safe, affordable places to live. More than that, we strive to foster communities where people feel connected with their neighbors and proud of where they live. We do this in small ways that have big impacts.

— Sandhya Seshadri, Apartment Syndicator, Skilled Asset Manager

There will be good days, great days, and the worst days. Those bad days make us who we are. Those thoughts of "Am I doing enough?" push us harder. Great things don't happen overnight or without hard work and dedication.

— Brian H. Ferguson, Father, Partner, Friend, Real Estate Investor

It's been an amazing adventure learning to follow the God whispers in our lives. Many lessons and life experiences have sprung from it, not to mention the challenges and adversity. One thing stands out to us in following God's whispers: every whisper required determination to press into the unseen future, an unseen future which held the possibilities, potential, provision, and power to change not only our lives but also the lives of others.

— Pastor Donald Rucker, Founder of Christian Development Center

Like sunflowers—which no matter where they are planted turn toward the sun—I too began turning in the direction that nourished me. This path has since become a way—no matter where I may find myself planted—to turn toward the sun, the light.

– Lalah Delia, Spiritual Writer, Author of Vibrate Higher Daily

I had no idea the impact crypto would have on my family's future or the exciting paths it would lead me down. When I initially invested in Bitcoin, it was to buy low, sell high and hopefully make a profit, like it is for most people. But when I really dove in and figured out what blockchain was and the potential impact it would have on every industry in the world, I was hooked.

– Courtney Moeller, Entrepreneur, Speaker, Blockchain Expert

As I was questioning God as to why He let my phone break, I realized He didn't want me to see His beauty with the lens of my camera. He wanted me to see His beauty with the lenses of my eyes.

– Robert Commodari, Top Real Estate Agent, Author, Speaker, Podcaster

This technique helped me stay focused, gave me a sense of accomplishment when I deeply needed it, and changed my overall attitude in life. I was no longer asking myself, "What did I do today?" No, I was telling myself, "Look what I got done today." This simple technique of prioritizing with smaller tasks that I could accomplish in a day helped me in my work, my business, and my personal life.

– Kohshean Kuda, Real Estate Developer, Entrepreneur, Investor

Life is filled with gifts...and miracles. I've been given a gift with my leg, my miracle. I choose to keep moving forward... in wonder and giving myself the nod of encouragement.

– Sean Hackney, Real Estate Agent, Ironman Triathlete

The journey from mile marker zero to mile marker zero and back was much more than I could ever have dreamt of. I've lived many lives in one. As long as you have the drive to keep going and know where your north is, you'll get there. Planning is important. Executing is important. But the most important thing is being fulfilled with yourself, your mission, and making sure you enjoy the journey.

– Wagner Nolasco, Real Estate Developer, Investor, Volunteer

If you do the right things, in the right order, over time, good things will usually happen. Some things have a longer gestation period than others. But once you figure out what that is and what the principles are, if you follow those, the odds of success are dramatically in your favor.

– Kyle Wilson, Founder Jim Rohn Int, Marketer, Speaker

TABLE OF CONTENTS

DISCLAIMER

The information in this book is not meant to replace the advice of a certified professional. Please consult a licensed advisor in matters relating to your personal and professional well-being including your mental, emotional and physical health, finances, business, legal matters, family planning, education, and spiritual practices. The views and opinions expressed throughout this book are those of the authors and do not necessarily reflect the views or opinions of all the authors or position of any other agency, organization, employer, publisher, or company.

Since we are critically-thinking human beings, the views of each of the authors are always subject to change or revision at any time. Please do not hold them or the publisher to them in perpetuity. Any references to past performance may not be indicative of future results. No warranties or guarantees are expressed or implied by the publisher's choice to include any of the content in this volume.

If you choose to attempt any of the methods mentioned in this book, the authors and publisher advise you to take full responsibility for your safety and know your limits. The authors and publisher are not liable for any damages or negative consequences from any treatment, action, application, or preparation to any person reading or following the information in this book.

This book is a collaboration between a number of authors and reflects their experiences, beliefs, opinions, and advice. The authors and publisher make no representations as to accuracy, completeness, correctness, suitability, or validity of any information in the book, and neither the publisher nor the individual authors shall be liable for any physical, psychological, emotional, financial, or commercial damages, including, but not limited to, special, incidental, consequential, or other damages to the readers of this book.

Dedication

To all the mentors and influences that have shaped the lives of each of our authors. To our families and loved ones who fan our flames and inspire us. To all those who read this book and are inspired to next level their lives!

Acknowledgments

A big thank you—

To Takara Sights, our writing coach, editor, and project manager extraordinaire, for your endless hours of work and passion in this book! Despite the complexities involved with a project like this, you keep the process a pleasure and always provide first-class results. A thousand praises! You are a rockstar!

To Claudia Volkman, Joe Potter, and Anne-Sophie Gomez, who have put countless hours into designing this book. Technology and thoughtful design allow readers to receive the powerful wisdom of these authors. We are grateful!

To Gary Pinkerton, Adrian Shepherd, Jennifer Stewart, Justin Mendenhall, Roxanne Bocyck, John Obenchain, Aaron Nannini, Emily Houser, Jo Hausman, Mark Hartley, Tammy Hane, Courtney Moeller, Alan Neely, Dale Young, Chris Chickering, and Ethel Rucker for being our second eyes and proofreading the manuscript. We so appreciate it!

And to Brian Tracy, Phil Collen, Mark Victor Hansen, Olenka Cullinan, Kevin Eastman, and ALL the amazing mentors and world-class thought leaders who took the time to read this book's manuscript and give us their endorsements—thank you!

FOREWORD

by Denis Waitley

What does it mean to next level your life?

It means you are getting closer to the ideal you. The person you long to be.

A great question to ask yourself is, "If I had the time and the money, and if circumstance was not an issue, who would the ideal me be? What would my ideal life look like?"

Neuroscience has confirmed it is possible through repetition to jump over previous habits and create new pathways in your brain.

To switch any negative habit you have to a positive, you must apply these three things: Emotion, plus repetition, plus clarity, equals realization.

Emotion, with imagination, plus repetition, creates internalization.

If you are emotionally involved, you will get there ten times faster. But you must want it and own it.

And, it needs to be your goal, not someone else's that they want for you! Unless you own it, it won't have enough power to pull you.

That is why mentors and examples are important. They help pave the way! If they can do it, then you can do it!

That is what my long-time friend, Kyle Wilson, and his powerful group of authors have done for you in this book—given you examples and strategies to follow.

You are now in the driver's seat!

Get ready to take the wheel and next level your life!

To Your Greatness!

Denis Waitley

 Denis Waitley is a world-renowned speaker and the author of 16 bestselling classics including *Seeds of Greatness* and *Safari to the Soul*. His audio album *The Psychology of Winning* is the all-time bestselling program on self-mastery. Denis has worked with Olympic athletes, astronauts, and POWs and is in the SMEI speaker hall of fame. To learn more about Denis, visit www.deniswaitley.com. Follow Denis on Facebook @OfficialDenisWaitley.

"Creating the next level of results requires the next level of thinking."

— Rory Vaden

ROBERT HELMS

Finding Your Next Level

Robert Helms is a professional real estate investor and developer with past and current projects valued at over $800 million. As a former top-producing real estate agent, Robert ranked in the top 1% of sales worldwide. He is the host of the nationally syndicated radio show The Real Estate Guys™, *now in its 27th year of broadcast. The podcast version of the show is one of the most downloaded podcasts on real estate and is heard in more than 190 countries.*

The Roller Coaster of Reality

Life is grand, business is booming, people are amazing!

Sounds good on paper.

In reality, the trajectory our lives take is often like a roller coaster. Ups, downs, twists and turns, way too fast and often a little scary.

Yet every accomplishment you've made has likely been preceded by change. A change in your perspective, attitude, vision, circumstance, or belief. And usually accompanied by some fear and discomfort.

That's what it takes to reach the next level.

The Long and Winding Road

Today, the radio and podcast versions of our talk show reach millions of people each year in more than 190 countries. Quite humbling. But it didn't start there.

We began on a single local radio station in San Francisco more than a quarter century ago. Although I had been in college radio and knew basic production and announcing, it took my original partner and me a while to find our way. And we weren't super clear about our intention. While the show helped my credibility as a local real estate agent, at that point, it was really a hobby.

After stumbling our way through for a few months, we were ready for our next level—growing listenership, attracting sponsors, and holding live local events. Little by little, our audience expanded and people were resonating with our message. Many were interested in coming out to a seminar to meet us and learn more about real estate than we had time to cover in an hour-long show. The radio station helped get the word out and our sponsors were supportive. Within a few years, our sponsors were covering most of the costs of producing the show.

That's about the time that my co-founder left the show. Rather than stop, I decided to move forward, and the next level gave the program the chance to evolve. Rather than a new co-host, I started bringing several smart, local real estate folks to the studio each week. One of those revolving guests was mortgage specialist Russell Gray. Before I knew it, Russ was coming every week and eventually assumed the duties of co-host.

Russ brought a new dimension to the show from a content perspective, but also helped identify a path to creating a true business around my former hobby. We became more strategic about our outcomes. When our station changed formats, we were approached by a larger station with a stronger signal, increasing our impact.

For the next few years, Russ and I grew our listening base by adding additional radio stations, leveraging our program into other markets, and speaking at other people's seminars and conferences. Our sponsors were able to reach a larger audience, and pretty soon, listeners would actually travel to come to our live events. At last, we were making a profit. Not a living, but a profit.

Our next level was a result of the burgeoning podcast phenomenon. Podcasts were new, misunderstood, and outside the mainstream. As we started to establish a podcast audience, we thought of it as a supplement to the main thing, which was the radio show.

Yet, while radio listeners might come and go, podcasts gave folks a chance to subscribe and listen on their own schedule. Soon we discovered that the "narrowcasting" of podcasts was more effective for us than the "broadcasting" of traditional radio. Our base grew and so did our credibility... and our revenue.

As the podcast continued to grow, the next level was upping the quality of the production, landing notable guests, and continuing to expand and improve our live events. Soon, the increasing podcast downloads began to rival the radio audience. The argument could be made that the podcast listeners were more serious and engaged. And our star continued to rise.

The Real Estate Guys™ today is no longer a hobby, but a seven-figure business.

Along the way, we've been able to hit more and more levels of success... and so can you!

The good news is that it's easy. Easy, that is, if we use Jim Rohn's definition of easy: Something you can do.

It takes time, patience, persistence, and dedication... even when you can't see immediate results.

The challenge is that we can't always clearly see the next level in our life or business from where we are today.

So how can you put yourself in the best position to find your next level? Here are some thoughts....

KEYS TO GETTING TO THE NEXT LEVEL:

- **Start with Modesty** – The Bible tells us to not despise the days of small beginnings. Start from where you are with what you've got. Don't worry about what you can't do—focus on what you can.
- **Test Small** – You can take on the world but only after you've proven your point. Start small and make sure you've got something that can scale before you spend a lot of time and money trying to scale it.
- **It's Okay to Stumble** – Brian Tracy says, "Anything worth doing well is worth doing poorly at first." Be patient as you move through the four levels of competence (Unconscious Incompetence, Conscious Incompetence, Conscious Competence, and lastly Unconscious Competence.)
- **Be of Service** – Realize it's never about you but the people you serve. The more you serve, the better you'll do. Want to have more in your life? Serve more people. Zig Ziglar taught, "You can have everything in life you want, if you'll just help enough other people get what they want."
- **Seek Collaboration** – It's difficult to rely on yourself for everything. The next level requires you to develop your thinking and your team. Together Everyone Achieves More!
- **Expand Your Comfort Zone** – Your business can't grow if you don't. Don't get stuck in a rut. Step out on a limb... that's where the fruit is!
- **Ask "What If...?"** – Think in terms of possibilities, not limitations. Remain open-minded. Most of the great products and services we use today were once "impossible"... until they weren't.
- **Let Go of What's Not Working** – Be bold enough to look honestly at your actions and your results. Jim Collins says to "confront the brutal facts." Seek the truth and accept the feedback.

- **Focus on the Gain, Not the Gap** – Appreciate how far you've come, not how far you have to go. (Read *The Gap and The Gain* by Dan Sullivan and Dr. Benjamin Hardy) Be grateful for your achievements... even the small ones.
- **Take Control** – of your schedule, your activities, your thoughts, and your actions. Run the day, or it will run you. Successful folks are intentional and deliberate.
- **Up Your Tribe** – Want better results? Surround yourself with better people. It's always who you know. Start today.
- **Remain Flexible on Your Approach** – While keeping your goals—or targets—in mind, be ready for the path to achieve them to change.
- **Go Easy on Yourself** – Life doesn't move in a straight line. Sometimes it's two steps forward, one step back. But if you have something worthwhile that you believe in, then stay at it. The key is persistence. And time is a zero-sum game.

Some Final Encouragement

Becoming successful in any area of your life takes work. But if you're reading this book, then my guess is that doesn't bother you.

Here's some good news as you seek to reach the next level... bigger can actually be easier.

As you continue to level up, you also up your game. And as you do, you'll see that staying small is in many ways more difficult than scaling. Here's why:

1. Economies of Scale – As you and your business grow, you'll become more efficient. Many of your expenses are fixed costs that don't increase with more production or team. And things often run smoother with better volume. It only took us slightly more effort to be on two radio stations than on one. Same for three, four, etc.
2. You Can Afford to Hire Professionals – The fledgling entrepreneur has to bootstrap and cut corners. As you hit higher levels, you'll be able to attract better team members and vendors and will be able to justify paying them more.
3. Teamwork Makes the Dream Work – Scaling means bringing on more people (who don't have to be employees, by the way). Each person brings new energy, ideas, skill, and enthusiasm to the team, which actually makes doing the work easier.

4. Better Brainstorming – While it's great to brainstorm on your own, it gets better with each person you add as you riff off each other and build on ideas through collaboration.

So what is the next level for you? You can't make it to second base without leaving first base. Scaling takes work, but it's worth it.

My personal belief is that we never arrive, and there is always a next level. I can't wait to hear about yours!

Here's wishing you more and more success on your way to making a bigger and bigger impact on the world!

Robert Helms is the co-author of *Equity Happens: Building Lifelong Wealth with Real Estate*. Robert's annual Goals Retreat helps people unlock their potential and provides a blueprint for achievement in all areas of life. Listen to *The Real Estate Guys™ Radio Show* at www.RealEstateGuysRadio.com. To learn more about The Real Estate Guys™ programs and events, send an email to SuccessHabits@realestateguysradio.com.

Tweetable: What is the next level for you? You can't make it to second base without leaving first base. Scaling takes work, but it's worth it.

WAGNER NOLASCO

In Honor of Those Who Serve
My Ride Across the USA

Wagner Nolasco is the founder of Build 2 Rent Direct, one of the largest developers in Florida, with $700 million in delivered inventory. Wagner has over 5,000 hours of volunteer service with the United States Coast Guard Auxiliary. He received the Lifetime Presidential Achievement Award in 2017 from President Donald Trump.

You May Not Know

I was born in Brazil and came to the United States in 1993 when I was 13 years old. I worked as a parking valet, then I cleaned restaurants. Before I was 18, I got into the construction business as a supplier. Over the years, we grew into a company supplying large, luxury resort projects internationally. I became ambitious to become a developer and started in the construction business in Florida. What some people may not know is that motorcycle traveling is one of my biggest passions.

My Love for Serving America

I joined the US Coast Guard Auxiliary in 2006 as a volunteer, and I continue to serve to this day—over 5,000 hours and counting. Being a volunteer in the United States Coast Guard gives me the advantage of meeting amazing people. One of the people I met is the President of the United States Coast Guard Riders Association, Colin Eckert. He gave me an opportunity to become part of the association's leadership team. The more I connected with active duty or retired personnel, the more I noticed that a lot of them love motorcycles.

Around that time, a member of the active duty Coast Guard personnel passed away in a motorcycle accident. To help create awareness of the principles of motorcycle safety, to honor our military and all branches of service, and to challenge myself, I thought, *Why don't I do an extreme trip?* So, in 2017, I set out to ride The Ultimate Challenge in long-distance motorcycle travel—from the southernmost tip of the continental United States (Station Key West, Florida) to the northernmost tip (Prudhoe Bay, Alaska) and back. And on my round trip from Key West to Prudhoe Bay and back, I would make stops at Coast Guard stations around the country.

I rode my motorcycle, decorated with Coast Guard colors and prints for all branches of service, through New Mexico, Utah, Colorado, Nevada, Death Valley, and Route 66, all the way to California. I went up the California coast through Big Sur and the giant Sequoias. I drove to Seattle, through Canada, and then rode through Denali National Park, a wild part of the country, and north through the Arctic Circle to Prudhoe Bay on the edge of the continent. In 28 days during June and July, I experienced every season of the year. I started in the extreme heat of Florida in June, got snowed on in Crater Lake, Oregon, and rained on in Alaska. From semi-tropical to desert, it was amazing. I was experiencing everything I could.

I did daily posts with pictures and my location on Facebook, Instagram, and a group I created on Whatsapp. I slept when I was tired. I ate when I was hungry. I rode when I wanted. I stopped when I wanted. I knew my general direction, but I didn't have a route plan. I didn't have a maximum timeline to complete the trip. I just wanted to complete it. At every gas station, people stopped me, asking, "Hey, man, what are you doing? What is this? Where are you going?" I met a lot of Coast Guard personnel on the way, all kinds of people, all branches of service. I honored a lot of people on the way. I brought the message that whatever your dream, it can be done.

Being Humble

On the way to Monument Valley in Arizona, where Forrest Gump stopped running, I stopped at Four Corners, where you can stand in four different places at the same time. I stood on the spot with my feet in Arizona, New Mexico, Colorado, and Utah. How cool is that! Many have asked, can one person be in two places at the same time? The answer is no, but a person can be in four! It's amazing how much you discover about the world and yourself during experiences like this. Then, in the middle of nowhere, with desert all around, I saw a young lady who was blind running on the road with her guide. We met, and I learned she was a paralympic athlete in training. I'm like, this girl who cannot see is running competitively, training in the middle of nowhere! And I thought what I was doing was a big deal.

Later, in Alaska, I met a couple from Germany. They were cyclists, and they had come to Alaska by bike and ship from Europe. Next, they were planning to ride south through Canada, the US, and Mexico then ship their bikes to Panama to ride through South America (Panama, Colombia, Ecuador, Peru, Bolivia, Brazil, and Argentina) to Ushuaia, Argentina, also called "El Fin del Mundo" (the end of the world). By bicycle!

At the end of the day, I truly realized, I'm really nothing. However good you think you are, there's somebody else much better than you. I felt what I was doing was cool, but I always know there is more. What you think you're achieving, which is a major thing in your life, may not be as much for somebody else.

It's the Journey

By pure luck I was in Alaska on the longest day of the year—the summer solstice—so I was able to experience the midnight sun. Every day I drove north, I was thinking, *How is it going to be when I get there? The northernmost tip of the US, that's my destination. I'm gonna make it.* And, when I got there, it wasn't what I expected.

I don't know what I expected. I think I was imagining a paradise with icebergs. Maybe I dreamed it. In reality, Prudhoe Bay is an oil field in the Arctic Circle, the largest oil field in North America. More of a small work camp than a town, there's not much in the way of infrastructure. The hotel was shipping containers connected together. It was a very humble place. What I had created in my mind never existed. It wasn't anything fancy, but I've learned that it was amazing.

It was a great experience to get there and find out that the journey was more important than the destination. All the memories, all the days, all the views, all the experiences, all the people that I met along the way were really more important than what the destination was all about.

In life, I've learned that you always plan that the destination will be paradise, and the destination is never what you think it is. It could be better or worse, but it's never what you think it is. If you don't enjoy the journey, the destination doesn't really matter.

There Are Three Types of People

I don't like to label people because I think people are usually much more than whatever we may think they are.

However, I was able to meet many people on this trip, and from what I've seen, there are only three types of people in the world: people that wish they had done it, people that say they're going to do it, and people that do it.

There were the people that are now elderly, and they usually would say, "Hey, man, you're living my dream. I wish I was young and I could do this trip." There are people that live their lives and regret whatever they have not done.

Then there are people that keep saying they will do it one day and they keep planning.

And then, there are the people that do it. So who do you want to be? Do you want to be the person that constantly says, "I'm going to do it one day," and that day never comes? Do you want to regret things that you haven't done that you should have done? Or do you want to go do it?

It's very easy. It's all about your perspective. It's all about you identifying what is important for you and taking action. Old, young, it doesn't matter. It's never too late to live your dreams. I saw a guy more than 80 years old riding his motorcycle to Alaska too. There's always room. There's never an excuse. Your dream can be accomplished.

The United States. What a beautiful country, what a beautiful nation, what beautiful human beings. We are beautiful, beautiful, beautiful creatures. My trip was a life-changing experience, and I recommend whatever your goal may be, go for it and just enjoy the journey. Don't forget the people that are around you, how important they are, and be open. You never know what's coming.

It's the Little Things

I visited a city in Alaska called North Pole. I visited Santa Claus' house and recorded a video with Santa Claus for my daughters Valentina and Maria directly from the North Pole. I got to show my girls that Dad is friends with Santa Claus! They were blown away. That was magical.

You never know what you'll find out there, but I think life is a little bit about magic. I think life is about the small details. There's nothing big that surpasses the small details of a trip like this, or the moments you live. Maybe you'll never take a trip, but having dinner with your family, taking a weekend off, or taking your kids to the movies, whatever it is that gives you the perception of being fulfilled, don't wait, just go out there and do it. I never know if tomorrow is going to come. And if it doesn't, then at least I know that I tried my best to be fulfilled. At the end of the day, it's all about the small stuff.

Lead by Example

On my way back south I stopped at the US Coast Guard Academy in New London, Connecticut to meet the 41st Superintendent of the Academy, Rear Admiral James E. Rendon. He was kind enough to take the time to receive me, talk to me, and take pictures. It was so powerful.

During my visit, I presented him with a Florida to Alaska banner with the Coast Guard emblem signed by every man and woman in uniform I met during the trip. He signed it for me and presented me with a Superintendent of the Coast Guard Academy Challenge Coin, which is a pretty big deal. I was honored. When I got back to Florida, I would present to the family who had lost their son in the motorcycle accident that banner with the signatures from Key West to Prudhoe Bay and back.

The moment of the visit at the academy that stands out to me the most was when the Admiral said, "I'm sorry, I have to go because I have a new class of cadets and I'm going to run with them.

I thought, *You are the highest-ranking officer in the Coast Guard Academy. And on their first day, you're going to go on a run with them?* I asked, "How long are you running?"

He said, "20 miles." I was surprised. He explained, "Yes, I'm going to run 20 miles with them. If I expect them to do something, they have to see that I can do exactly what I am asking them to do."

When you lead by example, you can change somebody's life. This is a man that didn't have to do that. His words and commands are extremely powerful and respected. How powerful is that, for him to lead the class on their first run? He was demonstrating that if he ever asks you to do something you'd better do it, because he won't ask you to do anything he can't do himself. I thought that was so powerful.

When you ask somebody from your company to perform a task, you may not be good at it, but you should be able to perform the task. A team is formed by different talents in different areas, but at the same time don't ask somebody to do something you would not be willing to do. Different skills apply to different people, but at the end of the day, you can only ask people to be accountable for what you would be able or willing to do yourself. If you lead by example, people have no excuse not to follow you.

Iron Butt, The Ultimate Challenge

Because I had a bigger purpose, everything I needed was on my motorcycle, aside from my family and friends. I learned how to live extremely humbly for a long time. I noticed that I don't need a lot to be happy. You don't need a million dollars. You don't need a huge house. As long as you have the basics, you can be fulfilled.

I remember feeling extremely fulfilled and happy every second because I had control, but I also had a lack of control. I had control of when to ride, but I didn't know when it was going to rain. I had control of when I ate, but I didn't know how many more miles I was going to be able to ride that day or what challenges I would face. Just like in life. You think you're prepared, and usually you are, but once you are on the ride life throws so much at you that sometimes you have to stop. Sometimes you have to just breathe and think, Oh my God, what am I doing here?

I made it home to Orlando and spent the night with my family. But that wasn't the end of my trip. I started the trip in Key West and I wanted to finish the trip in Key West.

I ended at US Coast Guard Station Key West, exactly where I left from. I was received by the Captain in charge of the station. It took 28 days, five sets of tires, and almost 17,000 miles to complete the trip.

I submitted all my progress, all the mileage, and everything that I did to an organization called Iron Butt, and I won a certificate for completing the Ultimate Challenge, which, at the time, only about 14 people in the world had accomplished. I didn't do the trip for the purpose of achieving that, but sometimes when you aim at the stars, you don't know what you're going to hit.

For people that ride motorcycles, that is a pretty big accomplishment, but the real accomplishments were more personal. It was experiencing nature. It was feeling how small we are. It was just seeing how many good people are out there and the many amazing people I met. It was such an amazing, magical experience.

On the journey from mile marker zero to mile marker zero and back, I experienced the views, the sunsets, the sunrises, the rain, the snow—it was much more than I could ever have dreamt of. I've lived many lives in one. As long as you have the drive to keep going and know where your north is, you'll get there. Planning is important. Executing is important. But the most important thing is being fulfilled with yourself, your mission, and making sure that you enjoy the journey as much as you can.

Wagner Nolasco is a developer, real estate investor, syndicator, and founder of Build 2 Rent Direct in Central Florida. Connect directly with Wagner Nolasco about real estate development, sales, and investment syndication.

(305) 684-2222
Instagram: wagnernolasco.official
Email: wagner@b2rdirect.com

Tweetable: The destination is never what you think it is. If you don't enjoy the journey, the destination doesn't really matter.

DAN ARMSTRONG

A Lesson From My Mom That Forever Impacted My Life

Dan Armstrong is the author of The Adventures of a Real-Life Cable Guy *and* Smart Dust—The Dawn of Trans-humanism. *A heart-centered speaker, multi-time guest of* The Los Angeles Tribune, *and other platforms, and performer of street magic, Dan challenges audiences to overcome adversity to pursue purpose and serve others in a hurting world. He is married and the father of four daughters.*

Shopping with Mom!

My brother David and I were in Christian Rock bands. We wanted to look the part, and the county where we grew up wasn't known for being a fashion capital. Fortunately, the big city of Philadelphia was less than a two-hour drive. It was a plan!

My roommate, Doug Drescher, would complete the trio for the adventure, that is, until my mother got word we were making the trip. She called me the night before and basically begged to come along. Admittedly, I wasn't thrilled at the idea of Mom coming along with three 20-something guys, but she was very persuasive.

The next morning, we pulled into my mother's driveway—she was so excited that she ran from her house and into the warm car without a coat. She was beaming ear to ear; she was with two of her sons and an adopted son for a road trip.

The drive to Philadelphia was filled with chatter among the three of us young guys, just talking about what was going on in our lives—perhaps a bit filtered since my mom was sitting in the back seat soaking in the moment.

When we arrived in Philly, parked cars lined the sidewalks bumper to bumper. There was absolutely nowhere to park. As we drove further away from the shopping district, we began venturing on side streets, zigzagging through one-way alleys until we finally found a spot over 10 blocks away from where we wanted to be. The excitement and, more than that, a radical experience that would forever rock my world, was about to begin.

From Poverty to Prosperity

My mother was born in Iowa. Growing up, she traveled with her family while my grandfather found work as a bricklayer. Times were hard, as she recalled many times. A tent was their home for a while in South Dakota. When she met my father, he was earning almost two hundred dollars a month. She thought she'd hit pay dirt! He was a hard-working man with a steady job and roots in Lancaster County, Pennsylvania, going back three hundred years.

They got married, had five children, and struggled financially. Dad never got past the 8th grade, but what he lacked in "book knowledge" he made up for in heart wisdom. He didn't earn a lot of money, but what he earned he gave to his family. This day was no different. My dad had given Mom money for the special day.

We exited the car and began to make the trek toward the shopping district. I don't think any of us were prepared for the culture shock. The sidewalks were polluted with cigarette butts, loose pieces of paper floating about, and splotches of sticky soda and even spit from a passing man who cleared his throat. If we tried to hopscotch over the debris, there was a good chance we would just fall and find ourselves on all fours.

The brisk walk kept Mom warm despite her refusing our offered coats. She responded, "Your dad gave me some money. I'll find something warm." Her voice was full of expectation.

After right and left turns through sketchy alleys, we arrived! An angelic choir sounded with a harmonious *Ahhhhhhh!* Nope, that was the air horn of a delivery truck barreling down on us foreigners in this strange land. Time seemed to suspend as each moment we were enraptured by a cacophony of the sights, sounds, and aromas of the big city.

My mother found a beautiful coat that blanketed her shoulder to her hip in warm wool. She swirled around in front of the large floor-length mirror, showing off the coat to her inner little girl from Iowa. Perhaps my mother was proud of how far she had come. "You look great, Mom," the three of us agreed.

We left the store, but it wasn't long before my mother looked down at her ratty shoes. She had enough money to buy a new pair, and that became our next mission. I remembered, as a child, when my mother took me shopping for shoes, it was due to the fact that the shoes were literally falling apart. After getting fitted, it was common for us to ask the store employees to throw away the old pair and wear the new shoes out of the store. Today was no different, her old shoes were discarded, and Mom walked out clad in style. A new coat and a new pair of shoes; she was living the life.

Mom Had Another Plan

The daylight was beginning to fade, and we knew the walk to the car would take some time. It was time to grab a bite to eat. I don't remember much about the meal together, only that my mother didn't finish her plate. She asked for a doggie bag—that's what it was called back then—and said to the waitress, "My husband gave me money for my new coat and shoes. The least I can do is bring him back some dinner."

With the leftovers wrapped, my brother David said, "It's getting late. We better start walking to the car. I sure hope we can find it before it gets dark."

Off we went. We were thrilled at the day's adventure in the big city. As we came around a street corner, I jerked back upon seeing a person sitting on the stoop of a vacant storefront. It was a woman. Her hands were cupped, hiding her face. Her long, black, filthy hair draped down to her elbows resting on her naked knees. The paisley dress she was wearing was paper thin and barely covered her. She looked cold and alone. I believe she was shivering. But what could WE do?

After we regained our composure, we picked up our pace. Making our way to the end of the ominous street, we turned left and then right towards our parked car somewhere in the distance. We three boys were busy rattling off what we liked about the stores, the cute girl behind the counter, and the great clothing we found when, for some reason, we stopped. My mother wasn't making a sound. We turned around and gasped. Mom was gone!

She was a small-town girl from Nevada, Iowa, and this was the bustling city of Philadelphia. The sun was setting, and the tall buildings made it seem darker. Finding her became like a rescue mission with the clock ticking. We began to run, looking frantically into the narrow walkways between the row homes, hoping she wasn't pulled into one of them by a nefarious mugger.

Speechless Moment in Time

And then, I saw her. She had gone back to the homeless woman. I ran to her side.

My mother was sitting beside the woman, embracing her, holding her close to keep her warm. *Am I really seeing this?* I peered over the bony frame of the sitting woman. Black toenails and shoeless, pale feet pressed against the hard concrete. I looked back over my shoulder as David and Doug caught up. I was out of breath and speechless. It was very cold on that October day, and I shivered empathetically. I could see the swells of mist coming from my breath and the cold chills on the bruised arms of the fragile woman.

My mother spoke, "Please come with us. We will take care of you."

The woman shook her head without showing her face and yet did not resist the warm hug from the complete stranger. After a few more tries to persuade the woman to come with us, my mother brought her close, almost like she was her own daughter. With her cheek pressed against the woman's matted, soiled hair, my mother whispered, "I want you to be safe. I want you to be warm and dry." Under the loving embrace, the frail woman shrugged and slowly shook her head. A stranger was touching her, embracing her, flesh against flesh, but to no avail; she remained unmoved.

I wanted to say, "C'mon, Mom, you tried. Let's go." But, not one of us could speak as we watched my mother love on this woman without expectation of getting anything in return.

My mother stood up and removed the brand new coat from her shoulders and lovingly placed it on the shoulders of the shivering woman. Then, my mother reached down and removed her shoes one at a time, left and then right. She placed them carefully between the woman's naked feet. The doggie bag of food she had been saving for my dad was the third gift. She placed it beside the woman. And the last gift was one more compassionate hug and a prayer.

We offered my mother a coat of ours. She put her hand out: no. My mother took the place of the homeless woman for ten blocks as she walked barefoot over the sidewalks polluted with cigarette butts, loose pieces of paper floating about, and splotches of sticky soda and spit from a passing man who cleared his throat.

A Challenge to Step Up Your Game

How can you stand there and not be affected? My parents had always welcomed people in need into our home. One time, a family of seven moving to the area for employment jammed into our house for a month. Many veterans of WW2 occupied a spare bedroom over the course of a dozen years. Foster children and friends who needed a place to stay could find refuge in the Armstrong house. But this was different.

We were not in our comfort zone. We were not inside the walls of our home. There were no doors to shut tight, no way to lock out the world. No, instead, this was my mother's heart bleeding and staining the street with her love. Could it be because my mother had been hungry at times in her life? Was it because she had lived in a tent? Or was it because she understood that we all are homeless without each other?

This chance meeting in the city of Philadelphia was like breathing for the soul of my mom, Jane Armstrong. This was a natural expression, like soft water gurgling in a brook over hard rocks. Her actions that day would be a fearful challenge to a tepid soul. Her natural environment was the neighborly, quiet sidewalks of her small Midwestern hometown, but time and wisdom had stretched her love and compassion beyond the easy thing to do—walk past a woman who was alone, cold, near naked, and probably hungry. The weight of doing nothing in her conscience would have been a burden. She was aware of who she was in a world that needed her.

At that moment, my mother knew her mission. She didn't need permission from her hosts. She didn't need to explain her motives. She left the parade to seek that which pulled her heart.

Watching my mother act without thought of compensation, without thought of ROI, without thought of gaining favor in the eyes of the community, I was challenged to leap forward in acts of service far beyond what I could have imagined.

I have emulated the heart of my mother privately and for my four daughters. And I have watched as my girls have demonstrated the exponential generosity my mother showed me.

Bullhorn of Service

I have told this story to thousands of people across the country, and every time, I can't help but get choked up. This is the first written record beyond the memorial service of my mother.

On my parents' tombstone, etched in granite, it says, "They lived Matthew 25:40." I hope it prompts people to find that old book and look up the profound principle. It was the Master Teacher Jesus who said the words, *"...whatever you do unto the least of these, you are doing it to me."* Jim Rohn often said, "I am not a Bible scholar, but it seems to me..." and then, Jim would offer the insight he gleaned from his reading. Here's mine —Whenever you serve others who need it, you are serving God. I will add

—Whenever you UP YOUR game, YOU are serving others! When you improve what you have to offer, you change the world.

When we watched my mother give her brand new coat, her brand new shoes, and the food for my dad, the volume of her actions became a bullhorn of challenge to thousands of people. One person took the time to take a leap of faith and set aside the familiar, the safe, and the comfortable, and the impact of that moment still resonates today.

Dan Armstrong is married and father to four daughters. He is a Certified DreamBuilder Coach, magician, author, and speaker. Dan is available for speaking engagements to empower YOU on your impact in the lives of others. Contact Dan at DanArmstrongAuthor@gmail.com or visit his website at DanArmstrongTheAuthor.com.

Tweetable: She left the parade to seek the mission that pulled her heart. The love and compassion practiced at the local level ramped up in a circumstance that expanded her boundary. Whenever you UP YOUR game, YOU are serving others!

LALAH DELIA

Shifting from Trauma to Impacting Millions

Lalah Delia is a spiritual writer, trauma-informed wellness educator, certified spiritual practitioner, founder and instructor of Vibrate Higher Daily School, and bestselling author of Vibrate Higher Daily. *She has been featured on film, in documentaries, and various media, including television, podcasts, and magazine.*

My Story

I grew up in the heart of South Central, Los Angeles's "war zone" neighborhood. In our community, gang life, liquor stores, hustlers, broken dreams, flashy street styles, and beautiful people with unrealized higher potential existed on every street corner. On a vibrational level, much was low, from the food quality to the education quality to the lack of wellness and self-development resources. The culture of lack within the inner cities such as where I grew up has a direct adverse effect on the cultural tone and overall quality of life for masses of people and their personal and shared experiences. South Central Los Angeles in the 1980s and 1990s was a new kind of struggle and negative vortex for pretty much everyone there. And as with most inner city communities still, it was common for us youth growing up in that environment to create peer bonds through our pain. We were all seeking affirmation and validation of some kind from one another.

I am grateful, through it all, that I had an advocate. I spent most of my childhood with my father, a man who was many things: an entrepreneur full of dreams, a transplant from New Mexico, and a practicing Buddhist, here and there. My father's ability to keep a positive mindset and his "pursuit of happiness" while in the midst of such an environment as South Central had a deep foundational impact on me. No matter what went on in the war zone neighborhood surrounding us, my father always created good vibrations and a positive atmosphere in our home. He had a way of energetically turning our home into a sanctuary and a safe haven.

My strongest memories about our home environment are of dancing in front of the television to Soul Train on beautiful Saturday afternoons, hearing lots of '70s and '80s soul records playing, laughing, the burning of incense, and feeling pure love. My dad knew how to turn up the vibes in this way and shift our atmosphere into something higher, lighter, and better for the soul.

My father did the best he could with what he had to work with. Using his Buddhist mindset and his joy for life, he taught me the skills for navigating our surroundings, and its potential traps. With a deep inner peace, a compassionate mindset, and a passion for progress, he instilled in me how to rise above our environment and the ability to see our situation and time there as temporary. Yet in spite of his most necessary, intentional, and urgent efforts to shelter me, including moving out of South Central, I was, on many levels, still affected by the negative elements around us. My initiation into the writing and work I do today was—like it is for so many others—through the path of pain and suffering.

Even though my parents did the best they knew how to protect me, deep pain had entered my life in four main ways. Over a short period of time, I was sexually violated as a child by a trusted teenage caretaker. At the same time, my parents had divorced, and I was not adapting well to it. I slipped into a state of depression, so much so that at the age of nine, I told my mother that I wanted to die because my family was broken. On top of all of this, at the age of five I had been diagnosed with a form of epilepsy known as petit mal. Every time I came out of a seizure at school, I'd "come back" to a crowd of laughing children, many of whom mocked and bullied me without fail. These painfully humiliating times happened all throughout grade school, until I eventually (and gratefully) outgrew the seizures at the age of twelve. And a very welcome healing it was.

In addition to these early childhood traumas, I also experienced verbal abuse from my mother's fourth husband. He was a white man from a small town in the South who loved my Spanish mother but could do without her half-black children. Racial slurs were a norm to him. This period strained my relationship with my mother—a woman who loved her children dearly but had deep unprocessed pain of her own that was clouding her judgment. She would detest her husband's behavior one day, with great apologies to me, and then dismiss it another day. I never knew which type of day it would be. This was the epitome of low vibrations versus high vibrations—in full effect.

These collective experiences created deep depression in me as a child, teen, and young adult. I experienced regular stomach aches, poor digestion, anxiety, shortness of breath, panic attacks, and fatigue, and I was underweight.

Dark Night of the Soul

By the time I was in my early twenties the damage—although I was unaware of it at the time—began to reveal itself. For instance, it showed up in the relationship I was in, which turned into a domestic violence nightmare of two years until I escaped in the middle of the night. I had internalized the wrong messages—that pain and abuse were norms. I already had a low sense of self-worth, which led me to accept an abusive relationship in the first place, but the effects of that abuse diminished whatever little amount of self-worth I had left.

After escaping that abusive relationship, I found myself disoriented and hopeless, to the point of trying to end my life. I couldn't figure out how to make the pain and negative patterns stop. But as fate would have it, my past, the pain, and the suicide attempt would not win, or have the final say. After I attempted suicide, I was unconscious for three days, and after regaining consciousness, my first reaction while in this dazed state was anger because I was still alive and, needless to say, unsuccessful in escaping the pain of my life. But then moments later, this other feeling and awareness rose within, and my focus shifted—into a comforting realization that my life had just been saved from ending in the tragic way it nearly did. The deep-rooted pain and duress that had been guiding and affecting my life for so long had not won.

Various spiritual teachings call this experience *the dark night of the soul*. It is a spiritual phenomenon that happens to people to intentionally shake them awake, to activate their higher purpose, and to convert them and their lives into something new. As a spiritual practitioner and wellness educator, I've seen it many times. It's a temporary period of inner or spiritual crisis (although you don't realize it's temporary when you're in the midst of it) when the life you've come to know no longer makes sense, is no longer tolerable—often to the point of isolation and depression settling in.

My life had a divine appointment to not die physically, but spiritually and conceptually. My suicide attempt called for the death of the lifestyle, mindset, and cycles that were no longer serving me. For other people, the dark night of the soul may look different. It can be a more subtle and less intense experience that includes some pain and frustration, but no life trauma or spiritual crisis. Both ways lead to awakening.

For me, this dark night reckoning was the beginning of something new. It led me to realizing that the slowly sprouting seeds planted deep within me all those years before—the ones that helped get me out of my unhealthy relationships and toxic life—were finally ready to break through and rise above the soil. Seeds germinate and grow only when the conditions are right, so having a new path that supported me in this way was essential.

Another Way of Being

After my dark night of the soul, I started looking for solutions to overcome my circumstances instead of feeling defeated by them. The depression and shame that I quietly journeyed with throughout my childhood and teen years, and into adulthood, had consumed enough of my life. This dark night experience was a fork in the road, a turning point, an activation.

I was led and inspired to begin living more mindfully and intentionally through my everyday choices. And it started with what I ate. Food became the gateway. After some time and consistency, the vibrational awareness around how I had started eating soon grew and transferred to the types of energy I allowed into my environment, to how I managed my thoughts, to how I treated others and myself, to how I lived in general, and to the type of work I did in the world—a better way for me. These various areas of my life had always been interconnected, but now I was living more and more aware of that interconnectedness, and I was more intentional in my day-to-day choices and decisions.

From mindful eating came awareness of bigger things. Thanks to a free Wednesday night support group for survivors of various forms of abuse, I learned to release my ego and my old way of thinking and surrender to necessary change—a wonderful thing for my soul. I continued deciding day by day and choice by choice to take my power and life back. Along the way, I had mentors, who each saw something more in me than what I—with my limited, yet changing, perspective at the time—saw in myself. I saw a victim and survivor; they saw someone overcoming adversity, a teacher and a hero.

My first full-on mentor was a calm, wise, older man called simply Dr. B. He entered my life by divine appointment, and my life has never been the same since. For more than a decade, I've passionately and diligently worked with this mentor and others on my spiritual journey and path to vibrational awareness. These important and positively impactful connections would eventually guide my being toward teaching others the path that has reconfigured me and my life, vibrationally.

Shaped throughout the reconfiguration process, I was able to grow, learn, and unfold into my more authentic self—over time. I turned my whole life in a more healing, holistic direction. Like sunflowers—which no matter where they are planted turn toward the sun—I too began turning in the direction that nourished me. This path has since become a way— no matter where I may find myself planted—to turn toward the sun, the light.

Over the next decade, my journey to deeper healing, transformation, and discovery beyond the life and pain I'd known would be through the path of what I call vibrate higher daily.

Things, people, and energies that were once painful memories or blockages to my higher well-being and development were neutralized, including the limiting mindsets, tendencies, and habits that I used to struggle with throughout my life. They no longer had power or authority over my life. Living from this reality has been liberating and life-changing.

Soul Work

Today, I no longer live in the consciousness that I used to; one where I identified as a victim who is stuck, powerless, and purposeless. This process led to the reconfiguration of my entire life, my physical health, even reconfiguration of my appearance.

This is the life-shifting power of vibration, which is always within you. No matter where you are planted, may you always turn toward the sun.

I emphasize the word *daily* in the term *vibrate higher daily* because this path is a process. The choices and the individual practices we adopt every day hold the power to shift us higher or lower. Through daily practices we are able to build a lifestyle that serves us and that supports our exodus from a life that doesn't serve us, personally and collectively. Just as running coaches will tell us that to become a runner we have to start slowly, with a mile a few times a week, so too we nurture vibrational-based living through small, incremental choices each day that build upon themselves. We are always creating our lives through each moment and with each choice.

As I reflect on my journey and the experiences I've had with trauma, despair, domestic violence, emotional pain, heartbreak, a limited mindset, toxic relationships, and the sticky places I've been in and out of, I send myself love, not judgment. I do so because at the time of those experiences, I didn't know about vibration. It was there all along, as it is in us all, but I wasn't at a place where I could yet recognize it within myself. I was living and experiencing life through a lower vibration and a limited mindset. And with those vibrations came the life experiences to match.

My intention and prayer for you is to rise above and beyond too— starting wherever you are. And for you to step into your empowerment and higher purpose. Whatever your story is, whatever your pain or disconnect from life may be, it's not allowed to have the final say in your life. Your story doesn't have to end where you feel it may be trying to end. Find your way through and beyond. Allow your pain and frustration to awaken and rebirth you into a new creation. From this inner space, you can create change within, reach your higher potential, and then help to shape a better society and world.

Each day you receive an invitation to vibrate higher. It is a lifelong practice, and it all starts within. There is no rush. Seek to journey in awareness, grace, and power each day, as you fervently grow and unfold even more into yourself and your purpose set before you. To all of the things that help set us free and vibrate higher daily, thank you.

Visit Lalah Delia's work and school at vibratehigherdaily.com, where you can work with and be guided by Lalah in her private and thriving sacred personal energetics and development community. Lalah's bestselling book and audiobook *Vibrate Higher Daily: Live Your Power*, with HarperOne publishers, is available everywhere books are sold.

Tweetable: She remembered who she was and the game changed.

ALAN NEELY

Tenacity
Becoming a Pilot and an
Apartment Syndicator

Retired pilot, real estate developer, investor, and syndicator, Alan Neely is constantly seeking the most direct and turbulence-free route to achieve steady passive income for himself and his investors.

My First Goal

Flying airplanes. Or as a backup plan, racing Formula 1 cars. That is all I ever wanted to do.

At Cascade Junior High, a teacher "strongly encouraged" me to attend an after-school event about goal writing. We were given a small notecard and simple instructions, "What do you want to do with your life?" We were told to write down where we wanted to go to college and what we wanted to accomplish by the time we were 20 and 30 years old.

Mine said, *Alaska Airline pilot by 30. Married, two kids. Float plane tied to the dock. Race car driver or Reno Air Racing pilot—Race Winner in a P-51.*

That simple task motivated me to ride my bike to the airport after school. I wear glasses. The Air Force would not let me fly airplanes. Our family had no money to pay for flying lessons. At 14 years old, I would ride my bike to Auburn Airport now and then. Occasionally, I would get a ride in an airplane.

To afford flying lessons at 16, I started cleaning machine shops after school and saved all the money for flying lessons. I went from my bicycle to a driver's license to soloing an airplane in the same week.

Along the journey, I was flying mainly old antique airplanes, which led to flying aerobatics, which led to a great job teaching aerobatics and eventually a job flying small airplanes in the great state of Alaska.

Mitigating Risk

In 1992, at 23 years old, I moved to southeast Alaska! Haines, Skagway, Juneau, and Glacier Bay became my stomping grounds working for Layton A. Bennett, an iconic aviation pioneer. I was like a kid in a candy store.

Layton must have seen me as an arrogant kid. He was 72 years old. Little planes are loud; Layton was deaf from 55 years of flying. When he spoke, he yelled! With spit flying, he could cuss, swear, and belittle you better than any notoriously foul-mouthed machinist I worked with.

He would encourage me to be better with kind words (cleaned up for publishing): "The next time you see your parents, you'll be in a pine box! And I am the one who has to call them and tell them you got there by being the dumbest pilot that ever lived!"

His favorite though was, "You'll kill all the passengers! You'll kill the whole town! I will have nobody left to fly around!"

He knocked me down a few pegs and toughened me up. He fired me a few times, always in front of passengers, but with a twinkle in his eye, he would always add, "If you do that again!" He also taught me techniques that are not in any books on flying. I used his wisdom often in my flying career.

When I moved on to MarkAir Express, I was based in Bethel, Alaska. They sent me all over the state to clean up messes caused by others. When they fired pilots, I was sent in to fill in the void. When they opened up a new base out of Kotzebue, Alaska, to serve nine villages, they called on me to move there for three months. When pilots refused to fly, because of bad maintenance, they sent me there to smooth it out. The work was very challenging, and I loved it. After a year working there, I was flying 19-seat De-Havilland Twin Otters and training newly hired pilots in seven-passenger Cessna 207s.

As much as I loved the job, MarkAir Express went into its second round of bankruptcy causing the Twin Otters to be repossessed. They transitioned me to flying Beechcraft 1900s and sent me straight to Dutch Harbor. I was "blessed" to fly out to the Aleutian Islands for November and December. We were serving small villages like Nikolski and Atka, far out on the Aleutian chain, where no sane person would choose to live. It was the most stressful and riskiest flying I have ever done.

My friends who lost their jobs at MarkAir got hired by other airlines within Alaska. They were pushed by management to fly in bad weather or fly severely overweight airplanes. They started crashing. Some died. My paychecks were not clearing the bank. MarkAir was in its third round of bankruptcy. The writing on the wall was bold print. I left the great state of Alaska broke but alive.

Marriage

Along my journey, when I was a young, impoverished pilot making $18,000 per year, I was lucky enough to meet my wife, Elena. She was a college student from Russia on a full-ride scholarship to earn her MBA in international finance. I met her, and within one minute, I'd made up my mind. No matter what, we were getting married.

For the rest of this journey, she was there too. We always support each other's schemes, refine them, subtly making suggestions, seeing things the other did not.

Transition to the Dream Job

All in all, I worked for six different airlines. Some went out of business; some were not safe. Along the way, many of the captains were previously Eastern Airlines, Braniff, PanAm, or TWA pilots. All of them had the same advice: When you get the real flying job and start making the "big bucks," don't spend it. If you're lucky, you will get a pay cut or get furloughed. If you're unlucky, you will lose your job or lose your license to fly for medical reasons. Find a side hustle to secure your financial future.

I hung in there. In the summer of 2000, I landed my dream job with Alaska Airlines.

After a few months working for Alaska, we took the first vacation of our lives. I was 32 years old, with $10,000 in the bank. Sitting by a swimming pool, I read *Think and Grow Rich*. The most important lesson: "Whatever the mind can see, it can achieve."

After much consideration, I believe it's true. I could see myself as a pilot, so that's what I became. I could see myself happily married, and that's what I am. That book really opened my mind to all the possibilities in life. Look around the room or out your window, whatever you see, somebody had to envision all those things long before they were created. Look at the tallest building in your city. Somebody envisioned building that—dreamed of it, set goals for it, until it became embedded in their DNA. Then, with the power of a made-up mind, they built it. Why not me?

That book changed me. There I was, a pilot for a great airline. But I was gone from home constantly. When our daughter, Natasha, was born, the chief pilot didn't approve time off so I could be there. I made sure to be there anyway. Just one more thing about the fabulous airline career nobody tells you about.

In the back of my mind, I was waiting for the airline to go bankrupt, like the other airlines I had worked for. In the back of my mind, I was thinking, *When I have a family and lose my job, what then? Start over at a new airline for little to no pay?*

Elena and I started investing in real estate with the purchase of our first rental property in October 2000. We bought our first home; it was by far the ugliest house in the nicest neighborhood we could afford. We had views of downtown Seattle between the trees and a view of the Olympic Mountains and Puget Sound from the roof. We spent a year and a half turning that 680-square-foot, two-bedroom home into a rental property. Then, we refinanced it and bought another house.

This house was, again, by far the ugliest house in the nicest neighborhood we could afford. It was 100 yards from Puget Sound with great views of the Olympic Mountains from the roof. This house was a crooked "beach house" built in 1904, last remodeled in 1936, and complete with original 1936 appliances. We leveled the house, jackhammered the basement slab, dug down one foot, repoured the concrete floor, and framed a bathroom and a bedroom in the basement. I did it all myself.

Then we set out to get plans for a building permit for a new house on the side yard. Ultimately, we ended up getting plans and permits for a two-unit townhouse on that lot. While we were focusing on real estate with long-term goals and a long-term outlook, the short-term economy was not looking good.

After the 9/11 attacks, the airline industry was decimated. United Airlines pilots lost their pensions and took large pay cuts. Delta, Continental, United, US Air... you could go down the list of airlines. Even the pilots who retired years previous had their pensions cut by 60% or more!

Turning Point

Then, May 1, 2005, it happened. I was in Oakland, California. At 4:30 in the morning, I walked into the hotel lobby and saw the captain. He looked horrible. With bloodshot and teary eyes, he gave me the news. We had been "awarded" by an arbitrator a 30% pay cut. This captain had just bought a new house, a new truck, and new off-road motorcycles for him and his son to bond over, all on credit. He had believed the union when they said the pilot group would be getting a pay raise!

I still remember that flight. That miserable captain's head was not in the cockpit. I was flying the plane, working the radios, and talking to the passengers and flight attendants as we flew to Seattle. After landing, we were supposed to fly to Sacramento, then back home to Seattle for a few days off. I looked at that guy and said, "Love you, buddy, but you're calling in sick. You are not fit to fly."

There were so many valuable lessons in that day and the years leading up to it. No job, no career, is safe from an economic downturn or an odd mistake that gets you fired. ALL of us are at risk of losing a job. Recessions happen. Depressions happen. It is simply a fact of life.

Not My Legacy

All those past captains who warned me about this were 100% correct. I committed myself to not having the same legacy. I committed on such a level that it became my DNA to succeed outside of the airlines. No matter what, I would have a happy wife, a happy daughter, and financial freedom.

We already had a rental property and a house. We also had a building permit in hand. We bulldozed our house, and I became a general contractor. Bigger idiots than me figured this out, surely I could too! Elena and I were addicted to new construction, and creating our own vision inspired us both.

Elena and I realized we wanted more from life. But to get more, we had to become more. We both started studying mindset and motivation. We attended seminars and grew ourselves. As we grew our goals, our ambition and desire grew as well. We started keeping journals of our thoughts. We changed. We sought out properties that were in great locations and bought them with great terms. And they were on expandable lots. Location. Terms. Expandability.

We also started a property management company, a general contracting company, and a real estate brokerage company. I was still flying for the airline.

And the Wheels Came Off the Bus

We are all told on a plane rule number one: Take care of yourself first. Put your oxygen mask on before you help others. I had a minor heart attack. While on vacation. On a cruise ship. Headed to Jamaica mon. Not the ideal location. I was blessed with 20 hours by myself in the cruise ship sick bay. I remember all my thoughts clearly from that time.

First, the great news: I would have Mother's Day off this year. I would be home for all of Natasha's soccer games and the play she had the lead role in. I would be home for Fourth of July, Christmas, and New Year's. I would be home for dinner every night. And I would get my Federal Aviation Administration medical certification and clearance back in about a year. That put a smile on my face. Also, I could use that year to build more townhomes and accelerate our path to financial freedom.

Adjusting the Strategy

Ultimately, my minor heart issue was the best thing that ever happened to us. We built a portfolio of build-to-rent townhomes. We also sold some land off with plans and permits. I even had the time to get plans and permits for a 46-unit apartment. We amassed a high enough net worth to retire.

But something was still off. Our cash flow on equity was a paltry 2.5%. Our rentals paid the bills and were appreciating much faster than inflation, but we could not retire on the meager cash flow.

We studied the market, sought advice from our mentors, and figured out that we had to get into apartments in landlord and business-friendly communities with appreciating and cash flowing assets. I spent a few years studying apartments and different markets. We did not want to lose everything we had worked so hard for.

We sold half of our Seattle properties over the next few years and moved the capital into Texas apartment buildings where we began to earn truly passive income. We learned about apartment syndication from the passive investor side. We leveraged other people's experience, time, and resources. After investing in over 1,500 apartment units and verifying it works well, I started telling friends about it. Soon they were asking, "Can we invest in apartments too?"

My answer is always, "YES! You can and you should!"

Your Dream Lifestyle Is Possible

Today, we have all we have because we set goals, adjusted course as necessary, and made up our minds. We are constantly seeking passive investments with cash flow and appreciation in well-chosen markets. We are constantly learning about new opportunities and new methods which provide a rising tide that will lift the boats of all our partners.

My wife and I own over 5,600 apartment units with our business partners. We spend summers working from our boat and winters working from Hawaii. We have one daughter in college, who is already investing in apartments.

We could retire, however, we really do not have much desire to. We are dedicated to helping others become financially free through passively investing in apartments. Besides syndicating apartments, we also host seminars on mindset, motivation, and apartment investing which allows us to inspire others to open their minds to what is possible, set goals for success, and achieve it.

Alan Neely is passionate about teaching others to expand their mindset, find motivation, and become financially free. A firm believer in the phrase *success leaves clues*, he is committed to helping others find the clues to success. To become part of his community, email: al@andoverholdings.com.

Tweetable: Every job, every investment, every property we've bought was always for tomorrow. With every decision you make, remember your tomorrow.

ROBERT COMMODARI

The Power of Moments

Robert Commodari is a passionate speaker, #1 bestselling author of Better Than You Think, *and host of the podcast* Chiseled. *He's spoken to thousands of people over the years, inspiring them to develop awareness to live a more fulfilling life. Rob leads a real estate group and has sold over 2,000 homes in his 21-year career.*

An Epiphany

I've been a part of a mastermind group for 11 years now, and in September of 2021, my two mastermind buddies and I headed off to Las Vegas to watch the Ravens play the Raiders and to visit the Grand Canyon.

I had never experienced this natural wonder, and I was full of anticipation. As we approached just prior to sunset, euphoria ran through my body. We walked past the tree line and saw before us the most exhilarating sight, one of the seven wonders of the world. The Grand Canyon!

In the moment, I could feel the spirit of it all! I could feel the sacredness of the moment. There was not much talking. Everyone was in awe.

My friends—Mark Brodinsky and Mark Pallack—and I walked some of the perimeter, talking in a whisper and enjoying the magnificence that pierced our eyes, our hearts, and our souls. I could feel the spirit, and I could see it and hear it too—if that makes any sense. When I closed my eyes and listened, there was this humming silence throughout the canyon, and when I stared into the vast view, it was as if I could see it. It was like a racecar driver seeing air to make a move in a NASCAR race, speeding at 150-200 miles per hour. I could see the air. I could see the spirit.

As a real estate professional for over 21 years, author, and podcast host, I'm a busy guy, and my phone is my lifeline. Pretty much anyone breathing has a phone, and one of the most common uses of our phones these days is taking pictures. At the canyon, we busied ourselves with taking pictures to capture every moment.

A few minutes later, as we were ready to watch the sunset and take more pictures of this sacred moment, Mark Brodinsky asked me to take a picture of him with the canyon in the background. I took his phone in one hand and thought I was putting my phone in my pocket with the other, only, it wasn't completely in. It fell to the ground a few feet away. It had a case, so no big deal. But when I picked up my phone a second later, it was broken. No matter how I swiped or what I did, I couldn't get into my phone. I couldn't even use my camera.

I was in a state of panic. All this way, all this anticipation, and I wasn't going to be able to use my camera to capture this moment. Not to mention, I'm a Realtor, and I was going to be gone for the next several days. I would need my phone to manage my business.

I looked up and asked God, *Are you kidding? I'm at the Grand Canyon for the first time, about to see this glorious sunset, and you're not going to allow me to take pictures?*

I wrote my book *Better Than You Think* to help people develop awareness and live a more fulfilling life. I've been reading and studying personal growth and development for over 30 years, and developing awareness is something that resonates with me. So, when the opportunity arises for me to become aware of something, I want to seize the moment.

I've learned over the years, there are multiple levels of awareness. The first is, after something happens, we look back and ask, *What was the lesson in that experience?* A higher level of awareness is when we can understand the lesson the moment it happens.

As I was questioning God, I realized He didn't want me to see His beauty with the lens of my camera. He wanted me to see His beauty with the lenses of my eyes. Although I was frustrated in the moment, I asked God to give me the courage to surrender to His will, not complain about not having my phone, and take in all the moments. The sunset was magnificent! I stood there, took it all in, and gave thanks for what I could see with my naked eyes.

A Glimmer of Heaven

The next morning, we woke up early and arrived back at the Grand Canyon for a 15-mile hike. My buddies had their phones ready to take pictures, and I was ready to take it all in. We stopped several times on the way down, and as my friends took pictures, I looked around in awe. I let myself feel the moment in my heart. I remember getting to the 7.5-mile point of Bright Angel Trail and admiring the amazing view. While Mark was taking a panoramic shot with his camera, I slowly did a 360-degree turn to see all I could see: the vastness of the canyon, the multiple colors of rock thousands of feet down, the beautiful sun, and the Colorado river flowing below. Absolutely incredible!

Later, the two Marks and I headed to the bar to grab a beer. Mark Pallack asked me what the hike meant for me. I looked at him, and the emotions began to flow. Through tears, I replied, "If this is a glimmer of what heaven looks and feels like, I can't wait to die to see all He has in store for me to see." Of course, I wasn't ready to die yet, but in that moment, that's how blessed I felt.

The Spirit Is Everywhere

The next day, I flew home and prepared to leave the following morning to watch my son compete in an Ironman Triathlon. We registered Robbie on Friday and spent some time hanging around the town. Then we would get up early Saturday morning for the big event.

We arrived at the starting area at 5 a.m. Off in the distance, there was a haze hovering over 2,500 bikes that were lined up for the second phase of the Ironman. I closed my eyes, reflecting on what I had seen and felt a few days earlier at the Grand Canyon, and there it was again. It was the spirit! It was that idea of being in the moment again and experiencing the spirit.

The energy was amazing. All the participants were about to celebrate a year's worth of training and preparation by putting themselves through the most grueling day of their lives. There were people of all ages, sizes, cultures, and genders. There was even a blind woman competing. A truly inspirational event!

There was a moment in the race when my son was in the middle of the 26-mile run. He was struggling and couldn't hold down any food or liquids. While running, he pulled out a note from the bag wrapped around his waist. It was a note of encouragement he wrote to himself. I learned later, it was the handwritten notes I had been writing to my children for years and the constant encouragement I had given them that inspired Robbie to write himself the note.

Every time we saw Robbie, we would all cheer and shout and encourage him. You got this! Keep going! At one point during the run, a woman approached us and asked if we would cheer her husband on when he came around the bend. She was the only one there to support him, and it would mean the world to both of them if he could hear us. We asked her what his name was, and she told us it was Dave. Sure enough, several minutes later, this guy came running around the bend, and the front of his shirt read, *I'm Dave*. As he ran by, we went nuts and cheered loudly for him. He stopped and hugged his wife, and they were both in tears as they thanked us for making this day special for them.

These are all powerful moments that should encourage us to become more aware. Moments happen in an instant, and if you are not aware of them in the moment, they will pass you by. We must realize the spirit is talking to us. We must listen for it and be aware of it, because when we do, we will experience deeper levels of joy and fulfillment in our lives.

Jailbreak

Years ago, I was approached by a friend of mine, Karen Storey, to be a guest speaker for a Toastmasters event in a prison. As I pondered what I would speak about while doodling on a napkin, I wrote "Jailbreak." This rush of energy overwhelmed me. I wanted to give these guys a message of hope and not some ordinary speech.

Minutes later, I began to second guess myself. How could I go into a prison and title a speech "Jailbreak?" Would I start a riot?

How often do we get a good idea and get excited about it only to then defeat it in some way? Then, I remembered what my friend told me years ago. He told me that a person goes to the next level in their life and business when they listen to the voice inside. I believe that voice to be the Holy Spirit. My friend's words led me to start focusing on that voice and becoming more aware of it. Over the years, I have learned to recognize moments when that voice is speaking to me. It's my belief that when we have a moment of inspiration, it's coming from God.

I went with my title, "Jailbreak."

On the morning of the speech, I pulled into the parking lot of one of the biggest and oldest prison facilities in Maryland. It was a cold and damp December morning. All around me were 20-foot high fences with razor wire from top to bottom. It was intimidating! There was that feeling again, that haze hanging over the prison. The spirit was here.

After passing through the gates and security, I entered a small room. There were 20 inmates awaiting the presentation. When we were ready to start, the president of the club, an inmate, walked to the front of the room and made the announcement: "Our speaker today is Rob Commodari, and the title of his speech is 'Jailbreak.'" You could see the curiosity rising in the room. Eyebrows lifted!

I looked out over the audience, and in a whisper said, "I am planning a jailbreak! Are you in or are you out?" I paused for what seemed an eternity, and then loudly, I said, "I'm not talking about the jailbreak where you break through walls, climb the fence, and run for your freedom. I'm talking about breaking down the walls that everyone in this room has inside our own heads. I am talking about breaking down the walls of fear, hate, jealousy, and anger! Now, I am going to ask you one more time. Are you in or are you out?" With that, all 20 of the guys jumped out of their seats. They were ready to hear the plan.

Throughout the speech, I made references to *Shawshank Redemption*. We were going to break those walls down using hope as our tool. I compared inmates being institutionalized in prison to how we are institutionalized on the outside.

When inmates first enter prison, they fear those walls. After some time, they get used to those walls. Finally, inmates begin to rely on those walls.

In that same way, when faced with a new challenge or change, most everyone will sense fear building in their mind. Day in and day out, we have this anxiety regarding fear. After some time, we get used to fear. Finally, we begin to depend on fear to get us through our day. Thus, we are institutionalized in our minds by our own fears.

I concluded with the vision of the guys getting out of jail the next morning and walking toward the entrance for their freedom. Going to bed that night, I wanted them to hear that jail cell door slam shut and think to themselves, *I am never going to hear that noise again. I wanted them to envision that long walk down the corridor toward the exit doors, hearing the echo of the guards' shoes, click clack, click clack*, and think, *I will never hear that sound again.* As they were approaching the door, they were to envision taking their last step out of jail, and as they did, they were to look up to the heavens, take a deep breath, and ask themselves one final question: *Do I get busy living or do I get busy dying?*

I ended the speech right there. All 20 guys jumped out of their seats hooting and hollering! It was a total success! I connected with these guys, and I could feel it. We can get busy living when we are present and recognize powerful moments.

Making an Impact

Ten members were to evaluate the speech. No sooner had they left the room to gather their thoughts that another inmate, not part of our group, came running down the hall with a bloody mouth. Lockdown! At first, I was nervous, but after a few minutes, I began talking to the guys still in my room. From our conversation, I learned their stories and why each of them was there.

The lockdown eventually ended, and we continued. One by one, they gave their evaluations. To make it easier for the inmates to look out over the audience and not at me sitting on the side, I decided to sit in the middle of everyone, as if I were one of them.

As the final participant stood to give his evaluation, he looked at me and said, "Mr. Rob, thank you for coming here today! Thank you so much for making us feel comfortable and thank you for looking like you were comfortable as well. Please don't get mad at me for what I am about to say, but if I didn't know any better, I would have thought you were one of us!" With that, all the inmates broke out in laughter, as did I. I knew in my heart this was a success.

I looked at the gentleman and said, "Thank you for that compliment. All you are telling me is I connected with you, and that's what I came here to do."

When I left the prison, I knew I left the guys with a feeling of hope—hope that one day when they get out of prison, they could live a life free of fear, hate, jealousy, and anger. As I pulled out of the parking lot, I looked in the rear-view mirror at the large fence and razor wire. I knew something magical had occurred. I could feel the spirit within me.

As you travel your journey, my hope is that you will become aware of all the powerful moments in your life and how they lead to deeper levels of joy and fulfillment.

To connect with Robert Commodari regarding real estate, visit www.talktorob.com. To learn more about his book *Better Than You Think* and to book speaking engagements, email him at rob@talktorob.com or visit www.robcommodariauthor.com. To learn more about his *Chiseled* podcast, go to https://spotifyanchor-web.app.link/e/Tpsv5xUWssb.

Tweetable: If this is a glimmer of what heaven looks and feels like, I can't wait to die to see all He has in store for me to see. If you allow yourself to live in the moment, you might experience a little bit of heaven.

COURTNEY MOELLER

Mom to Millionaire

Courtney Moeller is a US Navy veteran, investor, blockchain expert, and CEO of Invest on Main, a blockchain tokenization platform that will revolutionize the way people invest. She is also the co-host of the vodcast, Ladies Kickin Assets, *where Courtney hopes to empower people with the financial education they need to live the lives they want.*

My Time in the Navy

We pulled out of the port in San Diego early that morning in January. It was the first time I had ever gone to sea on an aircraft carrier, and I was in awe of this magnificent ship and its capabilities. The USS Nimitz was like a floating city that held thousands of sailors, civilians, aircraft, supplies, and much more.

I will never forget that first afternoon at sea. We were testing all our systems to prepare for our upcoming cruise to the Persian Gulf in support of Operation Iraqi Freedom. As I worked in my assigned shop, I heard this loud squealing sound. It got louder and closer, and then there was a large crash at the front of our ship. I literally thought we had been hit by a missile. Turns out, the shop I worked in was directly under the catapults on the flight deck that launched our aircraft, and when they're running, they are loud! It still makes me laugh when I think about it today.

My time in the Navy was incredible for many reasons. I was young and had so much to learn, but I have always had this strong desire to be the best version of myself that I could possibly be and to find ways to set myself apart. The Navy was a great place to do this. I was awarded medals for finding ways to lower costs and streamline our processes. I was great at repairing the electronic equipment we worked on, and I moved up in rank quickly. I thought outside the box and made this opportunity more than just a "job" I showed up for. I was even awarded Junior Sailor of the Year of the Southwest Pacific Fleet and a NAM, the Navy and Marine Corps Achievement Medal, in recognition of the amount of money I was able to save during my service.

I very quickly found myself in charge of one of the most important shops on board, which repaired critical equipment for the F-18s we were flying. I spent that cruise working with the leaders from all the squadrons on board. It was one of the most rewarding times in my life. This time in the Navy helped shape my desire to do better, to underpromise and overdeliver, to succeed beyond what people told me my capabilities were and truly set me up for success.

Life After the Navy

I loved my time in the Navy, but I could not make it a long-term career. I was a single mom with small children, and it was just too difficult to spend so much time away from them. So, after an incredible five-year service term, I was let loose on the world to find my way. During my enlistment, I was fortunate enough to meet my incredible husband. He was in the Marine Corps, and we were stationed in school together in Pensacola, Florida. We didn't marry until after our enlistments ended, but I knew he was my person.

I wasn't sure what I wanted to do, but I knew I would figure it out and I knew it would be great. I tried out several careers including selling real estate and nursing. Even though I truly loved them both, I knew neither career was going to last. Each position I held contributed to the philosophies and values carved into my being and shaped the way I did things as I moved forward.

My family comes from an oil and gas background. My father was a petroleum engineer and my brother worked on rigs as well. They were two of the most important people in my life. Growing up, we got to live in places like the United Arab Emirates and Pakistan as my father drilled his way around the world.

Unfortunately, about ten years ago, I lost them both in a short period. One to disease and the other in a car accident. It was a devastating time, and I was consumed by the sadness that losing loved ones can bring.

New Beginnings

About a year later, my husband and I knew we needed a change of scenery and decided to move our family from West Texas to the Dallas/Fort Worth area. This truly was the beginning of a bright and exciting future, and we were thrilled by the prospects of our new surroundings and community.

I always wanted my own company and to be my own boss. I wanted the freedom to do what I wanted when I wanted. When I inherited my father's oil and gas company after his passing, I also inherited the opportunity to work for myself while really figuring out what I was going to do and what the future would look like.

We continued drilling throughout Texas, and I learned to navigate my way around the oil field. But I really wanted to diversify into other assets. Oil income is great when oil is selling for $100 a barrel and not so great when the price drops to $30 a barrel or even goes negative.

I started studying different types of investments and how I could really get our money to work for us instead of the other way around. This led me into the blockchain and cryptocurrency space.

Learning to Fly

I had no idea the impact crypto would have on my family's future or the exciting paths it would lead me down. When I initially invested in Bitcoin, it was to buy low, sell high and hopefully make a profit, like it is for most people. But when I really dove in and figured out what blockchain was and the potential impact it would have on every industry in the world, I was hooked.

I started learning everything I could. Like a kid in a candy store, I couldn't get enough. And, in a short time, I had managed to take a six-figure sum and turn it into multiple seven-figures.

I couldn't believe how successful I had become in such a short time. I was overwhelmed with gratitude and wanted to share what I was doing with others. Most people weren't receptive, but I appreciated the ones that were. The very best text messages I have ever received were the ones thanking me for the success they experienced after we had a conversation about the possibilities of investing in cryptocurrency. I hoped I would one day be able to do this for many others, I just wasn't sure how yet.

I didn't really talk about crypto or blockchain to my friends. When I would bring it up, the subject usually got brushed off pretty quickly. At the time, most people hadn't heard of Bitcoin much less blockchain. Until one day... I was with friends including my great friend, Kara Helms, and a conversation on blockchain came up. I started rattling off all the things I was so excited about, which was a lot.

The next thing I knew, Kara suggested I come and speak about crypto at The Real Estate Guys Investor Summit on Sand in Belize. Wow! I was completely blown away, a little intimidated, and absolutely honored.

Spreading My Wings

I went to the summit not really sure of what to expect and hoping I would be able to bring enough value to the summit attendees. I could not believe I was sitting on panels discussing money with incredible people like Robert Kiyosaki, George Gammon, G. Edward Griffin, and Ken McElroy. Having dinner with Kim Kiyosaki, Tom Wheelwright, Mauricio Rauld, Robert Helms, and Russell Gray was an added bonus! I hosted daily round tables and even gave a solo presentation. It was absolutely, hands down, one of the most life-changing events of my life.

I had already started down a new investing path, but this event took me out of a golf cart and threw me into a beautiful Ferrari. It truly was incredible, and the people were just the best.

I left that summit energized and ready to tackle investments I'd previously had no idea were even options. This event opened up opportunities at other events, where I met people who helped me create things I didn't know how to build on my own. I learned about syndication and went on to raise $7 million in just under a year for several funds. Talk about next level!

I start every single day being grateful for everything I have, for the incredible people in my life, and for the amazing opportunities that have come my way. There have been great times and tough times, and I have learned so much along the way.

Our past shapes our future—the good, the bad, and the ugly. Those hard experiences, we find the value in them and use that value to do things better next time. The tough times make us stronger, smarter, and better. Nobody ever learned anything by having everything go perfectly all the time. It doesn't matter what you are working on or what your job is, do your best and do it better than everyone else.

You never know where your passions will lead you and what doors they will open. Two years ago, I was working on my own and figuring it out myself. Today, I have spoken on stages internationally, have been an expert guest on many podcasts, and am working hard to change as many lives as I can. I am partnered with incredible people and am now officially a syndicator, vodcast co-host, and creator of a real estate tokenization platform that will revolutionize the way people invest. My goal is to change as many lives as possible with financial education, allowing people the wealth and time to live the lives they want.

Contact Courtney Moeller to get information on her investment opportunities and projects at www.CourtneyMoeller.com. Check out her financial education content on her YouTube channel *Ladies Kickin Assets*. Connect with Courtney on LinkedIn (Courtney Moeller) and Instagram (csmoeller) for blockchain and investing tips.

Tweetable: Follow your passions. You never know where your passions will lead you and what doors they will open.

SEAN HACKNEY

The Unexpected Miracle of Endurance

Sean Hackney is a second-generation Realtor and co-owner of NextHome Northwest Living in Bellingham, Washington. Sean has completed 11 Ironman competitions after being told he could lose his leg. Whether in business or sport, Sean's story of resilience and persistence after a life-changing moment demonstrates that anything is possible.

Belief & The Nod

The blinking yellow light is about the only reason you'd slow down on Highway 47 southwest of Portland. But the town of 900 people was home.

The excitement of sprinting out onto the field in youth had given way to fear. High school football was different. This was old school, suck it up, survival of the fittest football. Hazing and initiation were norms. I was a small kid and I wanted none of it.

On a mid-August evening before my freshman year, the phone rang. I waved Mom off, trying to avoid talking to Coach, but she didn't buy it.

"You ready for tomorrow?"

I flooded him with a string of excuses. Coach McNulty had been my middle school coach and had just been promoted to the high school assistant coaching staff. He didn't let me finish my sentence.

"I'll pick you up at 6:45 a.m." The phone clicked silent.

I made it to the second week of hot August two-a-days constantly intimidated, but I had never pushed myself so hard.

The varsity offense needed a "dummy" defense, and the underclassmen got to be the dummies. Same play, same two running backs… over and over and over. Right at me… EVERY. SINGLE. TIME. I was tackling air as they ran by me… or over me if they wanted some fun. Play after play, they laughed, but the joke was about to be over. As soon as that final whistle blew, I'd be hanging up my cleats and walking off the field for the last time. I was done.

Then it happened. Again, the senior all conference running back got the ball, broke into the open and took aim at me. Somehow, by the grace of the football gods, I tackled him. It was an incredible rush of adrenaline. I laid there for a moment, basking in glory, until he rolled over, pinning me underneath him.

Nostrils flared and spit flying, he said, "If you ever do that again, you will regret it."

Why couldn't I have missed one more time, absorbed a little more ridicule, and been done? Completely defeated, I waited for the final whistle to blow.

Fifteen yards away was Coach McNulty. He had heard the whole thing. He saw the fear, the embarrassment, the defeat. I had the utmost respect for Coach McNulty. He didn't say a word but locked eyes with me and gave me a nod.

The whistle blew. The coaches granted a players-only meeting and the senior stood up to speak. There was silence as the coaches walked away—something that I'd learn over time usually meant something life-changing was near. I was terrified.

Using very colorful language, he went on a tirade that was obviously directed at me. I tried to mentally brace myself. I wondered what they would do to me and how much it would hurt. His final words changed everything: "...and THIS is who I want to go to BATTLE with."

I would go on to be a four-year varsity starter on both offense and defense.

During my senior year, I started to receive recognition and accolades. Scouts were showing up to games. The dream of playing college football started surfacing. There were many, though, who liked to remind me that I was still the small kid from a small school in nowhere Oregon.

Western Washington University

I walked into Carver Gymnasium for the first time as a Western Washington University college football player. I had defied the odds. In the trophy case was a football with the number 4,000 in white lettering, a date from the '70s, and a name. A testament to a 4,000-yard career rushing record that very few at any level have achieved.

At the first team meeting, I realized that everyone's resume epitomized talent, speed, strength, and size. You were in that room because you had talent and were recruited because you could play the game, but I knew what most were thinking.... *That is a small dude to be playing college ball.*

You've been here before, I reminded myself. I gave myself the Coach McNulty nod.

My freshman year I redshirted, which meant I practiced and suited up for a few games but never played. This preserved my four years of eligibility. I had a solid year and was awarded Offensive Scout Team Player of the Year. The defensive player who won this award went on to be an All-American linebacker. I was in good company and setting the stage for that 4,000-yard ball.

Change of Direction

As a running back, you're going to get hit. That's part of the job description. At my size, you have to be strategic. Split-second decisions are made at full speed. What I didn't know was that the next split second decision would change my life.

I took the handoff and broke into the open when our outside linebacker hit me. Unable to bring me down, but unable to break free, we found ourselves at a stalemate.

Instinct told me to go down. Lose the battle to win the war. Wanting to impress the coaches, I made the decision to not listen to instinct. I chose to stay up.

A wave of defenders crashed into me. Immediately, I felt a burst in my knee. Oddly, it didn't hurt.

As a second wave of defenders hit me from the opposite direction, my surroundings blurred, and I could hear someone screaming. As the bodies peeled away, I realized the screaming was coming from me. "My leg... I can't feel my leg!"

On the gurney and still suited up, I fought not to pass out from the nausea as they moved my leg around. They confirmed I had blown my knee. Historically, a ruptured anterior cruciate ligament (ACL) was always career-ending, but this would, surprisingly, be the least of my concerns.

There was swelling and still no feeling. And, more importantly, there was no pulse. Not knowing what more they could do, they put me in a brace and sent me back to the dorms. I was told to come back in a week.

Not the most patient of people, my dad made some calls, and I soon found myself in Kirkland, Washington, being introduced to the Seattle Seahawks head physician, Dr. Brad Shoup.

A battery of tests ensued over the coming days. Still, no feeling or detectable pulse in my lower leg.

They pieced together what had happened. The first hit had dislocated my kneecap. With my kneecap off to the side, there was nothing to prevent my leg from hyperextending when the second wave of hits came. My knee inverted, bringing the top portion of my leg downward towards my shin.

Days went by. They decided to inject dye and do further imaging. As the dye made its way into the lower half of my body, the doctors became silent.

A Temporary Salvation

I waited in Dr. Shoup's office, oblivious to what was about to come next.

There were a lot of words and terms. All I heard though was, "I have no medical explanation for why you have your leg."

Within hours, a vascular surgeon pushed a piece of paper across the large desk. The artery behind my knee was completely destroyed. In disbelief, I signed, giving them permission to amputate my leg during surgery if needed.

A week and a half before, I was living the college football dream and proving the critics wrong. As they rolled me to surgery, I stared at the white ceiling tiles. My mom hovered over me with tears streaming down her face. I heard myself saying, "I am your same son with or without my leg."

Two massive surgeries over three days would save my leg for the time being. The doctor did what he could to reestablish blood flow to my lower leg. Not a permanent fix. I was told it should help for the next 5-10 years. No one spoke of what would happen after that. Amputation isn't a topic you want to talk about.

Purpose Through Challenge

"I will live vicariously through you kids now," my mom said. After a brief remission, a six-year battle with breast cancer was back with a vengeance. This time it had metastasized to her brain.

Lou Tice, famed speaker, author, and founder of the Pacific Institute, shared a story about when his wife received a dire diagnosis. They chose to focus on a bigger vision and let that vision manifest, not the cancer.

Called the world's hardest one-day endurance event, the Ironman triathlon is a 2.4-mile swim, 112-mile bike, and 26.2-mile run to be done in less than 17 hours. It was November 2003. With the click of a button, I was signed up for Ironman Coeur d'Alene. If mom wanted to live vicariously through us, then we were going BIG. Mom booked her hotel room, and the stage was set.

But there was a problem. I had never learned how to swim. And it was still difficult to run for more than a few minutes at a time. I had six months to learn to swim, bike, and run for mom.

On February 6, 2004, with her kids at her bedside, a single tear made its way down mom's cheek before she took her last breath. Silence. The course of my life would again change forever.

The race had lost its original purpose. Now it was to honor my mom's legacy.

Training became my distraction and June quickly arrived. The day before the race, I met the legendary Bill Bell. Then 81 years old, he was the oldest Ironman triathlete at the time. Terrified about what race day would bring, I sought his advice. Without hesitation, he stated, "Keep moving forward."

Keep Moving Forward

Putting on my wetsuit that morning, I was sick to my stomach. A triathlon of any distance is daunting, and this was the granddaddy of them all. Swim. Bike. Run. 140.6 miles in total. Finish by midnight and I would hear the hallowed words, **"Sean Hackney, you are an Ironman."**

The person who enters the Ironman waters in the early morning hours is not the same person who crosses the finish line. You are stripped down to your core both physically and mentally. Thoughts of my mom made this process even more powerful… spiritual even.

140.6 miles later, those cherished words finally came, a title not many have. The honor of being called an Ironman.

I received the title of Ironman that day, but it was to honor a person with the best title of all, Mom.

Something's Not Quite Right

Mom's vicarious challenge turned into something even more significant. Over the next 12 years, I would complete 11 Ironmans and more than 20 half-Ironman races. Little did I know, triathlons would save my leg. Again.

In 2016, something wasn't quite right. Training for my 11th Ironman in Whistler, Canada, my leg felt off. I'd get off the bike and my calf would feel "full." During a run, the pain would become excruciating. My toes would go numb and the bottom of my foot felt like I was on hot pins and needles.

I finished my 11th Ironman, but by December, we still couldn't figure out what was happening. There were numerous doctor visits. After seeing my scars and hearing my story, a surgeon suggested we do a vascular study.

The vascular study started with the typical measuring of pulses, pressure readings, and an ultrasound. I then jumped on a treadmill to replicate what was happening. Within a minute, the tech's jovial good nature quieted. There it was again… Silence.

After an unprecedented 26-year run, the graft connecting my artery was finally failing. I was reminded of the reality of my leg.

A Miraculously Wrong Story?

My wife and I met a vascular surgeon in January 2017. It was obvious she questioned my story. There was no way an artery bypass had lasted over 26 years. There was no way I could do Ironman competitions with the story I shared. It was unheard of.

As my wife and I walked across the parking lot following the appointment, I felt foolish. Had I been telling people a lie all these years?

Following surgery, I noticed a change in the surgeon's demeanor. She showed us the video of the surgery. She marveled at what she had found. Despite a vein graft the size of a spaghetti noodle, all these years of training for and competing in Ironman had slowly been creating a web of new veins and collateral vessels to keep my leg functioning.

Nervously, I decided to ask, "My leg isn't what you'd thought it'd be, was it?"

She looked at us, smiled, and said, "I certainly can't explain it. Keep doing whatever you're doing." My story was, in fact, real.

Ironman World Championships?

The Ironman World Championships are held each October in Kailua-Kona, Hawaii. Only the top athletes from across the world qualify to compete in this legendary event. There is, however, another way in. Athletes who have completed 12 races are honored into the Kona Legacy Program. To qualify, I would have to complete one more race by the end of the year. Recovery had gone well. Inspired, I asked the doctors about racing in November to qualify.

Four weeks out from Ironman Arizona, my wife and I were in Kauai for vacation. I went for an 18-mile run through the sugar cane fields. It was magical. But within 30 minutes of finishing, I knew something was wrong. Really wrong. Unable to sleep that night, we cut our vacation short and booked a flight home. Upon landing, I headed directly to the ER and found myself being admitted for yet another surgery.

Waking up in the ICU, I was instructed to stay flat on my back and not move. I had a large blood clot in the artery graft. The reality of having flown home with this clot settled in. Three surgeries and four days in the ICU followed.

Over the years, I had become numb to my own story. It was just that, a tale from long ago. Yet, here we were again. I wasn't feeling equipped to handle this like I had when I was 20 years old telling my mom I was her same son with or without my leg.

The Ironman World Championships would no longer be a possibility. Football had been taken away from me and now it appeared triathlon would as well.

A dark cloud hovered over me. Each day I would wake up wondering if this was the day. *What will it be like without a leg? How will I cope?*

These thoughts lingered for the next several years.

In early 2022, I woke up to some discoloration on my foot, my lower leg feeling cooler and some tingling in my toes. Otherwise, I felt fine. I even went for a run. A couple days later though, I was headed into surgery again. We were running out of options, so I mentally braced myself for what was to come.

Following surgery, the surgeon told me, "I've got bad and good news." I had another blood clot and I no longer had an artery from the knee down.

The temporary fix has lasted for an unheard of 32 years, but I knew what this meant.

Then she said, "The good news is that you have a collateral vein that has tripled in size and it is taking over the work of your artery.

"Your leg continues to be a miracle," and with that, she walked out.

Gift of a Miracle

Miracle is a word that I hold to a high standard and one I do not take lightly. Dr. Shoup said he had no medical explanation. The vascular surgeon said my leg continued to be a miracle. These were the words of highly-regarded physicians and surgeons and they were not the language typical of the medical profession.

Throughout life, seemingly small decisions alter your life path and purpose. How you handle those define you.

Life is filled with gifts… and miracles. I've been given a gift with my leg, my miracle. I choose to keep moving forward… in wonder and giving myself the nod of encouragement.

To connect with Sean Hackney about his story, real estate, working by referral, or to book him to speak, visit SeanHackney.com You can also reach him at 360-303-0165 or email at Sean@SeanHackney.com.

Tweetable: Throughout life, seemingly small decisions alter your life path and purpose. How you handle those define you.

BRIAN H. FERGUSON

Next Leveling My Family Legacy

Brian H. Ferguson is a seasoned real estate investor. He grew a portfolio of over $100m by age 35 which all started with a $10k house flip and a determination to build his family's legacy. He is now focused on real estate syndication and helping others create and level up their family legacy.

Where the Journey Began

I always knew I wanted more, but I didn't know what that was for a long time. I just knew I wanted to one day give my family opportunities we didn't have and take care of those who took care of me. Growing up, we didn't have everything, but we had two amazing men in our lives who gave us what they could: my dad and my grandfather.

We started as a family of five: Dad, Mom, older brother, myself, and younger brother. Pretty standard structure for that time. We went to a private school in exchange for my mom working in the cafeteria, and my dad was an oilfield man who worked hard. The education at the private school was good, but being the kid that didn't come from money wasn't always fun. I would visit friends and think, *Wow, this is nice. I'll have this one day*. I remember the money talks, mainly how we didn't have it. Things were tight. Christmases were hard. But it could have been worse. Then, things changed.

My dad was severely injured, almost losing his right arm. Shortly after, my parents divorced, and my mom moved away. I knew then, I would never let that happen to my family!

This spiraled into me skipping school, hanging with the wrong crowd, and eventually spending quite a while in juvenile detention. During that time, I knew this wasn't my path and I would change it. I utilized the time in detention to complete most of my high school education and eventually, with good behavior, came home.

Things were good for a while. I was attending a half day at high school, working a minimum wage job at Taco Bell, and staying in line. Then working became an issue for probation and for the hours I needed to help around the house. That's when things went the wrong direction again. I ended up back in jail for a short time, but this time it wasn't Juvi. I'll never forget my probation officer telling me, "You are with the adults now, things are different." I knew then, I had to make a change, and it had to be permanent.

The Start to Building a Legacy

At 17, I started selling motorcycles. Then, a customer recruited me to come sell cars. I went from top salesperson to sales manager to finance manager in what felt like overnight. The money was great, and I was dating someone who I saw a future with.

It worked for a while. Then the long hours started to pile up. I knew I wanted a change but didn't know what. Watching flipping TV shows really intrigued me, and after lots of looking at listings and talking with different people, a group of friends and I bought a house for $10,000. We don't see many of those these days!

One house led to three, and three led to ten. Before long, I left my high-paying job and partnered with a friend to start our own investment company. It was tough at first. We had to find loans and money to repair the properties, and we had to do this with no salary, no income other than savings, and no family with money to lend.

This was 2007-2008, and because of the down market, everyone we talked to told us we were crazy. We pushed through, and before long, the market was doing better. We were flipping hundreds of residential properties a year in the middle of a recession and expanding into other ventures such as apartments, new construction, and more. We even owned a bowling alley for a time. Things were great. I married and started a family, having two amazing sons. My life was as I had always pictured.

Then, the working hours grew longer. Weekends became dedicated to showings and contracts. After some time of this, my wife left. And then I was a single dad. I had sworn I would never let this happen. This wasn't on my vision board, and it hit hard.

I blamed work and stepped back some, trying to find my next step. I shifted my focus to my sons and being the best dad I could be. I made sure I didn't miss a practice, school plays, Wednesday morning chapel, or anything else. This gave me a true appreciation for being a parent and brought me closer than ever to both my sons. After a while, this new focus went from being hard to being second nature. Some days I still find it hard to be present, but no matter what, I show up and take in every moment.

If It Was Going to Be, It Was Up to Me

After some time, I met Sarah, my soon-to-be wife. With her, I found new ways to enjoy life and continued to raise my sons. That was everything I wanted.

The companies were doing well, and my teams could handle most of the day-to-day on their own. For a little while, that was where it stayed. It was the perfect arrangement, or so I thought.

While everything was great and more or less on cruise control, I just felt like I wasn't fulfilling my potential, like I wasn't following the path set out for me. I really started to reflect on my childhood and felt a strong desire to make sure I changed things so that my children would have a different experience and different opportunities. And I wanted to do that not only for my children but also for future generations. I realized it was up to me to create generational opportunity and start a legacy my children, their children, and the children of their children could continue to carry forward.

The Days Ahead

I started searching for what was next. Growing what we had made sense, and that's where I started. I started flipping more, buying more apartments, and building more new construction.

In the middle of this, my daughter was born. Bringing her into the family opened a whole new world for all of us. We were now the family of five, the one I had growing up. I embraced the unspoken challenge and knew that family, work balance could exist. And that's what I started chasing.

We started traveling more, doing more kids sports, and really taking it all in. I did this while still growing professionally. I learned to sing my children to sleep, spend quality time with my fiancé, and still get to work early and catch up at night when the need arose. I truly believe anything is possible in this world, and it is up to us to take advantage of that.

Coffee with Dad, Always Inspirational

I was recently visiting with my father over a cup of coffee in my new office building. My dad was watching everyone walk by my window. After a few minutes, he looked at me and said, "Son, do you ever look around and think of what you have accomplished?" I honestly didn't know how to answer him. That evening I thought about it a lot, and the truth was that

I didn't think much about what I have achieved. I don't. More often, I stay up at night wondering if I'm doing a good job... if that day I was a good enough dad, a good enough partner to Sarah, a good enough leader at the office... if I did enough... if I was enough....

My dad's question led to lots of sleepless nights. Am I doing a good job? Is it enough? I wish I had an answer, but the truth is, it all depends on the day. I still wonder if I'm doing a good job, but each day, I truly believe that I can become better. I get better by trying a little harder—by trying a little more as a parent by letting the kids be kids even when we are stressed, by trying a little more as a spouse by watching her favorite TV show with her even when I have piles of work to do, by trying a little more as an employer by listening to my team members first thing in the morning even when I have many of my tasks to handle. Doing a good job isn't something we can do and then be done. It is a daily task of waking up and choosing to be your best you each and every day.

Where I Am Now

Today, I am fortunate to have the most amazing family of five with Sarah, our 10-year-old and seven-year-old sons, and our three-year-old daughter. We live in our dream home. I run multiple companies and have had the privilege to employ, teach, and hopefully help grow hundreds of team members. We are growing daily and excited to now open investments to passive investors and investors who want to learn. I hope I can help someone like me start their journey.

One day I hope to see my children carry on this legacy for years to come and into future generations. If I can help just a few change the next generation, then I will have left this place better than I found it. My goal is to leverage my nearly 17 years of experience to open opportunities to people looking for ways to achieve financial freedom and retirement while I also help others like me get to the next level!

There will be good days, great days, and the worst days. Those bad days make us who we are. Those thoughts of "Am I doing enough?" push us harder. Great things don't happen overnight or without hard work and dedication.

I am truly blessed and living a life that many dream of. I look forward to the days of helping others to accomplish the dream! I hope I never stop dreaming or asking myself if today was enough. When I'm sitting in a rocking chair at 80, I hope I still ask myself if today was enough. Did I kiss my bride good morning? Have I talked to the kids today? How can I be better today?!

 To reach Brian H. Ferguson, founder and CEO of Altunas Capital and Fergmar Enterprises, about starting your real estate career or beginning the path to investing your way to a passive income retirement, email him at Bferguson@Altunascapital.com or register at Altunascapital.com.

 Tweetable: Our past doesn't define us and neither do our bad days. Anything is possible in this life if we are willing to go after it and take it.

SANDHYA SESHADRI

Creating Wealth While
Building Communities

Apartment syndicator, underwriter, and hands-on asset manager Sandhya Seshadri is a Dallas resident with an immigrant mindset of extreme gratitude to this country and, especially, the Lone Star State. Sandhya is passionate about serving her residents and building wealth for her investors by creating neighborly communities and impacting lives.

Video Killed the Radio Star

I have vivid memories of the 1980s, when MTV came alive and the world of music videos exploded. Having grown up in India, it was my first trip to the United States and my first trip overseas.

How beautiful and amazing is the USA? In the mid-1980s, I arrived in New York City with its skyscrapers, bridges, and waterways. Thanks to a kind uncle, I was able to have this summer vacation as a teen. I was going to help him with his kids and get a glimpse of what life would be like if I lived in the United States.

The summer trip ended too soon, but the memories would last my entire life. Standing at the top of the World Trade Center, I remember looking down in awe and gratitude and deciding that I would do everything in my power to experience more of this amazing country. *But how can I turn this dream into reality?*

My parents are highly educated, and we were living a comfortable middle-class life in India. However, due to the exchange rate, the salary they made in India was about $50 per month. College in the United States was going to cost me at least $10,000 per year. My parents would not be able to afford to send me to school in the United States even if they gave me their life savings. So, I knew if I wanted to come to the United States for college, I had to get a scholarship.

Mission Possible

When I returned to India, I worked hard in high school, made the best grades I could, and excelled in competitive tests to get admission to a school in the United States with a scholarship to pay the tuition. I landed in Dallas, Texas, with two suitcases and never looked back.

I had the honor of attending Southern Methodist University (SMU) in Dallas to study electrical engineering. I fell in love with the beautiful campus and experienced my first taste of southern hospitality. The Lone Star State welcomed me and made me feel at home. Soon after my graduation, I was offered a job at a local Fortune 500 company. I was well on my way to the American dream.

From Corporate America to Trading Stocks

The company I worked for was kind enough to pay for my tuition to go back to school and earn a part-time MBA. That's where I got all my financial acumen and "crushed it" in both the business world and the technical world, while also playing the stock market successfully. I belonged to multiple investor groups, and we discussed stocks and traded on a regular basis. The insights from acquiring that business background served me well for many years both in the corporate and entrepreneurial worlds.

What I didn't realize back then was that as much as corporate America served me well and helped me with a salary plus benefits, it was my investments that made me wealthy. As Jim Rohn says, "Profits are better than wages. Wages make you a living; profits make you a fortune."

But then, I ran into a problem. Between corporate America and trading stocks, I was not doing anything that would reduce my tax burden.

Stock Market to Large Apartments

I knew that 90% of all millionaires become so through real estate. I analyzed single-family rental income and didn't find it to be lucrative enough to justify a recourse loan and the headaches of being a landlord. The hassles associated with the four T's—tenants, toilets, trash, and termites—were not appealing. There was no economy of scale in single-family rentals to justify paying a third-party property management company. A weekend seminar I attended led me to apartment investing as a way for me to not only invest while reducing my tax burden but also stay intellectually occupied and interact socially with peers.

Today, less than four years after beginning this journey in apartment investing, I have invested in over 4,000 doors which I either syndicated as a general partner or invested in as a passive investor. Between the tax savings and profit earnings, I was easily able to exceed my salary in corporate America, while having the flexibility to choose my schedule.

I was shocked that so few people knew about this avenue for investing in real estate passively. Why is only the stock market promoted everywhere as the vehicle to invest our 401K money and investments in general? The market is so volatile and subject to fluctuations from various political factors well beyond anyone's control. Apartment investing is such a great way to diversify one's portfolio from Wall Street to Main Street.

This led to my multifamily journey with Engineered Capital, where today we engineer the capital of our investors to make money work for them while they sleep or pursue other exciting adventures.

I am keen to give back to this wonderful country and the state of Texas that welcomed me and made me feel right at home. I am focused on improving communities in the Dallas area—one apartment complex at a time.

The Neighborhood, Cul-De-Sac Feel

The best part about my apartment investing business is that we provide safe, affordable places to live. More than that, we strive to foster communities where people feel connected with their neighbors and proud of where they live.

We do this in small ways that have big impacts. We have regular resident activities such as our Easter egg hunt, back to school bash, popsicles by the pool, Mother's Day roses, free Thanksgiving turkeys, and Halloween costume contest. We are building communities. This apartment complex is their home. I want the feeling there to be what I feel when I think of a neighborhood cul-de-sac. It's where their memories are made. I feel a strong drive to bring the community together in the places I invest just like a community in any other neighborhood because safe and surrounded by a loving community is the way I want to feel when I'm at home. And we, my company and I, are here to do that, whether that's by way of crime watch, social and financial awareness and assistance, or block parties.

What Is the ROI?

How does our focus on community activities make a difference for an investor? Here's an example. During COVID in 2020, when the world shut down, we delivered goodie bags to our residents containing hard to find items such as toilet paper and hand sanitizer. Some residents had lost their jobs and could no longer pay their rent. Due to the relationships we had already built with them, they came forward and worked with our leasing manager to fill out applications for rental relief. Our delinquency was almost negligible, despite COVID. This translated to better financials and an astounding return to our investors.

Most of us think of ROI as *return on investment,* but there's also a *return on impact.* When we build communities and residents refer their friends and family to our apartments, we tend to have better retention. Our renewal rates are higher which means that our turn costs are lower and therefore our economic vacancy is also reduced. We spend less in make-ready costs that we would have to spend when a resident moves out to get the unit ready for the next resident to move in.

With Gratitude

America is the land of opportunity that welcomes immigrants like me. I arrived here with two suitcases in hand, full of hopes and dreams. As a student, I lived in an apartment close to my college and enjoyed the huge highways, beautiful parks, magnificent campus, and the scene of Downtown Dallas. From my window, I looked out across the beautiful suburbs of Highland Park, which I still can't afford. But we recreate much of that neighborhood feel I could see there in our communities. It is not whether a house has granite countertops, but rather the heart and soul of the people that make a home.

When I focus on taking care of my residents as well as my investors, my two main customers, great things happen. We are fulfilling a vital need by providing shelter, one of the basic human needs that the government cannot provide alone. By taking these apartments to the next level, making them nicer, better, safer, and building communities—we are impacting the world.

To join Sandhya Seshadri in growing your passive income through real estate investments with a feel-good component of impacting communities, and to receive a free checklist for vetting a deal, email invest@engineered-capital.com.

Tweetable: You can do good and feel good about a business while building wealth. One does not exclude the other! And to do it hands-off while you sleep, with tax advantages! This is how you next level your life and build a legacy.

SIMON T. BAILEY

Giving Value in Service

Simon T. Bailey is an international keynote speaker, success coach, author of ten books, television host, and philanthropist. His purpose in life is to help you discover your brilliance. In his 30 years of experience, he's worked with over 2,000 companies in 50 different countries and helped countless people find their spark.

Childhood and Education

I went to Catholic school growing up in Buffalo, New York. In high school, Mom and Dad put me in public school, and my freshman year, I failed all of the classes. I went out for the football team and I got cut. I went out for the basketball team and I got cut. I went out for track and field, and they said, "You are too slow, you need to try cross country." My freshman year was a total disaster.

Sophomore year, Mom and Dad decided to transfer me to Bennett High School, where I met my English teacher, Ms. Rita. She said to me, "Young man, I want you to write a speech and give it before the entire school." That teacher changed my life. She saw something in me that I didn't see in myself, and I am forever grateful. She changed the trajectory of my life. She saved my life. That moment was the seed of my successful, 30-year coaching and speaking career.

I finished high school, and Mom and Dad dropped me off at Morehouse College in Atlanta, Georgia, where Dr. Martin Luther King, Samuel L. Jackson, and Spike Lee attended school. I enrolled as a mass communications major.

At the end of my freshman year, Mom and Dad called and said, "We don't have the money to send you back to Morehouse, nor do we have money to bring you back home, but we do love you."

I dropped out and moved into a drug-infested community in southwest Atlanta. I only had a mattress on the bright green carpet from the '70s and a black and white TV, with a hanger hanging out of the back, set on top of a couple of milk crates turned over. It was one of the lowest points in my life.

Discovering Reading and Becoming a Speaker

I transferred my credits from Morehouse over to Georgia State University. I was working during the day and going to school at night. I got a job at the front desk of the Days Inn Hotel making a whopping $5.10 an hour.

Lost as a goose in a blizzard, I was trying to find my way. It would take me about 10 years to finish my undergrad degree. It was during this rough time that I stumbled into reading. One of the books that really impacted me was *Think and Grow Rich* by Napoleon Hill. When I got a hold of that book at 19 years of age, I was like, *Whoa, this is incredible.*

Shortly after came another defining moment: I went and saw Les Brown. This was the '90s, almost 35 years ago. I was like, *Who is this guy? This is unreal.* He was killing it, and still to this day he does. I was mesmerized by his craftsmanship, his confidence, his positivity. It became a template. I thought, *Wow, I think I can do that one day.* I ended up joining The National Speakers Association. I was still working, but I was now moonlighting as a speaker.

Then I had a chance to meet Zig Ziglar before he passed away. Tom Ziglar invited me to have a private lunch with his father and who his father called The Redhead, Tom's mother. I was mesmerized. I had just started my speaking career, and I said to Zig, "What is it that I should tell people going forward?"

Zig said, "Always remember, if you help enough people get what they want, enough people will help you get what you want." It was a fingerprint on the canvas of my soul.

Disney, Thinking Big and Finding the Path

Disney started recruiting me in 1994. After a two-year period, 10 interviews, and a 10-page psychological analysis from Gallup, finally, they hired me. I had four different jobs while I was there from 1996 to 2003. One of the cool things I got a chance to do was go over to Disneyland Paris for a few weeks and work with a client out of London.

December 10, 2001, I got a call from a journalist. He asked me, "Where do you see yourself 10-15 years from now?"

I said, "I see myself as the president and CEO of the Walt Disney World Resort and eventually the chairman and CEO of the Walt Disney Company." And he put this in print.

At Disney, you never talk to the media unless authorized. The article came out, page 12, *Florida Business Trend Magazine*, February 2002. And there was my picture with the Mickey Mouse topiary behind me. My boss, Larry, called me: "What were you thinking when you did this interview!?"

I said, "Larry I work at this company whose motto is, *If your heart is in your dream, no request is too extreme for when you wish upon a star it makes no difference who you are…* but obviously, it does here," (Song by Leigh Harline and Ned Washington). That's funny today, not funny then. I was going for it. I was working at the happiest place on Earth. What the heck, right?

Looking back now, it was a lot of ego. I was way over my skis. It just didn't look good. HR showed up a couple hours later and asked me to sign a piece of paper that went into my personnel file. Disney didn't fire me that day, but about a year later, I could hear the footsteps coming and they were not singing, "It's a Small World." So, I thought it was probably in my best interest if I found my happiness elsewhere.

It turned out for the best. Leaving Disney sent me in a new direction, where I was meant to be. I realize now everyone has a cognitive bent, and my cognitive bent was leading me down this path. Meeting Zig and Les and seeing what I could become… sometimes a person gets a snapshot of their future before they walk into it.

Building the Speaking Business

Speaking is a tough business. It took me about 18 months to really get it off the ground. I left Disney when the country was going to war with Iraq for the second time. Corporations were laying off personnel by the thousands. And there I was, putting out a shingle saying, *I'm a speaker! I'm a coach!*

I cashed in my entire 401k with significant Disney stock. I had about a three year runway, and there was no plan B. My wife, the mother of my children, didn't work outside the home. I had Pampers to buy and a mortgage to pay. It was real.

My approach when working with human beings is always, how do we have that difficult conversation and grow from it but communicate from a place of kindness? That's the thread throughout our entire business. How do we always be kind to humanity, no matter how difficult it becomes?

Ten Books in 18 Years

The first book came out in 2003. I went to the National Speakers Association annual meeting, and they said, "Every speaker needs a book." I realized a book is a marketing tool that will reach people you may never meet and go places you may never go.

I figured out I needed some help. Sometimes I can get in my own way. And, I'm a perfectionist. I realize though, in some instances, it's to my advantage to leverage the talent of others. And that's how I started writing books more and more.

I would use the articles I was sending out via the newsletter. If I were sending out one article a month, that was 12 chapters that could go in a book. Over two to three years, I had 24 or 36 articles that I could cherry-pick stories, points, and how-to's from. We went on to write 10 books in the next 18 years.

I tried to keep on that schedule, but then it felt forced. It felt like I had to get something out there to sell. I want a relationship with readers. I don't want them to think that I'm just trying to pump and dump. I want to come from a place of service to humanity.

I'll never forget this. One of my mentors, may he forever rest in peace, a wonderful human being and phenomenal speaker, Keith Harrell introduced me to literary agent Jan Miller (Dupree Miller & Associates). At the meeting, Joe Tessitore, a senior VP of HarperCollins, asked, "Do you want to be a bestselling author?"

I said, "No, I want to be an effective author, and if I'm effective, I'll be bestselling." That's what I've stayed true to. I want to be an effective author. I'm not just writing to write it.

Ignite the Power of Women in Your Life

Ignite the Power of Women in Your Life: A Guide for Men was prompted for every person who has gone through divorce and doesn't believe they can bounce back. It's for those who have been drowning in debt. It's for those who have doubts about whether they will ever find love again. And it's for those asking, how do I continue to show up and be relevant in my career through years 40-50?

It took me three years to write. And I wasn't going to release it. It was too personal, too vulnerable. I just put it on the shelf.

I wrote the book after being married for 25 years. My then-wife said to me, "You give everybody the best of you, but you give us the rest of you, and I don't want the leftovers anymore."

I recognized that I had built a house, but I'd lost a home. I was chasing money but had no meaning. I was pursuing power but had no purpose. I wrote from that place of going to therapy and just doing the work. In fact, I'm still in therapy. I'm still doing the work.

One day, my wife Jodi said, "I really think you should bring this book to the world because it can really help people."

Since we released it, corporations have asked us to create an e-course called How Do You Ignite the Power of Women in Business? based on the book. It's created a lot of dialogue, helping men and women think about how we can ignite our potential.

A young 35-year-old business owner flew from South Carolina to Orlando after reading the book to say, "You wrote this book for me." I've heard from women all over the world who said, "I have read the book and could not put it down."

I heard from Dr. Jean Watson, a scholar in caring science at the University of Colorado, Boulder. Of course, I had incorporated some of her scientific research into the book. She said, "I read your book in one sitting. I could not put it down." To hear that from somebody I have admired, is like whoa!

We're hearing from people from all walks of life. I believe it's because I'm not trying to tell you, "Here's what you need to do." I just invite you into a conversation to ask, "How can you really think in a fresh way?"

Mentors and Mindset

I wake up every single day to hug people with my words. Words carry energy. I intentionally look for ways to connect, not just communicate. When I'm with an audience, they sometimes will feel that they're in a room of one because I'm talking directly to you. I discovered that a paycheck is given to people who show up, but opportunities are given to people who think and work beyond what they're paid to do. So, we are willing to do what others won't do.

I'm getting ready to speak to one of the largest franchise systems in the world. And I told my client that I want to interview the individuals who are part of the system. By the time we get done, the franchisees will feel like I work with them. That's what we do. Because excellence is early. Success doesn't just happen; it's doing those things that others will not do. And you know, it's not work, it's fun. It's joy. That's who we are.

I realized a decade ago, I'm not paid to speak. I'm paid to think.

Then, I discovered that corporations and businesses don't really care about your speech. They want to know if you can listen to their problem then create solutions that solve their problem. And they want to hear it in a fresh, new way. When I had that epiphany, I was like, *Oh my goodness, that's it. Stop speaking and start connecting. I am not paid to speak. I am paid to think.*

The last thing I'll say is that I'm a student. I don't work, I learn, every day.

Grateful as If It Were My Last Day

When I hear from people all over the world, that makes me happy. It will be just that day when I want to quit. I know we're talking about success, but I think we all have had a moment when we wanted to throw in the towel and say, *I'm done.* On those days, I will get an email, a text, or a post from someone that read my book. And they say, as a result, I was able to do X. Sometimes I forget. I will have had my head down, doing the work, just doing what is in my heart. And to hear from people who maybe years ago read something, and they're just now responding to say thank you, that makes me happy. It makes me think, *Okay, it looks like we'll live to fight another day!*

I have a lot to be thankful for, and I intentionally cultivate gratitude in my life. I started a little note in my journal entitled, "If this was the last day on Earth, what would I do today?" I am grateful for being healthy. I'm grateful for living in the greatest country in the world. I'm grateful for being a father and husband. Then I think about all the people who have impacted my life and who I get to serve every single day. I'm just grateful that I can serve in love from a place of gratitude, not need or desperation.

I think, after 20 years of doing this work, I'm going to continue to always live as if today were the last day.

Find speaker, author, and coach Simon T. Bailey on LinkedIn and Instagram. If you haven't yet, make sure to pick up and read a copy of *Shift Your Brilliance.* Visit IgnitethePowerofWomen.com to access a six-week course and a one-year, free, impact plan on how to really operationalize the book in your life.
SimonTBailey.com

Tweetable: Success doesn't just happen; it's doing those things that others will not do.

DEREK DOMBECK

From Small Town Construction Worker to Multi-Million Dollar Lender

Derek Dombeck is a real estate investor who loves creative deal structuring, lending, and educating entrepreneurs through his masterminds, real estate conference, and speaking engagements. Through thousands of transactions, with his wife Tracy and three children by his side, Derek has set himself apart through his love for helping people achieve success.

Just a Small Town Guy

It is an honor to help people change their lives with the knowledge I gained after losing so much.

I was born and raised in a small Midwestern town in Wisconsin in a blue collar, tight-knit family with loving parents, a brother, and a sister. When I graduated high school and received my PHD (public high school diploma), I went to work for the same company that my dad worked for in the construction trade. I learned quickly that a good work ethic could take me far in this world.

At age 21, I bought my first house with 20 acres of land, remodeled it, and made it my personal home. This was my first taste of using my construction skills to create equity.

I did not start investing in real estate until a few years later. I had zero education in how money works—until a multi-level financial services company approached my wife Tracy and me and showed us a glimpse of what our future could hold. That company was not the answer for us, but real estate was.

In October 2003, Tracy and I started our first acquisition company. We built our real estate portfolio like most people—buying fixer-upper rental houses and holding them long-term for cash flow. We were able to do this with extraordinarily little money out of our pockets because we had excellent credit and good jobs, so the banks would give us the purchase price, rehab money, and even more than that if the appraised values were good. The banks were also allowing us to get after-repair value appraisals to do these deals. This allowed us to build up a $4 million portfolio of 19 doors in three years. Some properties were in our home state of Wisconsin, the rest were in Florida, and they were managed by experts, *allegedly*.

I thought we were geniuses!

A Storm Is Brewing

While we were building our real estate portfolio, Tracy and I realized that we could not have kids naturally. In November 2005, we started an IVF process to have our first child. Our oldest, Makenna, was born in September 2006.

Soon after Makenna was born, we started to see the real estate markets turning. The challenge was, because the banks owned us, we had no control over our business. As we saw the market turn, there was nothing we could do regarding our finances. Banking relationships we had developed went away as employees were escorted out and banks were shut down. We were just a file to the banks, which was a huge, huge lesson.

We saw a very negative change in our income, but we went into two more rounds of IVF to try and have another child anyway. Both of those attempts failed and drained all our available cash.

2007 through 2010 was financially devastating. Our real estate portfolio had plummeted 75% in value, and we were officially financially destroyed.

We did everything we could to flip properties to make chunks of cash to pay off creditors. Ultimately, we took on a partner and used that partner's credit while doing 50/50 split deals. While we were struggling financially, I was still working a full-time job and running the real estate company every night and weekend. This was to the detriment of my marriage and my relationship with my young daughter. I barely saw my family while they were awake.

During that time, my father retired from the construction industry. He was six months into retirement when he was diagnosed with cancer. In the midst of multiple foreclosures against us, losing our property portfolio, and being unable to grow our family, my father lost his four-year battle with cancer and passed away. I lost my hero when I was 32 years old.

The main lesson my father taught me was: Always finish what you start, be true to your word, and never quit. By God, I was not going to let him down.

Whatever It Takes

Tracy and I never gave up the hope of building our family, and in August 2010, we started the adoption process for Robbie, who was named after my father Robert. We ended up using a private lender to secure the money needed to pay for Robbie's international adoption from China, because there was not a bank in the world that would touch us or give us a loan. That process took until February 20, 2012, our Gotcha Day, as it's called in the adoption world. This was our first taste of what was possible when we dealt with people instead of institutions. I had no idea this would shape our future in business.

During the years of negotiating with my banks and creditors, I noticed a trend. I was apparently the only person who was not blaming the rest of the world for my problems, and I got really good at relating to and helping other homeowners that were going through similar financial struggles. I sought out the most intelligent mentors I could find to learn alternative methods to buy or control real estate without using banks, and I became exceptionally good at it. However, I was still limited in the amount of cash I had available. I had not yet learned to leverage the power of building a network, until I met Jeff.

We met Jeff, our current business partner, in January 2013 while he was hosting a real estate investors association group in Green Bay, Wisconsin. Five months later, we started our first company together, and that is when I started to learn that lending itself is a great business. Jeff had never used a bank to fund any of his investment deals and only dealt with private individuals that he cultivated long-term relationships with. From 2013 through 2015, we were flipping properties while we continued to raise more and more private capital. It got to the point where we had more money than deals, so we started doing a little bit of lending on a small scale, maybe two or three loans a month.

Tracy and I were back on top of the world. So, in August 2017, we brought home a beautiful newborn baby girl from the state of Georgia. Lexi's adoption took less than one year, and God blessed us once again.

The Secret Sauce

Since meeting Jeff, Tracy and I embraced building a network of other successful real estate investors across the country. As we grew those relationships, opportunities opened for us to start and host our first mastermind, REI Circle of Trust, which was established with friends on an invitation-only basis. Shortly thereafter, we joined a second mastermind group. The immediate change in our lives that we experienced was mind-blowing. Tracy and I were educated on the process of building a vision for our personal lives, and after we had that piece designed, we changed our vision for our business. Most people work extremely hard to build a thriving business only to let their personal lives and relationships suffer. They lie to themselves and say things like, *I just want my family to have nice things,* or *Once I make enough money, I will be able to work less.* We focus instead on first living your vision for your personal life and then building a business to fit into the time you have left per week, and not the other way around. Try to imagine only working 5 to 15 hours per week while spending the rest of your days with your spouse, kids, and friends, working out, traveling, or doing volunteer work. That is the life we strive for every day now, and it is wonderful!

Two months after we added the goal of expanding our REI Circle of Trust to our vision, we were given the opportunity to take over an established real estate conference that we had attended for seven straight years. The Generations of Wealth conference was born and the REI Circle of Trust grew to three groups. It almost seemed like magic, but it was 100% because we had written it down in a document that we read daily.

As adults, expanding our minds can be hard. Most of us filter our dreams with negative thoughts like, *I do not have enough time or money.* After we got our heads right, Jeff and I made the decision to focus on growing our lending company. The dollar amounts that we wrote down for annual loan originations seemed impossible at the time. Now that dollar amount is a fraction of what we currently achieve.

As we have built our relationships and credibility with our investors, we have increased our lending business to an average of 25 loans a month only using private capital and without falling under the control of a bank or any other institution.

The returns that our investors receive have changed many of their lives.

We continue to help change the lives of distressed homeowners by creatively structuring our acquisitions to benefit all parties involved.

The business owners that we educate get to avoid the pitfalls we experienced.

Tracy and I have built a beautiful family with children from around the globe.

None of this would have been possible if we had quit trying and not finished what we started. There is not a day that goes by that I do not thank

GOD for everything I have been blessed with because of what we lost. As my father instilled in me, always finish what you start, be true to your word, and never quit.

Derek Dombeck co-owns a private lending company called Best REI Funding (BestREIFunding.com), a national mastermind group called REI Circle of Trust (REICOT.com), and an annual advanced strategies and networking conference for RE investors called Generations of Wealth Voyage (GOWVOYAGE.com). Contact him at Derek@BestREIFunding.com or on Facebook and LinkedIn.

 Tweetable: You only lose in life if you quit trying.

ROBIN BINKLEY

Set Apart and
Living on Mission

Robin Binkley is a wife, mother, former long-term care administrator, podcaster, real estate investor, and syndicator. She is passionate about sharing what she has learned in investing and helping others reach their potential. She can help you take the next step in your journey to financial freedom.

In the Blink of an Eye, Your Life Can Change

February 16, 2022, was a typical Wednesday morning. At 9:45 am, I was driving home and needed to stop for gas. I've lived in the same community in Houston for 30 years but had never stopped at this particular gas station just two miles from my house.

I put the car in park and pulled my credit card out. I left my phone and purse in the car and put the credit card in the machine. I opened the gas tank and turned back to get the gas nozzle and then there was a man with a gun at my waist. He said, "Give me everything you've got and give me your car!"

I actually turned around, thinking he was talking to someone behind me. But no one was there.

I heard a voice very clearly say to me, *He will shoot you*, and I could feel where in my body.

Again, but with anger and a louder voice, the man said, "Give me everything you have and give me your car."

I had my keys in my hand and I threw them down and ran. It was flight instinct that kicked in. I ran towards the convenience store and looked back briefly. The thief was working to get my car started. Our eyes locked. I opened the door of the convenience store and was hysterical, crying, and barely making any sense to the man inside.

Then, again, I heard a voice say, *Don't go in the store, he will shoot you.*

I immediately turned and began to run towards the street while the thief drove off in my car.

As I was running, crying, and screaming along the trafficked road, no one glanced up from their cars to acknowledge I needed help. I was in a sea of people, yet I felt alone and helpless. I encountered two men walking. They were the only people who offered to help me. The two men, in a moment, understood between my tears and heavy breathing that my car, purse, and phone had been stolen, and they flagged down a police car at the intersection.

As I recounted my story to the police officers, I was shaking and crying. I had no recollection of phone numbers except my husband's. A Hispanic lady approached me and lent me her phone. I called and sent text messages to my husband not realizing they were translated into Spanish.

I felt terrified, alone, stranded, helpless, and broke. I had no way to call for help, no mode of transportation to flee. I was dependent on the kindness of strangers. It was the people I least expected who helped me, and I will never forget this.

The police officers flew into action and left looking for the armed thief. After repeated calls, my husband called me back and he and my daughter were onsite within 15 minutes.

My daughter Kirsten had, just three weeks earlier, been onboarded as Chief of Staff of my real estate investment business, and with her assistance, we shut down my credit cards, bank accounts, and other accounts.

Following this frightening incident, I was afraid to be alone. I was jumpy every time I saw a black shirt or sweatshirt or if anyone walked up unexpectedly beside me. I would close my eyes at night and so clearly see the gunman's face.

As I began to connect with people and share my story, I realized I was connecting with people so differently. I heard stories of tragedy, and I felt a connection on a sensory level, a knowing of fear and terror, an odd bond of sorts with the people who opened up to me.

I realized I had been given a chance to reset. I had been given a gift of time with an unspecified end date. Time: the most precious commodity. There are only so many hours in a day, month, a year. You cannot recreate the past, and you cannot foretell the future, but I do control my now.

This incident was an epiphany, my intersection in life. I feel stronger, bolder, and on mission. I no longer waste my days or my moments. In fact, just the opposite. I work tirelessly, pouring myself into my business and doing the things I have "talked" about, working my goals and declaring what's next. I'm just pressing in and seeing where it takes me.

This year, in 2022, I have worked on a couple of syndication projects with my husband and business partner, Brett Binkley: a multifamily, 200-

door apartment complex outside of Atlanta, Georgia, and a Bitcoin mining fund. Additionally, I started a podcast and joined a couple of mastermind groups where I am being mentored by world-class thought and industry leaders. My husband has been a constant encouragement in all of these different lines of business. The power of unlocking dreams and taking action has transformed and propelled me.

I feel true passion to mentor women towards financial literacy and education. I want women to feel confident to make financial and investment decisions, and most importantly, TAKE ACTION. I have emerged on fire with drive. I recognize my life was spared for a reason and I don't want to waste any bit of it.

Dear Younger Me

I was born in Lakeland, Florida, in 1969 and have one sister named Tamara. I was raised in a very traditional family, including two parents who remained married for 39 years—just one month shy of 40 years when my mom passed away in 2005. I was raised Southern Baptist, and we attended church three times a week and then some. God and faith were very much part of my upbringing. We moved a little due to my dad's role in the military, his graduating college when I was five, and the relocation of his job in the farm credit industry.

When I was 15, my mom was diagnosed with rheumatoid arthritis and our family dynamic drastically changed. Her condition was so severe that she was bedridden for many months at a time and she was taking very strong medications that deconditioned her immune system and muscles, resulting in other health problems over the next 25 years.

I had to grow up rather quickly and do things you take for granted from a parent, such as shopping at the grocery store, cooking, cleaning, and doing laundry. This caused me to feel angry, worried, and helpless. I had so many other compounding feelings. It took some time and maturity to work through all of this. Periodically, I still recognize something in myself that dates back to that season that I need to work through. My dad worked while my sister and I were in school. My mom would do what she could when she could, but it was very hard on her and hard on each of us to watch her suffer in pain.

I met my husband, Brett, while in college at Texas State University, and we dated for six years. At the age of 24, we married, and by 26, I had my first child, Ashton. During this time, I started working in a nursing home as a social worker, and I fell in love with geriatrics. I developed a desire to help those who didn't have a voice or a family. I eventually moved into a role in healthcare administration as a Nursing Home Administrator where I worked for 24 years.

Eventually, we added two more babies to our growing family, and we ended up with three amazing girls, Ashton, Kirsten, and Jordan. My husband would often say he was a "minority in a sorority" in our home. During these years, we were investing in real estate by traditional means, thinking this was a way to really grow wealth for our family.

Rewire

Throughout my 24 years in healthcare administration, I worked in a couple of different nursing facilities, and I even opened a new facility from the ground up. The stress of a job that never stopped was extremely taxing on me mentally and physically. It was 24/7 and beyond. I felt robotic and exhausted.

Throughout the years, there were a lot of peaks and valleys in my home life. When my marriage was in a difficult spot, neither my husband nor I had given our marriage the time, energy, and nurturing a marriage needs to thrive over time. Busy and in survival mode, working and raising three girls, we were passing ships. We both decided to work through our hurts and forgive one another—no easy task. You have to pivot and be willing to change, and that includes forgiving yourself and others. Three years of tough self work and "dating" my husband resulted in my falling madly, passionately in love all over again with the same, but different man.

About five years ago, I resigned from my healthcare administrator position and had the privilege of devoting my time and energy to only my family. Though present in body in previous years, my mind was often elsewhere as I was always on the phone solving issues and grievances. Being able to focus 100% of my time on my family was such a blessing I cherish.

At this time, Brett and I had been investing in real estate financially and educationally, and we were finally able to put into practice what we read about in *Rich Dad Poor Dad* by Robert Kiyosaki. We learned the differences in the cash flow quadrants and realized which quadrant we were in and where we wanted to move. This was a rewiring moment that began the momentum in our investing. Throughout the next couple of years, we bought a commercial building, a couple of self-storage facilities, and several single-family homes. We were involved in lifestyle investing, international markets, and developments.

Though I had not worked as a nursing home administrator in more than five years, I continued to renew my license, just in case. In May 2022, by choice, I did not renew. My backup is no longer this former profession, but that of real estate investing and syndicating.

Proximity

Two years ago, after attending a goal setting retreat, I had to take a really hard look in the mirror. I had to evaluate my friendship circles. Did they have drive, vision, and ambition? Were they working on self-improvement?

In a lifetime full of people, I felt alone. Yet, I still had deeply meaningful relationships.

I have learned that you become the sum total of the five closest people you surround yourself with. I have been actively working to surround myself with people who have goals, mission, vision, and who are harnessing that to help others. People who are *investing*. I am hanging out with people who not only work on self improvement but also take massive action.

In the last few years, I have done a complete 180, and I look forward to what is ahead. Where do all the other relationships in my life fit? Certainly, keep your friends close but strive for more and seek out those who build you up and support where your mind is growing.

Be Who You Are Becoming

To be a successful entrepreneur, I need to learn about it, do it, and continuously improve. I actively attend seminars, engage mentors, take action, and am a part of several mastermind groups. Most importantly, I am doing my part to change my thinking, broaden my mind, and put myself in settings where education and entrepreneurship collide. This creates a cocktail for the best version of myself. I am continuously refining this. What you put in is what comes out.

I heard this idea in church: you'll never fulfill your calling if you do not have the courage to be set apart. If you have the right belief, it affects your behavior. This may mean saying no to the good to usher in the great.

We are called to a strategic location for a significant purpose, and I believe my purpose is to give back and pour into the lives of others. I am passionate about sharing with others how they can create streams of passive income, create generational wealth beyond themselves, and implement tax strategies for any financial opportunity. I am working to educate my adult children regarding financial stewardship and investing beyond themselves.

I love to empower women with the financial education they need to live the lives they choose. "To whom much is given much is required" (Luke 12:48). We are responsible for what we have, and we are to use our gifts, talents, and resources to glorify God and help others. This takes courage to be set apart and to take action. Today, my calling requires me to live on a mission.

God is not done with me yet, and I imagine there is a lot more refinement and chiseling that is to occur. I am excited about the people and places along my path that will help me transform.

Robin Binkley is a wife, mother, podcaster, real estate investor, and syndicator. To connect and learn more about real estate investing, passive income, and generational wealth, email NextLevel@realequityip.com or visit Realequityip.com, Ladieskickinassets.com, or RobinBinkley.com.

Tweetable: It is never too late to usher your God-given dreams into reality. This is what matters, that you work on your dreams and help someone else with theirs.

STEVE NABITY

Heading West
How to Buck the System and
Bring Your Next Idea Alive

Steve Nabity is a serial entrepreneur who has launched eight-figure companies from scratch. Steve creates high-performing teams to do the unexpected. He is also champion of the unexpected in his personal life, ranking 10th in the world for the Ironman Triathlon ages 60 to 64 and winning his division in the Ironman South American Championship.

It Started with a Fail

Quilts. I knew nothing about them, but there I was working a trade show booth with our team at the 2006 International Quilt Show in Dallas, Texas. Some of our staff at AccuCut suspected our hand-operated die cutting machine, popular with teachers and scrapbookers for cutting paper, would be a big hit in the quilt market. By the looks of it that day, they were right.

After just a couple of hours, our booth was full of people waiting to order product. With a big smile on my face, I cruised through the crowd to talk with them. Many were getting restless, so I created a handful of on-the-spot "ice cream number tags" and handed them out. "Take a number for fast service," I announced like a circus barker.

One woman stepped toward me and asked a technical quilting question related to our machine. Smiling inwardly, I thought to myself that this was just like a contract we had won several years before. At that time, I hadn't the slightest idea what a telecommunications wire harness was, but I "faked it" in my proposal, believing I could figure it out. We won that contract, and we did figure out how to make the part and make it well.

I looked that quilter in the eye and began implementing my "fake it till you make it" protocol. Two sentences in, she scowled and jabbed her finger toward my face.

"I see by your name tag that you are the CEO of this company. And I can tell you don't know *anything* about quilting. We are not scrapbookers. We are quilters. You should be ashamed of yourself for pretending."

In this case, it appeared faking it till we made it would not work.

A Gut Punch and a Gut Feeling

In spite of our apparent lack of quilting knowledge, we sold an unbelievable number of die cutting machines that day. After the show, I hopped on a plane to fly home, tail between my legs as I thought about the woman's words. I was happy to have flight time to think. I felt sick about the reality she had forced me to face. But, I kept thinking, if *that* many people would come to our booth and wait *that* long, there had to be an opportunity.

The quilters' passion was shockingly strong. The woman who chewed me out was a case in point. And if there was one truth I learned at the show, it was that as much as quilters love designing and sewing projects, they just as passionately *hate* cutting.

The cutting process takes away some of their joy. It is the most grueling, time-consuming, unfulfilling part of making a quilt. If only we could help them solve that dreaded problem. Before I left the plane, I had decided. In spite of the shame of being "outed" at the booth, there was indeed a great opportunity there, and I needed to learn everything I could about quilting.

Just as with the wire harnesses, I was convinced we could figure it out. I felt it in my gut. So did my team. But would that be enough to ensure our success?

All we could do was start running toward the goal. The success of any entrepreneurial effort begins with getting up every morning and taking action.

So, we ran.

"Heading West" in the Face of Adversity

With a sense of hopeful anticipation after the trade show, we returned to our Nebraska manufacturing plant and engaged the services of a highly recommended Dallas brand consulting firm. We would use information from Dallas and Chicago focus groups to design a machine customized for quilters. I would split the company in two—one branch to manage die cutting paper for schools, churches, and daycares and one branch catering to fabric and quilters.

To our dismay, the report was not what we expected. It indicated no market interest in a new die cutting product for quilting, and the consultants recommended we discontinue our efforts.

Another moment of truth. Should I believe the data—or my gut? In the end, the team decided together to fly in the face of all the negatives and "head west" anyway. This became our motto: "Head West!" Any time we felt discouraged or unsure about what was to come, we looked at each other and said, "It's okay —we're heading west anyway!"

Like explorers Lewis and Clark, we were energized by the idea of discovering what was over the next hill. We didn't have all the answers, but we figured we were smart enough to figure them out on the way. No one else was doing this in quilting—there was a clear market opening. In addition, all this was going on during the 2007/2008 financial crisis and many companies were leaving the market rather than launching new products, widening that opening.

There would be no other time like this to launch a disruptive product "no one wanted" that the experts told us wouldn't succeed.

Many successful new products began this way. Years ago, when carbon paper customers were asked if they'd like a copy machine, they said no—they would really like a carbon paper pack with five layers instead of three. But when they got the machine, they were overjoyed. The manufacturers ignored their customers, listened to their gut, created the machine, and the rest is history.

Getting to Work: Creating a New Product Category

My embarrassment at the quilt show reminded me of how 13-year-old me felt when he didn't make the eighth-grade football team. As I pedaled furiously and tearfully home from the field that day, my humiliation became fuel for a new, God-given determination that would last the rest of my life. I became the kind of person who isn't about to let detractors stop me. I went on to be a competitive athlete the next year and throughout college. I still am.

When I was in my late 50s, I got the itch to not only complete an Ironman Triathlon but to race in the Ironman World Championship in Kona, Hawaii, by the time I was 80. I worked hard and made it to Hawaii in my second year of competing, in spite of my age and some medical challenges. Not only that, I went on to win the Ironman South American Championship and was ranked 10th in the world in my age bracket.

I love living life this way because lessons learned along the way create immeasurable growth worth the effort of overcoming the challenges.

Hearing that professional consultants thought a die cutting machine for quilters was a bad idea tapped into my built-in determination and spurred me and the team on. Yes, some days we wondered if we'd done the right thing. But we all had the same gut feeling that we were on the brink of something special.

So... we invested millions of dollars in the product launch to give it the best chance of succeeding. Sometimes a powerful combination of conviction and confidence trumps any negative assessment or obstacle in your way.

Fighting to explore and progress like Lewis and Clark made me and my quilting product team smarter and more resilient. It gave us the nimbleness to change course quickly while maintaining our vision. With every new day, we moved further down the road, achieved small wins, and received more positive feedback. It became more and more apparent that, yes, this was indeed something worth going after.

We really buckled down and researched our market. We hired quilters to teach us, and we learned everything we could about their pain point and how we might solve it. We talked with hundreds of customers and quilting experts, tested products, attended more shows, made many quilts ourselves, and cross-referenced the successes and failures of similar products. We spent days, weeks, and months learning, preparing, and positioning our product.

The result was a quilting product no competitor could touch because we knew quilters so well. I have to admit, the day we noticed our first die cutting competitor in the quilting market, my heart sank. But, at the same time, it fed the fire in my belly. Competition can be daunting for anyone, even a crazy-competitive man like me, but as a team, we learned to welcome it because competition made us better—more humble, appreciative, innovative, and reliable.

Over the years, we beat back multiple competitors. It made us tough, and in the end, most of them left the market because they couldn't match the strong connection we had to the quilting customer. The more competitors we faced, the stronger and bolder we became.

I knew my unnamed disbeliever at that first show would be proud of us. In the end, adversity was our best motivation. We used it to our advantage. When we got knocked down, our response was to get up and start running again—to change how we did things and forge a path to the win. We are living proof that the power of feelings, such as embarrassment, frustration, and loss, can be transformed into *determination*.

Building a High-Performing Team

Ultimately, I hired a new CEO and got out of the way. She drew on the strengths and expertise of our excellent team members, and it all came together into something very special.

When you're heading into the unknown, one of the most important steps is to build a high-performing team. You should always insist on team members who match your culture and passion—who have the same burning desire to win. A certain type of personality can't wait to explore like Lewis and Clark and discover new things. The worst thing you can do is hire someone who is very smart but doesn't fit your culture, because it will be like a cancer eroding your good health.

Once you've populated your team with the right people, communicate your vision, lay out goals and expectations, help your team develop. Then, give them meaningful incentives and step away, letting them take ownership as you all "head west" toward your collective vision.

We did the work, learned the lessons, and didn't give up. In December 2021, we sold the company to a private equity firm.

The team and I looked back in amazement. We had created a number-one brand in fabric cutting, a product that experts told us nobody wanted, during a financial crisis, all because an unnamed quilter decided to chew me out and I was determined not to lose.

What if she hadn't said anything? I'm convinced we wouldn't have been as passionate. We might have lazily approached this market without the level of determination it took to achieve success.

Lessons Learned: Buck the System, Start Running

I know not every entrepreneur will find a product opening like the one we found in the quilt industry or have the guts to spend millions on something everyone tells them won't work.

But our story offers lessons for just about any entrepreneur, in any industry, with any product:

- Believe in yourself
- Look for inspiration in unexpected places
- Don't always listen to the "experts"
- Listen to your gut
- Let adversity motivate you
- Move in where everyone else is moving out
- Let competition make you better
- Build high-performing teams
- Never give up

Overall, building businesses is about managing risk. At AccuQuilt, we learned the hard way how to do this and always kept moving toward our vision. Now, I love sharing my business and life story, so others don't have to learn the hard way.

Over the course of my career, I built more than a dozen companies and learned truly valuable lessons from both successes and failures. Today, I work in syndicated real estate investing, showing others how to achieve passive income, save on taxes, increase wealth, and diversify their portfolios. When people realize they can do this while working at their regular jobs, their eyes light up the same way mine did when I saw potential in the quilting market.

I love leading others to that feeling. Great things happen when you believe in yourself, change your mindset if necessary, and keep heading west—for your family, for your future.

I have to humbly thank the woman who chewed me out at the quilt market. If only I knew her name and how to reach her, I could thank her and let her know how much she meant to the formation and success of AccuQuilt. You never know where inspiration will come from. The key to turning it into something tangible is recognizing it and doing something about it. Don't ignore inspiration when it hits you. It's there for a reason.

If you want to earn passive income, save on taxes, and diversify your portfolio—all while doing your day job—contact Steve Nabity of Skyline Point Capital for speaking engagements on real estate investing and overcoming obstacles in business and life.
Email: steve.nabity@skylinepointcapital.com
LinkedIn: Steve Nabity

Tweetable: Has an "expert" told you your idea won't work? They might not be right. Do the work and go with your gut. Steve Nabity's wildly successful company was built in the wake of naysayers.

RANDY HUBBS

Follow Your Passion, Pursue Your Why, Live Your Dream

Randy Hubbs is a real estate broker/owner, investor, and fund manager. He and his wife Jana have 71 years of experience in education and 90 years in real estate investing. As co-founders of Legacy Investors.US, they are using their unique skill sets to help others with their mission to **solve the special needs housing crisis in the US**.

Finding My Path

I grew up in Richland, Washington, one of three towns that make up the Tri-Cities and home to the Hanford nuclear project. It was one of two facilities built for the purpose of developing the atomic bomb in 1943 under the code name "The Manhattan Project."

The demographic of the area consisted of scientists, technicians, engineers, and skilled tradesmen and women. There was a huge emphasis on us boomer kids to "go to school, get good grades, and go to college so you get a good job like a doctor or lawyer." Scientist or engineer was also part of the local narrative.

My love for music showed up early in my childhood. I listened to music anytime it was playing and followed the traditional route through the school music band programs until high school. I quit after one year due to my unmotivating band director who seemed to hate his job. Fortunately, I was already a member of the Columbians Drum & Bugle Corps which elevated my interest in music.

Even though I loved music, I was also good in math and science and, because of the attitude in the area, was destined to become an engineer so I could work on the Hanford project and make the big bucks.

Pursuing My Passion

I loved being a part of the drum corps and made great advancements as a musician, ultimately landing the coveted position of drum major. This allowed me to discover a new love for teaching music! The drum corps is also where I met Jana, my wonderful wife of 41 years.

After graduating high school, I entered Columbia Basin College (CBC) to pursue my degree in engineering. Spring quarter, I visited the university everyone recommended I attend for mechanical engineering. After touring their department and campus, I was disappointed and began to doubt whether I had chosen the right career.

When I was venting to my girlfriend, she interrupted me, saying, "You don't seem all that excited about engineering, so why don't you change your major to music because that's what you love?"

That hit me like a ton of bricks.

The following week, I visited Central Washington University's campus, fell in love with the place and the vibe, and never looked back!

My poor experience in my high school band inspired me to become a great band director. I swore to myself that I would never be the cause of anyone not wanting to pursue music if that was their desire.

Pursuing My Career While Discovering the Power of Real Estate Investing

I graduated from college in the fall of 1978 and returned home to the Tri-Cities working as a substitute teacher in music. I also worked side jobs with my friend Warren whose father owned a flooring store. One day, Warren told me that he was going to buy his aunt's house, fix it up, and sell it for a profit. The term flipping had not been invented yet nor were many doing it. Warren asked if I wanted to move in and help him. I jumped at the chance to get out of my parents' house and participate in my first flip.

I wasn't unfamiliar with real estate. My grandmother owned a hotel when I was young and owned several rental properties. My parents also had a couple of rental properties but were less enthusiastic about them and often were taken advantage of by their tenants. In addition, Jana's father was a Realtor who owned several rental properties. We didn't yet know how important these experiences would be in establishing our real estate education.

In the fall of 1979, I landed my first teaching job in the Tri-Cities at Pasco High School. I was 22 years old, only four years older than my students in the senior class.

Jana and I were getting serious in our relationship and had several discussions about how we were passionate about our careers but didn't want to retire on a teacher's salary. Once I started my new job, I reached out to her father about finding me a house to flip. Within one month of starting my job, I closed on a small two-bedroom home that needed significant work.

That first year of teaching kept me busy learning the ropes and getting established, so I let the house sit vacant until the following summer. Once school ended, Jana and I strapped on our tool belts and spent the entire summer remodeling.

Young and naive, we were unaware that existing home sales were on the decline in the rest of the country. The Tri-Cities market was still booming but by fall, the crash caught up to us and we witnessed several people we looked up to get completely crushed. It was a lesson that helped us formulate our future investment philosophy.

Stepping Stone

Jana and I were married in June of 1981 and lived in that house for two years. We were able to keep it as a rental and purchase a larger home to live in and immediately realized the benefit of extra cash flow. We purchased two more rental homes over the next couple of years.

We continued to put our main focus on our careers. Jana taught life skills at Kennewick High School for three years. This was a class designed for special needs students to transition out of school and live independently. We didn't know it at the time, but this would later become the focus of our legacy project. Jana was so successful in this position, she was recruited into an administrative position that later evolved into her becoming the Director of Special Education for the Pasco School District.

I taught at the high school for eight years and had a leading edge due to my drum corps experience. I have to give credit to my sophomore class because they completely bought into what I was trying to accomplish with them. By their senior year, we were the sweepstakes winner for the King Bowl Marching Band Festival Championships and played for the Seattle Seahawks halftime show on national TV. Our jazz and concert bands were also strong, which led to many more awards in my career teaching high school, filling two huge trophy cases in the main hall outside the gymnasium.

In the fall of 1987, I earned a position as the Instrumental Music Director and Associate Professor of Music at Columbia Basin College. It was a welcome move for me. Jana was pregnant with our daughter Janelle, and the extra time requirements associated with the high school were now off my plate.

I spent 28 incredible years at CBC and loved every minute! My master's degree was in music composition, so I had the opportunity to teach Music Theory, Applied Brass, History of Jazz, and all of the bands.

Teaching at the college also allowed Jana and me to spend time with our growing family. In 1991, our son Ryan was born. We enjoyed camping, snow and water skiing, and taking our kids to the various sports and musical activities they participated in as they were growing up.

Ramping Up Our Financial Future

In 1997, we began to focus on acquiring more property. I happened to find a book on flipping houses and was completely blown away by the information it contained. It made me aware of how little we knew about real estate investing. We purchased a home, followed the guidelines in the book, and sold it for a substantial profit. We were hooked once again.

I ran back to the bookstore, excited to see what I could find on real estate investing. When I walked into Barnes & Noble, there was a huge display of the new book *Rich Dad Poor Dad* by Robert Kiyosaki. I figured the book must be pretty good if it had such an impressive display. I bought it, and like so many other people, went home and read it cover to cover.

We were already convinced that buy and hold was a smarter strategy than flipping, so we decided to use flipping as a means to gain the capital to invest in our first multi-unit property. In 2001, we closed on a five-duplex portfolio just a few blocks from our home. We loved the financing we could get with Fannie Mae and Freddie Mac and continued to buy duplexes and single-family home rentals until we hit the maximum number of properties we were allowed. By 2003, we realized that I was out of the rat race. Thank you, Robert Kiyosaki!

Surviving the 2008 Crash

We had already witnessed many ups and downs in the real estate market and were learning to pay attention to cycles. In 2007, with the purchase of our last single-family home, Jana and I hit the limit for conventional financing. It seemed like everyone was jumping into real estate investing and leveraging their properties and themselves to the hilt. Prices were steadily climbing, and people appeared to be panicking to get into the market. Jana and I decided it was time to move to the sidelines and see what we could learn about commercial multifamily investing.

September 15, 2008, on CNN, Jana and I witnessed the devastating collapse of the Lehman Brothers and the mortgage crisis being blamed for what became known as the Great Recession. We looked at each other and agreed that a great buying opportunity was about to begin.

After many hours of listening to podcasts, we decided to attend a three-day bootcamp offered by Anthony Chara of Apartment Mentors. Within six months, we closed on our first 32-unit apartment complex in Texas. More apartments followed in several different markets.

The Tribe

In the spring of 2011, Jana and I decided to spend spring break in Orlando. A few weeks before we left, The Real Estate Guys™ announced a one-day workshop called the Secrets of Successful Syndication. We had already attended their Dallas and Memphis field trips, so we knew this was going to be an event we couldn't miss.

As a real estate investor, you eventually run out of your own money, and we were nearing this point. We changed our plans, rented a car, and drove to Fort Lauderdale to see what we could learn. As the seminar finished up, we were invited to attend the welcome cocktail reception for all the "Summiteers" as they prepared to climb aboard a cruise ship for The Real Estate Guys Annual Investors Summit at Sea.

For the first time, we experienced being part of a "tribe." It looked like old home week as friends who hadn't seen each other for a year were embracing and getting caught up with each other. We were surrounded by so many successful real estate investors, entrepreneurs, and mentors—all of whom shared an abundance mindset.

Jana and I were heartbroken to be climbing onto a plane for home the following day instead of spending the week with this group of amazing people.

After attending our first "Summit" in 2012, Jana and I began exploring exit strategies from our jobs. Although we loved our careers, we also realized that our lives were taking us in an exciting new direction. It was time to put our energies towards scaling our business. I told my dean it was time to start finding my replacement. I applied for and received a sabbatical to focus on developing an online course for jazz history.

Also, during that year, I was advised by one of my close mentors, the late, great, Bob Helms, to get my real estate license so I could legally be categorized as a real estate professional by the IRS. This allowed us to capture passive losses from our portfolio. It also helped develop our brand as a broker specializing in investment housing.

The following year, I moved to a part-time position teaching my new online course from home, and Jana retired so she could work full-time on our real estate investment business. I retired the following year and we were now full-time real estate investors!

From Teaching to Syndication

I was known throughout the community as the music guy. Throughout our careers, Jana and I seldom mentioned to anyone that we were also investing in real estate, although those closest to us were well aware. Some had already invested with us. I now had to establish myself as a real estate guy in the community as did Jana.

In an effort to grow our syndication business, I joined The Syndication Mentoring Club Inner Circle. Both Robert Helms and Russell Gray were extremely helpful in guiding me through the process of reestablishing myself as a new brand in our local community. Jana and I continue to participate with this group today and have worked with our investors to raise millions of dollars for multifamily apartment buildings and luxury resort properties. I was also recently invited by Anthony Chara to be one of his gold coaches for Apartment Mentors.

Creating a Legacy

People often ask Jana and me how we like retirement. In reality, we're still working, but we're doing our life's work and living our legacy. We wake up each day with a mission and a sense of purpose. Our elder mentors and those we admire appear to live a much longer and happier life because they have a sense of purpose, and we hope the same will be true for us. We get to choose what we want to do, and how and when we do it. We also have the financial wherewithal to do so.

Today, we are immersed in our legacy project, solving the special needs housing crisis in the US. This is our big, hairy, audacious goal (BHAG).

Specifically, this population is composed of physically and developmentally disabled children and adults. In other words, those who were identified for and went through special education programs in school.

We refer to this as a crisis because today's market rents make it completely unaffordable for individuals to team up and rent a place on their own. Most all efforts to solve this problem have been through the creation of nonprofit organizations. This model doesn't work because of money limitations. Every city in every state has a long waiting list for people who need housing. Some of these people have to wait as long as 15 to 20 years to get placement, if they ever get it.

We have designed a "for-profit" model that outperforms standard monthly rental housing. This model presents a unique opportunity for real estate investors to create a portfolio as well as for parents and guardians who wish to provide affordable housing for their loved ones.

Everyone knows someone from this population group. This model creates an opportunity to create a portfolio and make a positive social impact in the community. Our 45 years of experience in real estate investing, combined professional teaching backgrounds, as well as Jana's special education knowledge, make us uniquely qualified to guide those who are interested through this process of creating these unique and vital properties.

Jana and I are very excited about the future. We feel that we've gone full circle. We followed our "why" from the start by going into teaching so we could make a positive impact on students. Determining your why comes from the heart, not the brain, which is why many people look back on life with regret. I thank God I followed my heart.

With their extensive backgrounds in real estate investing and teaching, Randy Hubbs and his wife Jana help others learn how to become financially free through real estate.

To get a free copy of their eBook: *Solving the Special Needs Housing Crisis in the US*, contact: Randy@legacyinvestors.us or visit www.legacyinvestors.us.

Tweetable: Follow your heart, pursue your passion, and live your dream. By doing so, you will have the freedom and ability to leave a lasting legacy.

CRAIG MOODY

Find Your Why!
From Depression to Obsession

Craig Moody is a serial entrepreneur, bestselling author, podcaster, and business coach. Craig built and sold a contracting business and is a student of leadership programs offered by Darren Hardy, John Maxwell, and Kyle Wilson. Craig and his wife enjoy supporting Northern Arizona University Athletics, boating, camping, and encouraging their three kids.

A Way Out

Over my 20 years of personal growth and development, I have invested tens if not hundreds of thousands of dollars in business education. Early in this newfound love, I would sign up for conferences, buy books, take notes, and try programs. And when I really liked the speaker or author and wanted to emulate their teachings, I would try and do too much. I would get home and have a list of 18 things to work on. Ultimately, I would get frustrated and not work on anything.

I flew to the East Coast dozens of times for seminars, conferences, meetings, and more. Drinking from a fire hose, I had to learn to stay focused.

One day, on a flight to Florida, I asked myself, *Why am I doing this? My business is stagnant. I am not putting in the necessary time and energy to receive results from these seminars. It's just too much.* So I told myself, *Just bring back one thing—one good thing that I know will make myself and my business better.* From that weekend on, I adapted that motto. *What is the one thing that will make my world better?*

The Beginning

In 2003, I bought into a contracting franchise: just myself, a briefcase, and a dream. Ten years later, I exited the franchise system and started my own brand. In 2021, I sold that business. From 2003 to 2021, I had gone from just myself to as many as 25 employees, from just one vehicle to 15 vehicles and three trailers, from one computer to 13, and so on.

That entire time, deep, deep down, there was a little, tiny piece of me, a voice, screaming out that this was all a lie, that truly, I was a phony. I gave this voice a name, Satan. It probably was him; I don't know. For several years, I believed myself a failure. A phony, a fraud.

Work hard, save everything you can, and probably even then it won't be enough. Don't get your hopes up, don't go for your dreams, because you will be disappointed.

Yes, self-doubt and risk avoidance owned me. I thought it was just me. I needed help but was too scared to admit it. I believed only psychos went to therapy. And I was no psycho.

About 12 years into the business, I was fortunate enough to have put together a good management team. One day, we were discussing an issue, and the conversation kept coming back to me being the reason for this issue. I could not wrap my head around it. Finally, one of my managers said, "Craig, maybe this is just part of your ADHD."

I said, "Excuse me, ADHD? You're saying I have ADHD?" I went home and told my wife, "My team says I have ADHD. Can you believe it?"

She laughed and said, "Yeah, everybody knows it but you, Craig!"

Strength in Numbers

I was blessed to have an amazing mastermind group, an informal board of directors, if you will. After telling them my dark days story repeatedly, one of them said, "Craig, your childhood and early 20s has often come up through the years, and I believe you suffer from PTSD." Post-traumatic stress disorder. It was an amazing realization.

By the way, my retired military friends who work with rehabilitating soldiers, are lobbying to get rid of the D in PTSD. Because if 51% of us have dealt with PTSD, then it is no longer a disorder. It's the norm. When my past pain was given a name, I could recognize it, categorize it, deal with it, bury it, almost all of it. Satan tries to remind me that the old Craig is the real Craig. *Nope. No way!*

Once I admitted I had a problem, sought help, and forgave myself, that is when I started to flourish and make positive gains in my life. I was no longer living for myself; I had a family to lead. Inspired by King David, I prayed for the knowledge to be the best leader possible. I prayed for wisdom, knowledge, and energy to be a better husband, a better father, a better friend, and a better employer.

Good People

One day, during one of my mastermind meetings, we were reviewing our current life balance and recognizing the number one issue that we each had to deal with. For one it was his relationship with his spouse, for another it was their relationship with their employees. For me, it was my health.

I remember the moment I decided I was going back to personal training. I saw success with it years earlier. I had it in the back of my head for months, if not years, but my excuses outweighed the positives.

A few weeks after I started personal training, something amazing happened. I found an old friend I had completely forgotten about. I was so embarrassed; I couldn't even remember his name. In the past, we had spent many days together and had great times and memories. Has that ever happened to you? You had a friend, and they were cool. Then they moved away, or you moved away, and then you cannot remember their name?

I started running into this friend after my workout. I worked out religiously every weekday at 5 a.m. I would see him as the sun was coming up and I was getting into my car, having just burned 500-700 calories, depending on the workout. I was like, What was his name? A few weeks later, I was like, *Oh, I remember his name! Endorphin, that's his name, Endorphin Release.*

Endorphin made me feel so good about myself and so did my trainers. I developed a relationship with most of them and won them over, like they were on my management team. Once they knew more about me and what I was trying to accomplish, they went the extra mile for me. If I lost 10 pounds in a month, they would celebrate. I believe they felt more fulfilled in their work. Developing that relationship was key.

In moments of pain and struggle, I would picture my why. Each morning, when my alarm went off at 4 a.m., I thought, *What? Wait, I just went to sleep. Do I hit the snooze button? Or do I 5-4-3-2-1 feet on the floor?* The voice of Hal Elrod, the author of *The Miracle Morning*, was shouting at me in my mind.

Ok, just get to the toothbrush, toothpaste on, and sit on the tub and brush those teeth. I want to see Endorphin today. He makes me feel so good about myself. Then I'd have two dogs fighting over my free hand for good morning affection. Then I was getting dressed in my workout clothes quietly in the dark, trying not to wake my wife. Then the dogs would remind me it was snack time. Next, I was listening to daily scripture on my headphones, drinking my coffee I prepared the night before. *I can't wait to see Endorphin today. He is a great enthusiast; he makes me feel so good about myself.*

The Fruits of My Labor

Eighteen months after I made up my mind, I was 50 pounds down. For those of you who are like I was and are already dismissing this as fluff that won't work for you, hear me out. Several years later, after all the joy of now living a healthy life, I realized something. There was something harder than changing my daily habits, putting in the work, and becoming a student of health. Curly said it in the movie *City Slickers*: What is the one thing? Finding my why was the one thing.

The excuses are endless, but the why is for real. For those struggling with health, find your why! Ask yourself, why do I want to do this? Just study on your why, then start. When you feel like giving up, think of your why. It was much harder to find my why than it was to lose the weight. Losing the weight was the easy part. Finding my why, admitting I work better with accountability, swallowing my pride, and stepping on that scale in front of my trainer once a month with a goal in mind, was much, much, much easier than eliminating the excuses, and changing my bad habits.

Exercise without food control will not work. You must make your diet part of your why. There are hundreds of diets out there. You need to find one that works for you. I tried several, but Keto was the one I got to stick.

I am a huge fan of Brian Buffini, owner of the largest coaching and training program for Realtors in North America. He has a mantra he often repeats on his podcast, "The power of a made-up mind." I would say that to myself every time I felt weak. When I wanted to eat dessert or something that was not Keto, like chips, beer, or my favorite Mexican food, I thought of my why and said to myself, *I have the "power of a made-up mind."*

My knees thanked me. I started sleeping much better, like, all night without waking up. I eventually started waking up naturally around 3:55 a.m., right before my alarm went off. I was so happy to start my day. Thirty minutes of prayer and devotion, 15 minutes of meditation, then off to work out. I would return home and read or write.

The results were so amazing. I learned to wakesurf. Skiing was much more enjoyable. Mountain biking has always been among my favorites. I began road biking, walking the dogs, hunting, and hiking steep mountains. I was not out of breath any longer. The one thing I did NOT do was tell people that I was trying to lose weight. I let them tell me. I never posted it on social media because life is about cycles and change. Just because I lost it, does not mean I won't gain it all back.

Don't Go Alone

Good personal trainers are amazing. They don't see a fat blob walking through the door. They see a project whose life is going to change. And, in the end, seeing six-pack abs doesn't drive them, seeing a complete personality, demeanor, and lifestyle change, and happier families does.

Everything improved as I began my journey to lose weight, most importantly, my relationships with my wife, kids, employees, and friends. I was five times more productive. My business revenue increased by $2.3 million over the next few years. The endorphin release from daily exercise is so important in my daily life. I almost remember what it was like to be a kid again.

I often see my old self in others. Holding onto pain, mistakes, self-doubt, and self-sabotage—reliving a dark past that almost everyone else has forgotten about or never knew existed—it's truly only a story you're telling yourself.

I never dreamed of being a contractor. Since selling that business, I have focused on my dream of coaching, speaking, and writing. Recently, I began a podcast that focuses on assisting small business entrepreneurs and leaders in Northern Arizona.

I have also been fortunate enough to help my daughter with her new business and my oldest son with his post-military music and professional careers. I have much more freedom and more time to focus on my why, my strength, and my routine.

Please, forgive yourself for your past. Leave it there. I had to. Only look forward. Fix what needs to be fixed, surround yourself with good people, distance yourself from the negative, never stop learning, study the greatest leaders and motivational teachers in the world, and find your why!

You can email Craig Moody at craig@thebizclimb.com. For business coaching and mentoring, podcasting, social media, his skin care company, or to view Craig's books, please visit craigmoody.co.

Tweetable: When you feel like giving up, think of your why. It was much harder to find my why than it was to lose the weight.

APRIL MARLEWSKI-HUDZINSKI

Built for More
Entrepreneur, Investor, Mentor, Mom...
and Still Evolving

April Marlewski-Hudzinski is a professional real estate and business investor whose mission is to educate and empower others. She leads national mastermind groups and coaches those wishing to next level their life. She hosts a weekly podcast and is a believer in good karma.

Feeling Stuck

Have you ever felt like you were built for more? As if there was way more available in this life than you were tapping into? I have.

In 2010, I was newly married. We had just purchased our first home, a duplex, and I was working my way up in my career. But something felt off.

I knew I needed a change, but didn't know what.

I began mulling on where my life was going and what I truly wanted. When I looked to the future, I felt uninspired. I craved more depth and wanted to feel like I was living life on purpose instead of just marking time. I wanted to have more time freedom, to raise a family intentionally, and to thrive in a fulfilling career that made an impact on people's lives.

Cast Vision—Set Your Intention

After seeking advice from those who seemed to have their life figured out, I set my sights on becoming my own boss and creating streams of passive income. I hadn't owned a business, nor did I know where to begin looking for passive income, but that didn't stop me. I knew that if I wanted a change in my life's trajectory, it was up to me to make it happen.

I looked at what I already knew and my skill set and dove in. My father was a DJ, and I had worked at radio stations, so starting a mobile DJ business seemed like a logical first step.

I spent my nights and weekends building the business and was quickly reaping the benefits of having a side hustle. Soon my weekends were filled with weddings, and I realized I had a problem—I had created extra income but was robbing myself of time freedom. Armed with the knowledge of starting my first business, I set out to try again, this time on a larger scale.

Learn From Those Ahead of You

Growing up in a tourist town, I spent many summers bartending. Much like Tom Cruise in *Cocktail*, I fell in love with the energy of a well-run establishment. I had never managed, nor owned a bar… but felt called to go for it.

What better way to prepare to open a bar than to tour the drinking state of Wisconsin bar hopping?! My husband Tony and I spent the next year meeting with bar owners and doing market research (which consisted of going to bars and taking notes over a drink or three), and eventually, we began the process of deciding where and exactly how to open a bar.

Along the way, I received a piece of advice that eventually would alter my trajectory even more: Don't rent a bar, own your own building. After searching the state for the perfect location to begin our new adventure, my husband and I found a cute, old building in the center of a sleepy downtown. It had multiple tenants, one being a bar, and it was for sale! It was run down, smelled awful, and felt perfect.

The Business Was a Huge Success!

We regularly hit capacity and often had a line down the road of patrons waiting to come in and tear it up. I was living a dream—hosting a party every day, being self-reliant, and enjoying the time flexibility and abundance that came with being an entrepreneur.

Simultaneously, since we had purchased the building where our bar business operated, we technically had started two businesses, the second being the mixed-use building that our bar business rented space from. This began our path of being commercial real estate investors, which years later, we've grown into a thriving investment business.

I'm Making What?!

Five years later, I had built multiple successful businesses, including the bar and DJ business, an ATM route, real estate investments, and I had reignited my past profession of life coaching. I had built an incredible team and grown leaps and bounds as an entrepreneur, but I found myself feeling resistance once again. I had two young children and was struggling to find balance.

Late one night, I was analyzing the financials of two of my businesses—one being a rental property with multiple commercial and residential units and the other being the bar business. As I reviewed the numbers, I received a wake-up call. I was making almost the same from the rental property as I was from my bar business! I hadn't considered myself a real estate investor—just a girl who had a few rentals. But there it was. I was generating as much from a building that required little attention as I was from the business that called for a significant amount of my time. That was a game-changer!

That realization changed my trajectory. I quickly began educating myself on real estate and investing, going back to the goal I had set before I even opened the DJ business: create passive income. As a parent with little ones at home vying for my time, the concept of not having to exchange time for money made my mouth water!

I spent the next year recalibrating my businesses so I could focus more on investing and being strategic with my time (and money), and eventually decided to sell the bar business so I could grow more quickly. By this point, I was actively coaching other budding entrepreneurs and teaching business bootcamp courses at a large university. I was growing my real estate portfolio and had embarked on my next chapter of life—a chapter geared toward living a more intentional life: a healthier lifestyle, more presence with my young children, greater focus on investing, and becoming more strategic with my time and priorities.

A Hole in the Ground. And in My Heart.

You never know when those life-changing days will come. On July 10, 2018, an explosion ripped apart our downtown.

That property that nudged me into recalibrating my businesses and life... a gas line was hit and the building filled up with gas. It exploded.

The aftermath was something out of a nightmare. I recall watching the whole thing unfold on national news. Shock and then trauma set in. Life was lost. My tenants had nowhere to live. The businesses that operated there were gone, including three of my own. Properties, including two of my buildings, were destroyed.

Picking up the pieces was a slow journey. As I navigated the unthinkable, I grew considerably in my business experience, but the lessons went far beyond business.

What Will Your Story Be?

Not long after that shocking night, I had my third child. The combination of working to replace significant lost income, navigating the aftermath of the explosion, and having a new baby put me over the edge. I found myself in a dark place and was diagnosed with postpartum depression, anxiety, and PTSD.

I felt like I was in a hole, unable to climb out or see the light. Thankfully, I had the support of a loving husband, who sat me down and said, "I need you to take care of yourself."

I had been so busy caring for my family and businesses that taking care of myself hadn't been a priority. I was in a deep fog, and that realization triggered a spark. I realized I had a choice—to recalibrate my whole life or allow this dark place to be how my story ended. Thankfully, a stubborn voice inside was not okay with the latter.

When you ask yourself, *What will my story be?*, the question allows you to gain perspective on what's important and what you wish to create with your time here on Earth. I knew that whatever I set my sights on could be achieved if I stayed focused and surrounded myself with people who were a few steps ahead of me on the journey.

Truly Taking Life to the Next Level

Since 2018, I've been on a journey to heal. The powerful lesson I had to embrace was **when you take care of yourself, everything else becomes easier**. Healing hasn't been easy. In fact, turning inward and really diving into personal growth and self-care has been far more challenging than I thought possible. But, as I've learned about and tried new things, I've experienced incredible growth, and as a result, I've watched my life and businesses thrive.

I set aside inhibitions and tried unconventional healing techniques beyond western medicine. I met people who were very different from me, yet we were all on a similar path—to feel more alive and enjoy life. Through my healing process, I've curated a collection of tools to rely on when I'm feeling overwhelmed, when I experience fear of failure or inadequacy, or when the stories in my head begin to overpower the purpose I'm working toward. I openly share those tools with my coaching clients and on a weekly podcast as a way to help others.

Cheers to Good Karma

Getting "sick" pushed me to assess and recalibrate my life. I found that time freedom, being of service, and living intentionally were most important to me. Armed with these values, I set out to create a life where self-care and being present took priority.

After significant time dedicated to healing my mind, healing my heart, and rebuilding my businesses, I found myself reflecting on my experience. I realized one of the greatest gifts I had during a difficult season of life was time freedom and abundance thanks to my investments and passive income streams. I developed a firm belief that if others had that same gift, their lives would feel easier, allowing them to live a more full and happy life. I felt so strongly about this that I set out to help others in the best way I knew how.

Using my background in personal development and project management, I launched **Paradigm U**. Paradigm U offers education and empowerment through group and individual coaching programs as well as retreats and monthly masterminds, all geared to help you live intentionally, grow your mind, expand your paradigms, and enhance your life.

As a real estate investor with a heart for teaching, I wanted to create an opportunity for people interested in investing in real estate but unsure how to start. I created **Good Karma Capital** to help people build wealth using the same processes I have used to create passive income streams—those same income streams that allowed me to step away from obligations and dedicate time to healing when I needed it.

Paradigm U and Good Karma Capital are designed to help you create a life that impresses you—that lights you up and brings out your best.

These days, when I'm not leading a mastermind or overseeing our investment properties, I spend much of my time mentoring others who find themselves wanting more from life.

I have three kids that have the gift of parents who are free to be intentionally present and who model how to create and manage businesses that offer time freedom. From giving me flexibility to coach my kid's sports teams and chaperone field trips to traveling our beautiful planet, being self-employed has offered my family incredible gifts, *and I will forever advocate for others to explore the same opportunity.*

April Marlewski-Hudzinski hosts a weekly podcast, leads national masterminds, and offers coaching to new entrepreneurs. She's an active investor and offers investment opportunities to create passive income through Good Karma Capital.

To learn more about April Marlewski-Hudzinski, visit: www.ParadigmU.com.

Tweetable: Accelerate your success by learning from others. Those who inspire you will be happy to help. Rising tides raise ALL ships. Take the leap and build your wings on the way. Cheers to good karma!

GREG JUNGE

How You Can Change Your Habits and Become UNSTOPPABLE

Greg Junge is a full-time investor, focusing on buying and selling businesses and several different niches in real estate. He was a full-time Realtor® for six years and today is also a #1 bestselling author in Success Habits of Super Achievers, *a life-long personal development student, and a health enthusiast.*

Success Is Trusting the Process

Success! That is the result everyone wants when setting goals. But both successful and unsuccessful people often set the same goals—so what makes some thrive where others fail? Earn money? Travel more? Lose weight? I have found that creating positive, long-lasting habits allows you to achieve the goals you set!

I used to think that achieving my weight loss goal was best accomplished by using willpower, toughing it out, or doing without. As a former fat guy who is no longer fat, I can attest that these approaches didn't work for me. And I know they haven't worked for a lot of others as well.

I became a real estate investor in 2012, met my wife Mandy in 2013, and left my W-2 cubicle job in 2015 to become a full-time Realtor®. That was a fun, but busy time in my life. Juggling investing, a blossoming relationship, and a new career was challenging. My habits and routines helped me accomplish many financial and business goals that I set for myself, but this came at the expense of my health.

In the summer of 2019, I started learning about personal development and mindset. Before then, I dismissed both and didn't think I needed them to maintain my success. Boy, was I wrong!

That summer, I started surrounding myself with people who consumed personal development content often, had a positive mindset, and attended events where other like-minded people gathered. They seemed to be happier, more successful, and more optimistic about life. Could this correlation be something more than a coincidence? I was curious.

Change Is About to Occur

In January 2020, Mandy and I attended The Real Estate Guys Create Your Future™ Goal Setting Retreat. My life truly changed when I heard Robert Helms ask, "Are you interested or are you committed?"

This felt like a gut punch. I knew I had to be brutally honest and ask myself some tough questions. I realized that when it came to weight loss, I was just interested; I wasn't committed. After this event, I committed to learning about nutrition, working out more, and not allowing myself to make any excuses, no matter what!

How Can I Optimize My New Environment?

When COVID-19 hit in March 2020, my days went from going out to client lunches and happy hours to the confines of my house. I embraced this change knowing a different environment can create life-changing habits. This was definitely the case for me.

When I stopped eating out, I adopted new, healthy eating habits at home. This was a game-changer. I raised my standards and leveled up my diet and nutrition.

I dropped some pounds, but more importantly, I was studying and learning habits, systems, and the importance of raising my standards. Once I saw and felt the results of my clothes fitting better, I wanted to continue and increase my efforts. Systems and processes drive results. Standards set the level of quality of your habits and your results.

Mindset Is Powerful, Even Through Tragedy

In May 2020, my father passed away. It was devastating. He and I had a very close relationship. He was the patriarch of my family and he was loved by so many in his community.

When someone close to you passes away, it makes you reflect on many things: the life of that person, the impact they had on you and others, the memories you created together, the great conversations you had, the personality traits you share, and your own mortality.

In my head, I had always labeled him as "Dad," but I realized after he passed that he was also a great friend and mentor who led by example. It took him passing for me to realize just how much impact he had on me and my life.

I could have easily gone back to my unhealthy eating habits after such a loss. Emotional eating is a real thing, and I've engaged in this activity in the past. But this time, I stayed on track.

How? I was so set in my new routines and habits that it didn't even occur to me that indulging in unhealthy food was an option. Looking back, my mindset had changed. I stayed the course that I set for myself, even on a subconscious level, during this really tough time.

Get to the Hospital

I was cruising along with my healthy habits in place, my systems were firing on all cylinders, and my standards were pretty high, or so I thought. In my mind, I had achieved my weight loss goal and all was well. Boy, was I wrong!

One day in April 2021, I felt a dull but constant pain in my stomach and thought, *Hmm, what's going on here?*

After a trip to urgent care and a visit from my naturopathic doctor, I was told that it was likely either my appendix or diverticulitis. Either way, I was told to get to the hospital right away. These are never words you want to hear!

I was hoping it was my appendix, which I would have had removed and continued on my way. But I was told I had diverticulitis. Today, I'm thankful that it was because this diagnosis opened the door to the next journey that changed my life.

The way I describe it, diverticulitis occurred because I wasn't eating enough fiber, which caused issues with my digestive system. I knew in the back of my mind that when I went back home, I was going to commit to (not be interested in) raising my standards to an even higher level regarding my diet and nutrition. I was optimistic and confident that I had the right mindset and people in my life to overcome this health challenge.

Avoiding Pain and Running Towards Pleasure

In the hospital, I wanted to avoid as much pain as I could, but the severity of my diagnosis was out of my control.

Motivation comes in many forms.

Fear can be a great motivator; I'd be lying if I said that I wasn't experiencing fear in the hospital. I was afraid of something that I didn't know much about, diverticulitis. *Is my case severe? How seriously will this impact my life?*

When I asked doctors at the hospital how I could correct this illness, they kept talking about surgery. I didn't want to exclude surgery as an option, but I knew that this was diet related and that it could likely be fixed with changing my eating and nutrition habits.

I asked every medical professional that came into my hospital room, "Can diet be an effective tool to get my health back on track?"

They all said, "I don't really know. Maybe."

Success is also a great motivator. Once I found out that my case was relatively mild, I eliminated my fearful thoughts and started focusing on success. It was like a game that I was playing, and now I knew how to win!

I started to ask better questions and thought, *Who? Who do I know that is way smarter than me when it comes to diet, nutrition, and the human body? Who is in my network that has this knowledge and is willing to help me?*

I didn't have to think very long.

Enter my dear friend Dr. Amy Novotny. She's a physical therapist and breathing coach, and that's just the tip of the iceberg when it comes to her talents. She has become my trusted health counsel.

The very next day, after my hospital release, Amy and I were on a call talking about my situation, diet and nutrition, and what next steps I should take. While she's not a gastroenterologist, she seemed to know more about diverticulitis than the doctors at the hospital. It goes to show, wisdom and education are two different things.

Amy confirmed that diet and nutrition would absolutely help me get back on track and optimize my health. She was confident and confirmed my belief with science and her experience that diet and nutrition could reverse my mild case of diverticulitis. She believes in fixing the root cause of the issue, not just the symptoms. I wholeheartedly agreed with her approach and knew I had the right doctor in my corner. Thank you, Dr. Amy, for your continued honesty, expert guidance, and friendship!

After our chat, I rushed out the door to my local health food store and came back with fruits, veggies, and vitamins. If it was on Amy's list, I bought it. I just knew this was the change I needed to make, which included going to a plant-based diet.

I decided to put my health before anything else.

How can I turn a mild case of this illness into a strength? How can I make this a turning point in my life? How can I further optimize my health?

I use this word *optimize* a lot. I was tired of being average, or more accurately, below average. I wanted to, and continue to, optimize and make the most out of my health every day.

From this moment forward, I dove into learning as much as I could about how to best optimize my health and nutrition. I never thought I'd voluntarily learn about the biology of the body, but it's fascinating to me because it's so complex and yet so simple.

I adopted the mentality that I should be playing the long game and the short game when it came to my diet and nutrition. Sure, pizza tastes great, but for how long? Five or ten minutes? Afterward, I would physically feel bad and I'd mentally beat myself up for making a bad dietary choice. Now, I think of both the short-term and long-term effects of the food that I eat. *Will this food make me feel great now AND be good for my longevity?*

I'm not saying that plant-based is the best diet for everyone, but it works for me. Each person is different, so you have to find what works best for you based on your desired results.

For me, diet and nutrition was a lot of trial and error, and it still is. *Let me try this food or technique. How does it make me feel? Is it healthy? How can I turn this into a daily positive habit?*

As I learn about diet and nutrition, I give myself permission to change my views and opinions, as long as they're based in science. I also listen to my body because it's pretty smart and is the first to know when something doesn't feel right.

Committing to the Process and Not Caring About the End Result

I had to get my mindset right before seeing results. The first step was committing to the process and not giving up, no matter what. I didn't allow myself to make any excuses.

Now, I focus on the process: the habits I create, the systems I put in place and continually adjust, and the standards I set and can raise anytime I want. I am in control. This is the fun part! Eating healthy, getting in movement and exercise every day, meditation, and breathing are my foundational habits. These habits are non-negotiable items on my daily checklist. If I do everything right in my process, the results will show up. They have to!

My old way of setting a goal was, "I'd like to lose 50 pounds." That's not a bad goal, but it's really just a wish. Plus, it looks very intimidating. Fifty pounds, yikes! It has no plan behind it, and it leaves a lot of room to make excuses.

Knowing what I know now, I solely focus on the process and get specific. "My goal is to work out five days a week and eat 30 different types of fruits and veggies every week." I'd then come up with a plan of attack by asking myself questions: *How am I going to track this process? What types of workouts am I going to do?*

Change Your Mindset, Change Your Habits, Change Your Life

Today, Mandy and I are on our health journey together. We offer each other support and share what we learn about nutrition, health, and habits. This allows us to work together to achieve all our goals and continue to focus on the processes.

I share my story to help others struggling with their diet, nutrition, and habits. I want to pay forward what I've learned so others can realize that they too can achieve their goals by changing their mindset, embracing education, and creating the right habits.

I've become a person who knows that I can overcome any obstacle and achieve every goal I set for myself. This fact alone makes me very happy and proud of who I've become and what lies ahead.

> *"Happiness comes not from what you get but who you become."*
> — *Jim Rohn*

Connect with Greg Junge to learn more about his story, investing in real estate and cash flowing businesses, and habits, health, and nutrition:
Greg@sevenfigurecapital.com
www.SevenFigureCapital.com

Tweetable: I've become a person who knows that I can overcome any obstacle and achieve every goal I set for myself.

J. TREVOR MILES

Across the Miles
A Passage Through Time

J. Trevor Miles is a serial entrepreneur whose love of business and geopolitics is superseded only by his love of country, family, and the great outdoors. Trevor's passions and experiences are quite diverse and have spanned multiple disciplines. He is now the founder of Bragga Occidental Capital Group, a private firm serving a small family office.

In the Beginning

Life for me began in a typical "Leave It to Beaver" suburb of southeastern Pennsylvania. My father worked two jobs, leaving home well before sunrise and returning home late, just before bedtime. My mother, heralding from humbled nobility, was surprisingly quite successful at being a stay-at-home mom. With her "Breakfast at Tiffany's" beehive hairstyle, pointed heels, and tightly buckled waistline, she mastered all the customary trappings of the 1960s household and managed our little, nuclear, family home like a Renaissance chateau.

My role as firstborn was much easier—basically, mowing the grass, bathing the dog, cleaning the gutters, and delivering my father's dinner to him each evening as a precondition to getting a bicycle. My free time would otherwise be spent engineering the coolest hidden forts and treehouses, exploring the deepest parts of the nearby forests, and cajoling every pet shop owner within the lower Delaware River Basin to carry my line of frogs, salamanders, and crayfish sourced fresh from the neighboring creek. (Upon the sale of the family residence 20 odd years later, remnants of escaped inventory could still be found throughout the house.)

Irreconcilable differences eventually took hold, and my parents decided it best to separate. My mother, with two small children in tow and one small suitcase each in hand, left everything behind and caught a turbo-prop plane back to the tropical Caribbean Crown colony of Belize, then known as British Honduras. Belize, an on-again, off-again love child of the United Kingdom for over 200 years, remained unchanged, in a vacuum, untouched by the elements of time and the modern world.

My mother, sister, and I settled into a shared room under the roof and protection of her brother and his young family. Streets in the old bay colony were dusty, and the old colonial homes, masterpieces in their own right, were desperately in need of paint and basic maintenance. Electrical blackouts were all too common, and homework was learned alongside the shadowy, flickering flames of kerosene lanterns. At the end of each day, town residents would quickly bathe, enjoy a light evening meal appropriately called "tea," then hurriedly sit by the radio and tune in to the BBC's soap opera broadcast "the Colgate special." Who in Belize could ever forget the intriguing tales of the illustrious Dr. Paul?

I quickly adapted to almost everything in Belize. Hand-pumping water from tall, wood-staved vats, English comic books, Smarties candies, and sports like rugby and cricket were all strangely foreign to me but not as strange, feared, and foreign as the Roman Catholic Church. The Catholic nuns were notorious for their creative forms of corporal punishment, and I can attest that I, a by-product of the US public school system, mastered them all. Many a night, I lay in bed, plantation-style windows and doors wide open, pondering the fact that I was destined for hell because I was not a Catholic.

Daylight, however, always arrived, and with the new dawn, I was gone. Like buccaneers before me, I learned to hunt, trap, and fish the jungle rivers and estuaries and to sail, dive, and spear the coral reefs and atolls. Some of the best bushmen and marine captains in the country taught me life lessons I believe have benefited me tremendously.

We eventually moved to a remote jungle fishing lodge which we would ultimately end up acquiring. Every evening as the sun set behind darkened palms and the smell of sweet pipe tobacco filled the air, I would sit on the porch and listen to stories, laughter, and conversations by the likes of Ed Dodd, Chauncey Loomis, Lefty Kreh, Hemmingway (the son), and a hodgepodge of lawyers, politicians, and captains of industry like Aldrich, Dillard, Johnson & Johnson, Procter & Gamble, Gerber, and so many more. Belize was their hidden playground after the fall of Cuba, and they enjoyed keeping it that way. It was a simple time when men were men, and their handshakes were their word. I was taught to respect privacy, never to discuss business unless it was first initiated, and then, to be brief and unobtrusive.

By the time television arrived in Belize shortly after independence in 1981, I had already crisscrossed the four corners of Belize. I spent the next few years of my life swashbuckling through most of Central America, the southern United States, and the Eastern Seaboard from upstate New York to the southernmost point of Key West. I came into my own during this time and tapped into an inner peace that has stayed with me to today. Travel is an excellent educator. It removes blinders, encourages tolerance, and forces you to question everything.

By age 19, I was beginning to realize that I wanted more out of life. On the porch one night, a nonagenarian war veteran leaned over towards me, eyes gleaming through his toughened exterior, and said, "Son, the world is your oyster! It's great to travel and to enjoy all the niceties that life has to offer, but it is extremely important that you do the things NOW that are necessary to get the things you want in the future." I took his words to heart and soon thereafter met a dark-eyed, dark-haired divorcee with three little girls. We've been together since, over 35 years.

Taking the Helm

Immediately, I realized that I needed consistent cash flow. The odd job or idea to carry me over peaks and valleys would no longer suffice. I've never been keen on working for others, so I started to look for a unique opportunity in Belize that I could call my own. The Internet and cell phones were yet to be invented, and Belize, being an end of the Earth, needed to source everything from abroad. I became a trusted, go-to source for ideas for both the public and private sectors and was able to find and deliver whatever goods and services were needed. I had a tremendous relationship with the US Embassy, and they had an incredible library that no one ever used. The old Thomas Registers became my closest allies, and business grew.

Still, I needed more and set out to find another niche. People in Belize were still painting on the wall by hand, and graphic artists were almost non-existent. I took a leap of faith, leveraged all we had to obtain a huge loan, and imported all the equipment to run a successful modern-day sign shop, the first of its kind for Belize. The gamble paid off, and we were busy! Every sign, banner, decal, graphic, awning, license plate, or traffic sign in Belize was made by us. We handled political conventions. We worked with the government. We worked with foreign advertising firms and launched a series of rental billboards throughout the country. As word spread, we eventually began supplying wholesale raw materials to the nearby Mexican states of Quintana Roo and the Yucatán.

The years quickly passed through various leads and lags, and in time, the first set of kids grew up and moved away for school or marriage. The answer to empty nest syndrome was to have three more children, and no, they are certainly not cheaper by the dozen! We've been extremely lucky when it comes to children. All are highly independent, competitive, and successful in their own right. The three older girls have gone on to become incredible wives and mothers, two of whom operate their own businesses.

I on the other hand remained unsettled and continued to want more, perpetually leveraging all we had to expand our portfolio and product offerings. Belize is a small country with a small population, and it's next to impossible to live on just one income. We expanded our businesses to include marine freight services between Belize, Honduras, and Guatemala, a commercial hard hat diving operation, crane and rigging services, construction and engineering, agriculture and aquaculture, fine flavored chocolate, housing, rental properties, and real estate development, not to mention maintaining our core businesses of signs and light tackle fishing. As long as my life insurance was paid up, I had the blessing from home to take on the world!

By 2006, we had parlayed our investments enough to secure a nine-figure mortgage, and we set about recruiting a core commercial real estate development team. The list of extremely talented team members read like a who's who in the development world. The first question anyone asked was, "How in the world did you ever put together such an incredible team?" The goal was to build a new, master-planned community for Belize: a residential, destination resort complete with world-class golf, a full-scale marina, club-style living, and all the amenities you would expect.

By October 2007, however, we received a call from our bank. It would be impossible to proceed as planned. They were not entirely sure what was coming down the pipeline; all they could tell us was that it would be bad. We let everyone finish their contracts, paid them in full for their services, and mothballed the development. Surely, we were out a lot, but not as much as we would have been if we had been a year early and had accepted all the funds. The glass is always half full... never half empty.

The years thereafter became a time of study and reflection. I immersed myself in the teachings of Lee Kuan Yew, G. Edward Griffin, Jim Rickards, Victor Davis Hanson, and so many others and finally accepted a voluntary position on the board of governors at one of the most prestigious schools in

Belize, an offer I had turned down several times due to time constraints. It was a great board, and collectively we worked late into the night to make sure the school was internationally competitive and sustainable. Additionally, we were able to ensure that students had a one-in-three chance of obtaining a full scholarship to top tertiary-level institutions within the United States, something previously unheard of in Belize.

Closer to home, we used this time to simplify our lives. We sold off a few businesses and marginal assets, stabilized returns for stakeholders, built a few homes, and spent much more time together as a family. The girls, now coming of age, traveled with me countrywide and into some of the most remote Mayan villages existing to help identify fertile lands and trees. They fondly remember listening to the Mayan villagers talking amongst themselves in their native tongue, jumping off waterfalls into deep river pools, seeing extremely large poisonous snakes, dancing to Garifuna drums, and dining with the village Alcalde eating "caldo soup" out of calabash gourds.

The quality of life is exceptionally high in Belize! I've always maintained that you must keep a place in the country and a place at the Caye and have the ways and means to get to both. Anything else should be considered an investment. The COVID-19 pandemic would soon put this theory to the test.

Stormy Seas

We began following the news of the virus in January 2020 after my return from a quick jaunt in Medellín, Colombia. My daughter was pursuing her degree in the Netherlands, and we were overly concerned about her safety. We stocked up on supplies well in advance when no one else was buying and outlined an action plan that my daughter would implement should things continue to escalate. The day her plane touched down in Atlanta was the very same day the US closed all flights from Europe. Thank you, Chris Martenson, and the team over at Peak Prosperity for all the hard work, time, and dedication you provide in bringing relevant facts and research information to your readers.

The scourge continued to circumnavigate the globe. Our son was now a front-line physician in the US and in the thick of it all. Concerned, we discussed the virus and its ramifications in great detail. I gave him the option of coming home where it would be safe and before the borders closed. He shot my suggestion down immediately stating, "Dad, how could I ever abandon what I am doing here?" Nothing more had to be said. We all understood. It was little comfort to two concerned parents, but from birth, we've always known he was called to a much higher purpose.

Eventually, Belize closed its borders. All cash flow stopped: no guests, no reservations, no sales, no orders, no showings, and no commissions. Tenants lost their jobs and rental incomes waned. We circled the wagons and realized that absent someone needing urgent medical care, we could survive in Belize. For how long? Indefinitely!

My early childhood training re-emerged. We could source fresh fish, conch, shrimp, and lobster from the reefs and rivers, and we could hunt a plethora of game meats and exotic fruits from the jungle. Decades of land banking paid off, and we had an overabundance of clean, cool water from deep underground. On the surface, we had chickens, eggs, turkeys, geese, pigs, and ducks, and a host of tropical fruits, nuts, and vegetables. We armored our immune systems with citrus, turmeric, garlic, ginger, lemongrass, spinach, and Cuban oregano which we imbibed daily like clockwork and made quarts upon quarts of thick, rich elderberry elixir. Everything was grown on the farm by our own hands.

With the entire country shut down and no real work schedules to speak of, we spent the bulk of our time at the farm or at the Caye fending for ourselves and our staff... all of whom we kept on without any governmental assistance. Resilience prevailed, and as my youngest daughter will attest, farm life, sun, salt water, good food, and fresh air are all excellent therapeutics.

Distant Horizons

Today, I find myself pondering the basics of grasses and topsoil as much as I do the complexities of modern-day economics. I was weaned on *Mother Earth News* magazine and have always maintained a greater-than-average interest in agriculture, alternative energies, recycling, distilling, green technologies, biofuels, and carbon. These interests have taken me to great places; I expect they will some more.

Well-informed erudites have forecasted the next nine years to be a time of unraveling, upheaval, destruction, and chaos. This will likely prove true, but it will also be a time of tremendous opportunity! Wealth will be exchanged, and a new financial system will be introduced. This will make way for the next cycle. A time of peace, prosperity, and creativity.

My efforts have now somewhat shifted from incessant hunting to planning, growing, and preservation—becoming the indelible conduit linking the last generation with the next, making sure both are adequately cared for yet vehemently capable of carrying a family legacy and generational wealth forward.

There is no better way to next level your life!

If living or doing business in Belize is on your immediate horizon, you can reach out to J. Trevor Miles at:
Email: trevormiles@braggacapital.com.

Tweetable: Travel is an excellent educator. It removes blinders, encourages tolerance, and forces you to question everything.

RONNIE SHALEV, MD

How I Became a Financially Retired ER Physician

Dr. Ronnie Shalev is a board-certified emergency physician, real estate investor, and entrepreneur. She is the co-founder of Shalwin Properties and has built a real estate portfolio of over 5,100 units with $178M in assets under management. She has been featured in Business Insider, MarketWatch, The American Reporter, *and multiple podcasts.*

Freedom at Last

As I walked out of the hospital that morning, I looked up at the rising sun and felt finally free. Ripping off my P100 respirator and taking off my white coat, I knew I had worn them both for the last time.

That last night shift in the ER was horrendous. I was one physician taking care of an endless sea of patients, nonstop ambulances, and by the way, *everyone* had COVID. I was on the other end of the shift, and this time it was for good. As I put away my weathered stethoscope, a weight lifted off my chest.

My name is Ronnie Shalev, and I'm a financially retired ER physician.

How It Started

My story began like many others: my entire life, I dreamed of becoming a physician. I wanted to help people. Science and biology fascinated me. I loved the human body and all its mysteries. I knew that I would be a great advocate for my patients and someone that could make a difference in so many people's lives. My goal was to have a highly-valued job that offered great financial stability and flexibility.

After years of staying home studying through nights and weekends while my friends partied, sacrificing college summer breaks and my social life, I made it to medical school. My dream finally came true. I was going to be a doctor. I just had to drink from the firehose of the medical curriculum and trust the process that would shape me into the doctor I would become.

When it came to selecting a specialty, I was very analytical. I knew I wanted flexibility in my schedule and didn't want to be tied to a pager or summoned to the hospital on my days off. I wanted clear boundaries.

I wanted to know when I would be working. As an ER doc, you know when you are on and when you are off. On the flip side, you work nights, weekends, and holidays, which seemed like a fair trade. I also knew I loved procedures and taking care of many different illnesses and patients. Emergency medicine seemed like a no-brainer.

Rocking ER Life

At first, it was a thrill to help people with whatever problems they had—heart attacks, stab wounds, sprained ankles, you name it—and I was really good at it! I was known as the doctor who could diagnose even the rarest conditions with the vaguest symptoms. I was also known as having a "dark cloud," meaning the worst tragedies and bizarre conditions would show up when I was working. It was a tough job, but I handled it well.

As time went on, seeing such horrific things day in and day out became very stressful and took a toll on my emotional well-being. When you're an ER doctor, you're part of everyone's worst day. I was constantly worrying and internalizing. *Did I do the right thing? Could I have done something different? Did I miss anything critical?* Every single day, every single patient —my mind never stopped.

I remember one shift where I was alone. I was the only doctor in the entire ER with no scribe and no mid-level. It was around 10 p.m., and I was treating two stroke patients at the same time, an asthmatic patient in respiratory distress, and a patient having a heart attack. The waiting room was full—there wasn't an empty chair—and you could see the pain and frustration on the faces of the patients and their families. On top of that, there were several ambulances lined up and waiting to get checked in. I looked up at the clock to see when my relief would come... eight more hours.

The stress level was unbearable. I couldn't breathe. I was responsible for all these people. You see, the administrators had cut physician and mid-level hours, leaving only one doctor responsible for everyone in the ER.

I had no other choice. I put my head down and did what I was told. I took care of everyone at the expense of my own health. I didn't eat, drink, or pee during that shift. I got home so exhausted that I collapsed on the bed, still wearing my scrubs, and slept the rest of the day.

When I woke up, I felt like I had been hit by a truck... every muscle in my body ached. My kids wanted to go to the park and play, but I had no energy and still had to finish those 50 patient charts. They didn't understand why I was so tired and disconnected. I was trying to recover, reserve my energy, and not fall behind on charting for the next shift. My family was frustrated with my absence. They didn't know that I'd taken care of 50 sick patients that night, with ridiculously limited resources, and carrying the burden of extreme liability. I mean, how could they? It's hard to fathom…. But what else was I supposed to do?

I still hadn't physically recovered when it was time for work again. I wanted to call in sick. But doctors don't just call in sick. It's not culturally accepted. Also, there was no one to cover my shift.

I realized I was a high-paid hourly worker. I was working my "dream job," but I had no energy, freedom, or time to enjoy the life I'd built with all the money I earned. I felt exhausted, burnt out, and trapped.

I was tied to my job and told by administrators with no medical education how to practice medicine and how quickly to see patients. I felt like I was working in a factory, pushing patients through the assembly line. My administrators would display my productivity numbers every month and made sure to tell me that I could be let go if they weren't happy with my numbers.

I started to wonder why I loved this job in the first place. I said to myself, *Something has to change.*

Money Mindset Shift

It was about that time that a friend told me about real estate investing. He owned a piece of a hundred 7-Eleven locations and received a check every quarter without doing any work. He called it passive income.

I thought to myself, *This sounds like a pyramid scheme. It sounds too good to be true… and risky… like I could possibly lose all my money.* But, I was frustrated enough with what was going on at the hospital, with my administration, and with trading my health and well-being for money, that I decided to give it a shot. I thought, *Why not? The likelihood of real estate's value going to zero is almost impossible.*

My husband and I decided to start small on our first investment. We bought into our first syndication—where a group of investors form a purchasing group to buy or build properties. It's difficult for individuals to buy big, commercial properties on their own, and syndications make it possible for a group of investors to fund and invest in large real estate projects together.

We were pleasantly surprised when it worked! We started getting checks every quarter and weren't doing any additional work. I thought, *If this works once, we should try it again.* So, we tried it again. And sure enough... it worked again!

As a passive investor, I received financial distributions every quarter, finally finding a way to make recurring income without having to do anything but let my money work for me.

I could finally see that real estate investing was the solution for my future I had been searching for. Like planting seeds, growing the harvest, and eventually harvesting the crops, it was a thought-out strategy with a predictable outcome. It was not a risky strategy like playing the lottery or buying stock in a company and *hoping* that the stock shoots up overnight. I wouldn't turn into an overnight millionaire, but with this strategy, I would definitely become a millionaire in the future.

Real estate investing is a long-term strategy. I knew it would take years of repeating this strategy to get me out of my golden handcuffs. So, that's what I did. I kept looking for different opportunities in various markets and asset classes and investing where it made sense.

More Than a Doctor

Today, I've been a part of over 35 deals, and I am always looking for new ones. The money I earned from syndications freed me from my golden handcuffs. The passive income allowed me to quit my grueling emergency room job and move into a less-demanding role at a medical device company. I am no longer tied to my job. I don't have to work, I want to work at the medical device company, so I can continue to use my medical expertise to help thousands of patients.

In 2020, I decided I didn't want to just help people with their health, I wanted to help professionals with their wealth too. I saw so many miserable physicians and other healthcare professionals who were financially trapped in their jobs and feeling hopeless, and I wanted to help them reclaim their freedom and design their own lives.

During this journey, I spent hundreds of hours and thousands of dollars learning how to invest in real estate which also equipped me to help others become successful passive investors themselves. My husband and I started our own real estate investment firm, Shalwin Properties, where we team up with other investors to buy apartments together. We find the deals, get them under contract, create and execute the business plan, and eventually sell the property. The investors put their money into our deals, and we grow their wealth alongside ours.

My mission is to share my knowledge and help those who are feeling stuck earn passive income that will allow them to take back their time and enjoy a more balanced, financially-free life. I am still helping people, but instead of helping with their health emergencies, I help with their financial wellness.

Picture a day when you go to work because you want to go to work, not because you have to go to work.

Picture a day when your spouse says to you, "You seem happier, you seem healthier, and I love the freedom that we have in our lives now."

Picture a day when you can travel if you want to travel, relax if you want to relax, or serve others if you want to serve others. That's what real estate investing can do.

Dr. Ronnie Shalev's mission is to help other professionals build and protect their wealth so they can reclaim their lives and freedom. To connect with her and schedule your FREE strategy call, email her at ronnie@shalwinproperties.com, so you can start living the life you've been dreaming of today.

Tweetable: Designing your life involves thinking strategically about what you want in life, being aware of what your life is like now, and taking proactive steps to get to the next level.

MOE ROCK

Lessons from Life and Self-Help Masters Along My Journey in Media

Moe Rock is the CEO of The Los Angeles Tribune. After a storied career as a producer and investor, he took over leadership of The Tribune with the intention to redefine how people see traditional news brands. He has executive produced programs that have featured Jack Canfield, Bob Proctor, Brian Tracy, Lisa Nichols, and Bill Gates.

A Life of Synchronicity

Synchronicity is my favorite word in the English dictionary. According to Merriam-Webster, it is defined as *"the coincidental occurrence of events and especially psychic events... (such as similar thoughts in widely separated persons or a mental image of an unexpected event before it happens) that seem related but are not explained by conventional mechanisms of causality."* The word was conceived by my favorite psychiatrist of all time, Carl Jung.

As somebody that has had a curious mind, hungry for knowledge as far back as I can remember, I have studied anything and anyone that offered insight into this magnificent phenomenon called the human experience. Along this journey of life, perhaps you too have had moments that seemed written for you by a force you couldn't see. Maybe you imagined a person or situation and that very same vision manifested itself in real life. Some call these "spiritual experiences." The words that work for me are "moments of synchronicity."

Throughout my life and career, I have had many such moments, and for the sake of context in this book, I will discuss how becoming the CEO of a national legacy brand, and the opportunities that sprung from that, led to a range of synchronicities and lessons that I will share with you today.

Do you pay attention to moments of synchronicity in your life and act upon them?

A Steward, Not a CEO

Over the course of the last few years, as my partners and I took over leadership of *The Los Angeles Tribune*, I have had the honor of being featured in many different media publications. *Forbes International* called me the

"Maverick of Media," *LA Weekly* did an expose on my journey leading *The Tribune*, and I also had an opportunity to be a speaker representing *The Tribune* alongside *USA Today* in Las Vegas at a media convention.

While these experiences are always insightful and humbling, whenever I am referred to or introduced as a CEO, it is not the term I see myself identifying with most.

I see myself as a simple steward. In other words, I see *The Tribune* as an entity that is larger than any single person. It existed in 1886 and will still likely exist in 2086. It may exchange hands, philosophies, and mediums, but the name will continue long after I hang my hat and walk into the sunset. In seeing my work as something larger than myself, I am able to step outside of my ego and see the macro picture.

I wonder, do you see your business (or purpose) as something larger than any single individual? If not, what would it look like if you started to focus more on legacy and less on the desire of the self?

Changing the Status Quo

Recently, I was interviewed by a magazine that published an article titled "Moe Rock on Building a Principle-Centered Media Empire," and one of the questions asked was, *"What advice would you give to someone just starting their own business?"*

I gave the following answer: *"Ask yourself the very fundamental question, 'Is my business changing the status quo?' If the answer is yes, proceed with every fiber of your being and be relentless in your pursuits. If the answer is no, go back to the drawing board."*

This is the centerpiece of every business endeavor I participate in. Changing the status quo is nothing new for *The Los Angeles Tribune*. Its first incarnation came in 1886 from the leadership of an eccentric figure that worked both in the private and public sector, Gen. Henry Harrison Boyce, soldier, politician, and publisher. At the beginning of the 20th century, *The Tribune* was led by Edwin T. Earl, the man who invented the refrigerated boxcar which affected and changed multiple industries. Decades later, in 1941, *The Los Angeles Tribune* was published by a female African American, Hallie Almena Lomax. This was something unprecedented and historical at that time. When I think about the historical implications of being a steward of this name, I recognize the responsibility to serve with integrity and to continue changing the status quo.

We do this in many different ways, such as promoting humanitarian causes, serving the local community, creating programs that connect the general public with professionals that offer pro bono services, and dedicating an entire division to the personal development industry. I made the decision to have our community outreach division focus on creating programs that uplift, educate, and inspire the masses—all for free.

I remember growing up watching programs on PBS in the early to mid-'90s and getting familiar with the likes of Les Brown and Wayne Dyer. Ironically, these programs resonated more with me than other made-for-kids TV shows. I recognize what a great community service it was to offer these programs to people who didn't have to pay a high ticket fee to have access.

As we entered a new world with the COVID-19 pandemic, I decided to launch this division, and we began curating programs with some of the biggest names in personal development. These programs have been seen around the world and have reached dozens of countries, all for free. I am proud of the fact that we are able to offer access to the world in the modern era of media and touch lives. Through this endeavor, I have had the honor of working with legends and icons that I looked up to for years. I had no idea that Bob Proctor would make his final public appearance at an event on our network, or that we would bring Les Brown, Dr. Joe Vitale, and Denis Waitley together for the first time live on the air. I have many stories from both in front of the camera and also behind the scenes that I have accumulated, and I will share a few of the biggest lessons and takeaways here for you.

How are you changing the status quo of your industry?

What Jack Canfield Taught Me About Responsibility (And Double Checking the Calendar)

We had just secured a deal to work with The Napoleon Hill Foundation and produce a program that revolved around the principles of *Think and Grow Rich*. In brainstorming who would be a great headliner, I thought of Jack Canfield. I don't imagine that there are too many people alive today that have dedicated as much time to principles of success and also impacted as many people as Jack Canfield. In my view, he is nothing short of a legend.

My mentor, Doria Cordova, personally introduced me to Jack and vouched for me to help start a working relationship. For me, this was an honor. I grew up on the *Chicken Soup for the Soul* books and have deep roots in the work. After being introduced to one another, we decided to set up a Zoom call so that Jack and I could speak directly about working together and the premise of this project. I was excited. I was so excited that instead of marking down 2:00 p.m. on my calendar for our meeting the following day, I marked 3:00 p.m.

I was just getting ready to log on to Zoom when I saw Jack sent me an email with the following subject line: *"Moe, I'm sorry we missed each other. I am booked the rest of the day."*

I felt like I just got punched in the gut. I pride myself on professionalism and I know the importance of a first impression, and I just did a no-show with a living legend that I had looked forward to doing business with. After a few minutes of feeling sorry for myself, I realized something profound in his email: *"Moe, I'm sorry we missed each other."* Jack started off his email to me with an apology. Why would he apologize to me when clearly I was the one at fault? I was amazed that this man whom I just unintentionally blew off sent me an apology before I had a chance to send one to him.

Jack practices what he preaches. In his book *Success Principles*, he discusses the distinction between being partially responsible versus being 100% responsible for everything that happens in life.

Eventually, we reconnected, and Jack was a big hit on the program. We actually discussed this incident live on the air and had a powerful dialogue about responsibility. To this day, I think about that as an example of someone that takes complete responsibility.

How would you have responded to someone missing a meeting? Would you have pointed the finger right away and felt disrespected or taken the Jack Canfield approach?

What Les Brown Taught Me About Spirituality

Les Brown is a regular contributor to our community outreach division. He has appeared multiple times and has been a big part of many of our programs. I have had the pleasure of speaking with him on numerous occasions. But one moment that has stuck with me is when I had a chance to ask him, *"Les, you are considered one of the greatest speakers of all time. If you had to summarize what makes you so great, what would it be?"*

Les answered without skipping a beat, *"Moe, I say the same prayer every time before I speak—Less of me more of thee."* I was touched, moved, and inspired by his answer to me. The idea of letting go and getting out of our own way was so brilliantly made clear in that prayer. Since that day, I have adopted his prayer, and before every program, public appearance, or even important meeting, I tell myself, "Less of me, more of thee."

How often in life do we get in our own way?

What Dr. Joe Vitale Taught Me About the Power of Showing We Care

We recently did an event that featured Michael Beckwith, Dr. Joe Vitale, and many other names who came together to make a global impact. At the time of writing this, there is a lot going on in the world. There is an active war in Europe, questions about the economy, and a crisis in the Middle East. In the country of Iran, there have now been months of protests that have led to arrests, deaths, and chaos.

Watching so much pain in another part of the world can sometimes leave us feeling disempowered. Sometimes we think to ourselves that there's nothing we can do about it and we go about our business. To me, this is the worst choice we can make when it comes to how we respond to unfortunate world affairs.

When Dr. Vitale was on the air with me, broadcasting to 17 countries, the two of us decided to do a public address directly to the people of Iran (a country both he and I have visited before). During this address, we acknowledged the people of the country, showed that we cared, and did a Ho'oponopono (Hawaii) healing prayer for the nation. This ten minute segment of a multi-hour program was then repurposed, translated, shared and re-shared to millions of people in the country.

Both Joe and I started receiving powerful, emotional, and very deep messages from people of the country about how that prayer helped heal them and gave them some peace of mind that they had not felt in months. It was a proud moment, and it only took a few minutes for Joe and me to do that, but the reverberation effects will be felt for a long time. Simply because we decided to show that we care.

How much of your life would be different if you simply showed people you care?

What Kyle Wilson Taught Me About the Law of Attraction

How many high school students do you know that would listen to Earl Nightingale's *The Strangest Secret* over and over again? In my case, I knew one. Myself.

Looking back, I can't quite remember how I came across that audio program, but something drew me like a magnet to both Nightingale's and Brian Tracy's work. I would listen to material produced by those two men over and over again until I memorized almost every word. It would have been a dream come true to work with Earl, but unfortunately, he passed before I had the chance. I often visualized and wondered what conversations would be like or what it would feel like to have meetings with remarkable people.

And while I never had that chance with Earl Nightingale, I did, however, get a chance to work with his mentee Denis Waitley. While working with Denis on *The New Psychology of Winning* tour, which was executive produced by *The Los Angeles Tribune* and ACE Productions, a company run by my talented friend Adora Evans, it was at that event I had a chance to meet Kyle Wilson. I had respected Kyle from afar and seen him as an important figure in the history of the personal development industry. Kyle joined the lineup and also helped facilitate a powerful moment that brought Brian Tracy to the program as a major contributor.

Years ago, when I made a vision board, I had imagined sharing the stage with Brian Tracy. It would have been a dream to work with him in some capacity as he was someone I idolized and looked up to immensely. When Kyle Wilson brought him to the event, this was a manifestation of the Law of Attraction from my perspective. I had a chance to collaborate with Brian and finally get that checked off my bucket list. Kyle taught me that the law of attraction is always working, and you just never know how it will show up for you. You just have to keep believing and taking action! In my experience, the key to the law of attraction is to combine your thoughts, your feelings, and most importantly, your actions together in sync, and then, amazing things can happen.

Some call that a spiritual experience, I call it synchronicity.

What events have occurred in your life that you attribute to the Law of Attraction?

In the words of James Redfield, "As we blossom or awaken, we begin to notice there is a force in the world that seems to be operating and leading us into a certain destiny. And it's very much a kind of detective effort on our own part to figure out what these things mean. The synchronicity is essentially a meaningful coincidence that brings us information at just the right time. While leading us forward, it also feels very inspiring and destined in a way. It feels like we're on a path of unfolding in our own personal evolution."

Moe Rock is the CEO and publisher of *The Los Angeles Tribune*. He can be followed on Instagram @MoeRockLovesYou—If you have a story that you believe is both transformational and newsworthy, or to contact Moe about business endeavors directly, he is accessible and can be reached via email at MoeRock@TribuneLA.com.

Tweetable: The most important question to ask yourself while you pursue your business endeavors is, "How am I changing the status quo of my industry." This is by far the most important fundamental question to ask to make a truly powerful impact.

CHRIS SCHWAGERL

How a Terminal Illness Uncovered My Superpowers

Chris Schwagerl is a licensed independent clinical social worker with nearly 20 years of experience in the mental health field. Ten years in, Chris bought his first duplex and started another journey toward financial independence. Today, Chris owns properties in several growth markets and helps everyday people, especially community helpers, experience the pleasures of passive income.

Facing a Dark Reality

When the doctor told me I had kidney disease that needed immediate treatment, I went completely numb. I couldn't hear what she was saying, and my mind dissociated from my body. I felt like I was watching from above. My mind was on my newborn daughter, Luella. I could see her chubby cheeks, smell her breath and feel the softness of her skin. I started crying. I didn't move. I couldn't.

I'd had a kidney biopsy a few weeks prior. I knew that any diagnosis was going to significantly shorten my life, and there would be pain along the way.

I was handed a pamphlet on IgA nephropathy and told the clinic would call me to schedule a follow-up appointment. I was told to pick up a prescription and stay away from sodium. I was told I could prolong dialysis if I followed the plan. The problem was I couldn't comprehend the plan because I was in shock.

I picked up my daughter from the babysitter and went home to tell my wife. When we arrived, she was in her car sobbing. "I can't do this anymore," she said. Postpartum depression was hitting her badly, and she was thinking about death a lot. I got her to turn the car off and come out of the garage. We all went inside, and I started making dinner.

While I cooked dinner, Kelly and I talked about my kidney disease and how in 10 years I would likely be on dialysis. In 20 years, gone. She cried all night.

She had been crying a lot lately. She was sleeping most of the day and incredibly depressed. I needed a partner, and Kelly needed me to be a rock for her. Instead, we were individuals living in personal silos of our own trauma.

All I could think about was Luella. She was three months old. I wanted to see her grow up—go to kindergarten, pursue interests, get her heart broken, graduate, walk down the aisle.... I roller-coastered between crying and being numb.

But I was determined. Something changed in me that night.

Suddenly, nothing in my life before this point mattered anymore. None of the trips, good times, parties, or desires. None of the insecurities or failures mattered either. And I was okay with that.

I was willing to trade everything I had once loved to give my daughter the support to find out what she loved. Luella needed a dad. She couldn't grow up with only a mom. And Kelly needed me too.

That night, I decided to do whatever it took to keep us together. If that meant being recast as a new person who could be and do these things, then that's what I would do.

When Life Was a Breeze

Just a few years prior, life was much different. My 20s were a carefree time of personal exploration. I met a ton of people, attended more than my fair share of parties, and generally went through life with a "go with the flow" attitude. I worked as a social worker mentoring kids who were on probation and had a second job as a bartender to make ends meet.

When I turned 30, I was living in a storage room in a friend's basement. I was finishing a master's program in social work and preparing to get a job in the mental health field. I attended classes on the weekend, worked full-time as a bartender, and had an internship leading therapy groups at a domestic abuse program. This was the first time in my life I had ever been busy. I was as type B as they come, so I struggled to keep my commitments and get assignments in on time. Instead, I loved anything spontaneous, a little crazy, and with a lot of fun attached. Unfortunately, my financial situation was worse than paycheck to paycheck. I was living shift to shift.

I started to feel isolated from my friends who had different jobs. They had the luxury of planning because they had consistent schedules, and they were able to go on much bigger trips because they made a lot more money than me. I frequently complained about unequal pay and the injustices of the world. Why was I paid next to nothing for working a job that greatly benefited the community while my friends got paid a ton more for being engineers, financial analysts, and salespeople? They were going on international trips on the weekends while I was picking up shifts to pay the rent.

On the flip side, one of the nice things about living in a friend's storage room is that rent is cheap. I was able to save enough money to attend a friend's wedding in Costa Rica. I took the red-eye flight down and packed extra food to avoid costly meals in restaurants. One afternoon, I was making a couple PB&J sandwiches and complaining that everybody else could afford the freshly caught fish when a friend finally had enough of my complaining.

"I'm so sick of hearing you complain about money! I work for a living, too."

"But my job doesn't pay me as much. It's not fair."

"If you need more money, why don't you do something about it!?"

We both sat there upset and stunned. To be honest, I never thought I could do anything about my financial situation. My family didn't talk about money, so I didn't have any prior training about analyzing an investment, using leverage, or reading a financial statement. All I knew was that cutting coupons and living cheaply was a constant.

But I had just heard something completely foreign to me—that I could do something about my financial standing. So, I took a chance and asked what I should do.

"I don't know," she said. "Somebody recommended *Rich Dad Poor Dad* to me. Maybe try reading that book."

Creating Wealth on a Social Work Wage

As soon as I arrived back in Minnesota, I found the purple book at the library. I devoured it, and a spark ignited in me. For some reason, it was baked into my existence that your lot in life was set, and you did your best to accept that. But after reading *Rich Dad Poor Dad*, the possibility of real estate investing and passive income started to sprout in my mind. Everything suddenly felt 3D for the first time. I decided to buy a duplex. And for the first time in my life, I wanted more.

Over the next year, I read countless books, saved money for a 3.5% down payment, and printed all the documents from *Property Management for Dummies*. I found a Realtor willing to work with me, and we looked at dozens of properties before I decided on one. It was a 100-year-old brick building on the east side of St. Paul that had been converted to a duplex generations ago. It needed a lot of work, and I didn't own any tools. But I was determined to buy it. My uncles showed me how to update the electrical system, modernize the plumbing, and buff up the wood floors. I lived on the main floor and rented out the top. I went from paying $250 a month in rent to breaking even. And I got the investment bug.

Around that same time, I met Kelly, and we started spending a lot of time together. About six months later, she moved in. That winter, I got on one knee in the living room and asked her to be my bride.

Before we got married, I called our loan originator and asked about the requirements for buying another duplex. He advised us to buy one in Kelly's name before we got married to take advantage of the 3.5% down payment for a first-time home buyer. She had never purchased a home before, so we bought a bigger duplex and moved in shortly after we were married.

We now had a small portfolio of three rental units, and we upgraded our own housing to the larger side of the new duplex. A few months later, we got the great news that Kelly was pregnant. In less than a year, we would be parents.

Kidney Treatment Starts

A few months after I got the news about my IgA nephropathy, I had a follow-up with my kidney doctor. She started me on steroids for three months, then four, then six, then a year. The meds made my face fill out, I felt angry, I was constantly hungry, and I couldn't sleep. I started a strict, very low-sodium diet. As a result, I spent a ton of time preparing meals, reading labels, and learning a new way to grocery shop. No more restaurants or convenience foods for me. I went hungry a lot.

During my steroid regimen, a friend invited me to a weekend retreat focused on building your life's vision. At that time, I was fixated on my mortality and pondering how much time I had left until things got really bad. Life on dialysis entails multiple painful treatments every week that leaves a body in a frail state. People need to rely on family and outside providers to survive. I was desperate to buy time to see my daughter grow up and support my wife.

That vision workshop was divine intervention. I had never considered the architectural design of my existence before, and I certainly had never spent 20 hours mapping my ideal life. I loved being able to relive some of my fondest memories: a dog sledding trip, meeting new friends while traveling through Europe, a six-week road trip through Canada with Kelly.... These were all times I had felt alive, free, and inspired. For the first time in my life, I created a vision for my future—full of health, travel, worldly experiences, community impact, and financial freedom.

I printed my vision and kept it in my back pocket for months. I read the first three lines so many times, I still remember them today. *I have the perfect body to kick kidney disease in the ass. I'm always there for Kelly, and she thinks of me as the sexiest man alive. I am a peaceful and playful father to my dear Luella.*

The New Normal

The next few years were grueling. I was constantly tracking my sodium intake and drank a gallon and a half of water a day. I had my blood drawn twice a month with monthly doctor appointments. Kidney disease was hijacking my schedule and my life.

I desperately wanted more time. I wanted passive income so I could spend as much time as possible with my daughter while I still had my mobility. I wanted to support Kelly in hopes her depression would improve. I tried flipping bank notes. I tried wholesaling. I tried working for other investors. Nothing stuck because I didn't get immediate results.

I was off steroids, and my body felt like mine again. But I had transformed into a type A, madly driven, stressed-out version of myself. I was always over-busy with work, making special meals, managing our properties, giving presentations, and attending investor meetups.

Through it all, my vision kept me grounded. I always made time for Luella. She was the very best part of my life, and her place at the top of my vision never changed. My life's greatest joy has been to watch her start to walk, giggle, run, play with animals, and develop her personality. She was a delightful distraction and the focal point of my universe all at once. Kelly and I endured ups and downs, yet we always stayed committed to our relationship and our health. And, despite challenges, my focus on creating passive income never wavered.

Along the way, I transformed. A novel feeling sank in. I was in charge of my future. Nobody was going to hand me my dreams—I had to create them for myself. My jealousy of others faded, and I started to realize I truly could design my life.

The Vision Manifests

Five years into my program, I sat alone in my kidney doctor's office. She walked in, holding a clipboard like always. But I could tell she had been crying. A tear fell down her face when she told me my lgA nephropathy had stopped progressing.

I had another six months of good numbers then six more. In the summer of 2021, my kidney disease was gone. I killed it! She said that lgA nephropathy takes 93% of its hosts. I'm one of the 7% that kicked it in the ass! I had manifested my vision.

My doc said I could go back to eating whatever I wanted, but I wasn't budging. I told her that I felt great on a restrictive diet, so I wasn't planning to change. All was well until I saw that food truck on the drive home. I walked up and ordered a porchetta sandwich. It tasted incredible. I stood there in a crowd of strangers choking back tears while I ate.

A New Dream Emerges

That summer, I took some time to reflect on my original vision I wrote years prior. Kelly and I were both in full recovery. Luella was enrolled in kindergarten. And we were living in our own newly-renovated house.

We sold one duplex to get working capital for a future business venture, and we completed a 1031-exchange for the other duplex. We diversified into new construction rental properties in growth markets to increase our passive income.

Some days, I wish I could go back to being that carefree, spontaneous guy of young adulthood. Life was simple then, but I was also scared—of commitment, of success, and of failure. A transformation was needed to keep myself healthy and my family intact. And I caught a glimpse of my true self. Thanks to a vision and some grit, a response to dire circumstances revealed my superpower.

Recently, I created a new vision for my future which entails a merging of family, friends, business, and adventure. I'm grateful that Kelly and I are partners in life and in business.

We are developing a campus of residential assisted living homes in Minnesota which Kelly will operate and oversee. We even got a puppy last year, and I've trained Rosy to be a therapy dog for our residents. I'm excited about the good our homes will bring to the community. So many members of our aged population are neglected or abandoned after transitioning to assisted living. I see our homes as a way we can learn about each resident and preserve their unique legacies. We are using our businesses to show Luella how to take calculated risks, treat people with respect, and live a life with integrity.

I also run Chris Connects, a real estate syndication company. We help everyday people experience the pleasures of passive income. I feel a strong need to help the community, and our syndication company is a way I can further support social workers, nurses, doctors, and other community workers. If we can improve a social worker's financial health, they will experience less burnout and be more spiritually connected to their clients. Combining real estate investing with a business that has a soul in the community, we're able to provide investment opportunities that feel great.

Chris Schwagerl is a father, husband, social worker, dog trainer, mentor, and speaker. He is also founder of Chris Connects, a real estate syndication company that helps everyday people enjoy the pleasures of passive income. Visit chrisconnects.co and schedule a call to see if our investment opportunities match YOUR vision.

Tweetable: Nobody was going to hand me my dreams—I had to create them for myself. More than that, I started to realize I truly could design my life.

CHRISTINA ALVA

Against the Odds
My Journey to Becoming a Boss Lady

Christina Alva is a career coach, USA Today bestselling author, and speaker who helps entrepreneurs and professionals achieve their goals. Christina is the CEO and founder of Amazing Books, LLC, and the co-founder of Elite Level Minds, a mastermind group for entrepreneurs. Christina also writes young adult fantasy under the pen name Chriss Bury.

I Want to Be a Boss Lady

When my mother learned she was pregnant with me, the doctors advised her to terminate the pregnancy. They informed her that I would have major deformities and most likely not live past the age of six. According to them, I wouldn't have much of a life. I would be mentally handicapped and unable to do things on my own. Against their advice, my mother carried me to full-term. Her version of the story is that God told her I would be just fine.

I made it to age six and then well past that. I was an active child with a creative imagination. I danced ballet, played the bassoon, ran track, and much more. I was also an honor roll student. I guess God was right.

When I think back to my childhood days, I remember watching and observing everyone and everything. I was always trying to understand why people did the things they did.

I watched my father work tirelessly for an organization that was stressful and demanding of his time. After fulfilling his obligation, he left that job for a more enjoyable opportunity even though he received less pay. I watched him pick up videography, his passion, as a side hustle to make a few extra dollars, but he treated it as a hobby. He never charged what he was worth and was always doing extra things for free, but he seemed happy.

I watched my mom open an in-home daycare and barely charge for watching other people's kids. During that time I'd often hear her say, "You can pay me next week." She had a dream of buying a big building to operate her daycare in. Her in-home business was not open very long, and she never bought that building to pursue her dream. I still wonder why.

Back then, I just watched. My father worked an average-paying job, and my mother, mostly a stay-at-home mom, worked odd jobs here and there for extra spending money, which was spent mostly on my sisters and me.

I thought we had a good life. Overall, I couldn't complain. At the same time, I wished we took family vacations to fancy places like Disney World like some of my friends or maybe lived in a bigger house where I didn't have to share a room with my sister. My parents made sure we had what we needed but I wished we could have done and had more, like the latest pair of basketball shoes or a Nintendo.

We had an aunt that would come visit. She carried a leather planner and a laptop bag. She was always checking her planner because she had places to be and people to see. She drove a nice car and traveled all around the world. She knew a lot of people and she always went after her dreams. She was a professional businesswoman. A boss lady. I remember thinking, *That's how I want to be when I grow up.* She looked like a lady who could do and have whatever she wanted.

How Did I Get Here?

Despite my affinity for my aunt's lifestyle, after high school, I found myself working odd jobs, getting married, and starting my own family. I told myself I was happy. There were moments when I wanted more. Even though I wasn't sure what exactly, I felt there was more I was supposed to be doing. I pushed that quiet, little voice deep down inside and focused everything I had on being the best wife and mother I could be.

Time went on, and slowly, my life unraveled one thread at a time. I found myself in an unhappy, unhealthy marriage. I shifted from living to existing. Walking away was one of the greatest challenges of my life. And once again, against the odds, I survived. I decided that I was going to live. This time it would be the way I wanted to live.

Hello, Boss Lady

My son and I left our home, moving from Texas to Washington, DC. I had no idea how I was going to survive on my own as a single mother away from my family, but I knew I would figure it out. I have always loved solving puzzles, and I viewed this challenge as another puzzle to solve. Through my connections, I obtained a job as a computer programmer and started to settle into my new life.

In corporate America, I realized my dream of becoming a boss lady. I shot up the corporate ladder like a bullet. I was on a mission. It wasn't long before I had my own leather planner and laptop bag, just like my aunt.

After my divorce, she and I became closer. Having lived a similar story, she became my mentor. She began to teach me how to ask the right questions and where to look for the answers. Most importantly, she opened my mind to new ways of thinking and officially introduced me to entrepreneurship.

I have always had an entrepreneurial spirit. When I was a kid, I sold candy, tutored, and picked up odd tasks to make a few dollars here and there. Like I said, I was observant. As soon as I learned that other kids would trade money for something I had, I never needed to ask for lunch money again.

Opening my mind to new ways of thinking was a game-changer for me. I joined a network marketing company where I learned about personal development, affirmations, vision boards, and networking.

After that, I wanted to be optimal. I wanted to be the best version of myself. You wouldn't buy an Apple Watch and just use it to tell time. There is so much more it can do to make your life more enjoyable. That is how I felt about myself. Even today, I push myself to see what I am capable of. I challenge myself to dream bigger and do more. I challenge those around me to be better versions of themselves too.

I started writing again, something I loved to do as a child. I started my publishing company, Amazing Books, LLC, to publish all the books stored away in my head. My first book, *Beyond the Job Description: How to Succeed in the Workplace*, opened the door to my business as a career coach where I help professionals land their dream jobs. As an author and publisher, I help others write books through ghostwriting and workshops. I also write young adult fantasy novels under the pen name Chriss Bury. I can't wait to see my books on the big screen one day.

I desire to use everything I have learned to help others the way my aunt helped me. Looking back, I wonder how my father's videography passion and my mother's daycare dream could have been different if they'd had someone to share ideas with and to challenge them to grow. This is why I created the mastermind group Elite Level Minds, a community of aspiring and seasoned entrepreneurs who come together to network, grow, and find solutions to challenges. A place where you can find an accountability partner and gain the perspective of others who have achieved success.

Boss Mindset

When I look back over my life and how I made it past my biggest challenges —escaping an abusive marriage, moving to a major city and making it as a single mom, and starting a business when I didn't know where to begin, I see that I needed four things.

First, I needed a vision. It was important for me to visualize who I wanted to be. That image had to be crystal clear to me, and I had to meditate on it often. I learned about vision boards and affirmations. This changed my life. I started saying what I wanted to achieve in every area of my life and posted pictures all around my house. At first, talking out loud to myself in front of a mirror felt weird, but then I started to get into it more and more each day. The first time I said affirmations, I said, "People are looking for me to be on their TV show." Six months after saying this affirmation, I was in LA shooting an episode of *Wheel of Fortune* as a contestant. After that, I was asked to be an extra in a movie.

Second, I needed knowledge. I needed an understanding of how to get to where I wanted to go. The problem is you don't know what you don't know. I had my aunt to start me down the right path. Later, I invested in coaching programs and courses. Mentors and coaches are a great way to learn what you don't know. They can also provide a clearer image of where you want to be. They challenge the way you think and help move you forward. You must be willing to be coachable. Be open to the idea that someone who has already achieved the success you are looking for knows how to help you get there. Success also requires you to get out of your comfort zone. The comfort zone is the final resting place of dreams. Other ways to obtain knowledge include taking courses, webinars, workshops, reading books, and attending conferences.

Third, I needed motivation. I had to have a desire that would drive me to act on a daily basis, even when I didn't feel like it. When I left my marriage, I felt like I had lost everything. I had to find myself. I had to reawaken that little girl inside me with all those big dreams. I had a strong desire to start living for myself and my son. Over the years, I began to surround myself with like-minded people who were investing in themselves and their dreams. Find others who will encourage you and hold you accountable for the goals you want to achieve. I started the mastermind Elite Level Minds so entrepreneurs could share what they know and learn what they need. You don't have to travel this journey by yourself. Your relationships can help you reach your destination.

Finally, I needed belief. I had to have faith that I could achieve the goals I set. It was easy to believe that I could be a boss lady because I saw my aunt all the time and she always encouraged me. It was harder to believe that I could start a publishing company, write a young adult fantasy fiction novel, and then win an award for it. I didn't see myself in R.L. Stine or J.K. Rowling. I found it hard to picture my book series as a best-selling motion picture. But I continued to go through the motions even though I knew I was missing something. I was disconnected from my dream. One day, my coach suggested I go to the Believe Nation conference. That was when I heard David Imonitie speak for the first time. He helped me find my missing link. His message inspired me to believe like never before. Now, I am dreaming bigger than ever, and I can't wait to see what my next level looks like.

You were created for a purpose. You can achieve any goal you set your mind to. Don't wait another day to start living your best life and achieve your next level.

For more info on Christina Alva and her coaching programs or to purchase her books, visit ChristinaAlva.com. To join the Elite Level Minds mastermind group, visit EliteLevelMinds.com. Follow Christina on Instagram and Facebook @ChristinaNAlva and @ChrissBury.

Tweetable: A mastermind is a great place to share what you know and learn what you need.

KOHSHEAN KUDA

Finding Balance in Family, Business and Finance

With over 20 years of experience, Kohshean Kuda is general operating partner of real estate management company Herbie Holdings and is passionate about helping people find balance as they juggle family, work, and finances. Kohshean, his wife Prianna, and their two boys live in Plano, TX.

Reality Check

I would wake up at 8:30 in the morning, make my way to the kitchen, pour myself coffee, change, and go play golf. I played so much golf that the golf course had a special rate for me. I would then come home and take a nap.

This was back in 2013. You would think I was retired! No. I would spend about an hour looking through job postings, and if it was the week for it, I needed to file for unemployment. I would then go hang out with my wife after she finished her work, eat, watch TV, and go back to sleep.

This was my daily routine. I was unemployed for over 13 months.

I had a real estate business, which I started part-time years prior, but my business was losing money. My wife and I were also struggling to have children. A sense of failure was pervasive, and I started to lose faith in my ability to overcome it.

Prioritizing My Time, Searching for Fulfillment

How did I get this way? Ignorance and too much pride.

I was very successful in tech and had a high-paying position, but I reached a point where I was feeling unhappy. I did not know it at the time, but looking back, I realize I was not living a truly fulfilling life. Without a specific plan, I decided to quit. I was sure I would quickly find work with a small tech start-up. Well, life has a funny way of knocking sense into you.

After months of unemployment, my turning point came when I began to let go of what I had achieved and focused instead on what I wanted to do next. It started with a simple step forward—taking the time to invest in myself. I decided to move to Boston to go back to school and immerse myself in the startup community there.

I said a temporary goodbye to my wife, booked a one-way ticket from Dallas to Boston, and moved in with a roommate, my new landlord. (I did not know it at the time, but my roommate was starting his own WeWork-type co-working space for startups in Boston.) I would wake up, attend classes all day, go to networking events in the evening, and spend the weekends meeting successful people who were volunteering their time to share their knowledge with us students.

I found a consulting position with a small startup and helped them with direct sales and in raising money from venture capital firms. It was exactly the environment I was looking to be a part of and a great learning experience. I spent seven months in Boston working with and learning from brilliant, successful people and working alongside startups—and I found I had my fire back.

The Climb Up

Back home, with new clarity and focus, I was committed to making my real estate business sustainable and helping it grow. I began to invest in myself, my education, my family, my knowledge, and my friend circle. I found myself overwhelmed with information and people pulling me in multiple directions.

One day I was listening to a series of documentaries on YouTube. One was about time management, and it provided a simple concept that drove exceptional results for me over time. Every night, I wrote down the three most important things I needed to accomplish the next day. In the morning, I went about working on those tasks.

This technique helped me stay focused, gave me a sense of accomplishment when I deeply needed it, and changed my overall attitude in life. I was no longer asking myself, *What did I do today?* No, I was telling myself, *Look what I got done today.*

This simple technique of prioritizing with smaller tasks that I could accomplish in a day helped me in my work, my business, and my personal life. More than that, the process of implementing this technique helped me make some painful decisions. I realized it was time to exit businesses that were not profitable and focus on preserving and investing in businesses that were profitable.

Exiting those unprofitable transactions allowed me to free up the time and resources I needed to invest in long-term business growth. In doing so, I realized that my strengths were in creating revenue while building effective marketing plans.

I also learned the importance of building repeatable processes broken down into small, simple tasks that when done take down a large, complex task. I learned to delegate these simple tasks so that I could focus on running the business. By making them simple and measurable, I could effectively hire and train staff. This, as well as understanding and then focusing on how I could learn and improve in areas where I was not as strong, helped me and my business become even more profitable.

It was not an overnight transformation, but in another four years I had amazing children, businesses that were generating good cash flow, and a path to stability through business growth.

In those four years, I exited partnerships and some real estate ventures, including the old hotels, reinvested in single-family vacation rentals, and built new partnerships. I found my current business partner, and I started developing assets from scratch—sourcing and finding land, zoning this land for commercial development, plotting lots, and then building. Working with the county and various commissions and charters to gain the necessary approvals for development, we saw our vision for these new-construction vacation rentals come to life. From the first guest that booked a vacation stay to looking at the yearly profit and loss statement and distributing profits to investors and ourselves, we all felt a sense of accomplishment.

Today, I am an owner of multiple healthy and successful business ventures that are profitable, and I am very grateful for what I have been able to accomplish. What changed? My attitude, my outlook, my focus and the desire to grow and have a mindset of helping others. That internal shift changed everything for me.

I learned never to give up and to keep moving, even if it meant prioritizing my time and taking only small steps forward.

Small Steps Make Great Successes

In my latest real estate venture, a wedding venue and event center, what started out as a fantastic purchase of land and pre-development work led to unexpected business conditions due to COVID. Those conditions were further exacerbated by supply chain issues and price escalations in everything from labor to materials, which resulted in our construction and project costs going up by almost 35%. This occurred against a backdrop of sharp interest rate hikes and high single-digit inflation. We had to take our revenue, cost, and services models completely apart and put them back together with new vendor partnerships and new package offerings that would allow us to create multiple revenue streams while reducing risk and shrinking our costs.

We looked at the business problem at hand and decided to break down the problem into smaller action items. We then started taking action on these tasks. This allowed us to decide what would help us increase revenue and reduce costs and what would not. Over time, these decisions helped us move the needle for our business.

Eight years ago, I don't know if I would have been able to directly take on this challenge, find a way to address it, and have the confidence to see it through.

Living in the Present with Balance

Today, I find myself driving forward with these lessons, with taking care of myself at the front. I make time to value what is important in my life and keep myself grounded. Having dinner with my wife, prioritizing my playtime with my sons, taking them to the park in the evenings, heading to an indoor play park on the weekends—these are just some of the things I am intentional about doing. Having a good mix of me-time, where I can think, focus on my work, grow my business, write out my daily goals, check up on my yearly goals from time to time, and do yard work when I can, keeps me grounded and sane.

In the past, there were three versions of Kohshean: Kohshean at work, Kohshean at business, and Kohshean at home. It was exhausting. The ability for me to be the same person at home, at work, and in business has allowed balance.

Balance in my life started with communicating. I brought people who cared the most in my life into my day-to-day—literally—my wife is my business partner today, my parents know my daily schedule, and I spend time with my sons daily. This has allowed me to achieve balance.

My mission now is to help investors starting their real estate journey who feel overwhelmed and are looking to grow their portfolio, achieve balance, and be intentional with their time. As they look to manage their cash, cash flows, credit, equity, and personal family time, achieving balance and having a sense of fulfillment is hard, but it is possible.

Contact Kohshean Kuda, founder of real estate investment company Herbie Holdings, LLC, to access his 20 years of experience in real estate investing and creating great value for investors and communities at kuda@herbieholdings.com

Tweetable: Finding balance with family, business, and finance started with managing my time. Every night, I write down the three most important things I need to accomplish. I then go about working on those tasks.

MARLIN YODER

How an Amish Farmboy Achieved Financial Independence

Marlin Yoder is a top-producing real estate agent and financially independent investor in Sarasota, FL. Equipped with an 8th grade education and a strong work ethic, Marlin works and invests with the sincere conviction that success comes from adding value to people's lives.

The Rush Requires Risk

When I was 19 years old, I crashed my motorcycle at 120 MPH. My bike flew 52 feet through the air with me right behind it doing somersaults into the ditch.

I was out cold for a couple minutes. When I woke up, I could not remember where I was or what had happened. I was lying flat on the ground with 20 people staring down at me, and nobody was saying a word. I was so confused. Why were they staring at me? And why was I laying on the ground?

I noticed one of the people staring at me was a good friend of mine, so I said his name and asked him what happened. "You wrecked your bike," he said.

That's when it all started coming back. I had been at a friend's house watching a football game that Sunday afternoon. After the game, on my way home with my motorcycle, I felt like blowing off some steam as I had done many times by cruising through the countryside at very high speeds. On Sunday afternoons, there was never much traffic, and my theory to offset the risk of my speed was to ride on the center yellow line of the two-lane road.

While this method had been successful in the past, I was presented with a new challenge that Sunday afternoon. As I rode the center of this two-lane road at 120 MPH, I found myself faced with four mopeds crossing the street single file in front of me. My only option was to take the ditch or hit one of the mopeds head on; I chose the ditch.

Fortunately, I walked away from this accident with only a couple of scrapes. My gear saved my life.

This was one of the defining moments in my life. I realized how easily my life could have ended that afternoon. This was a very humbling experience, and it birthed in me this certainty that my life had a purpose worth pursuing.

While it is not one of my proudest moments, I do believe there is a life lesson in this story. I could have ridden the speed limit and had some fun, but the adrenaline rush of going 120 MPH on a bike can only be experienced with the risk associated with driving 120 MPH. One of my favorite quotes is, "Life is a daring adventure or nothing at all." To be clear, the risk of riding a bike at high speeds is not one I have embraced since this accident. However, taking risks is something I have always embraced in life and is a large factor in my success today.

Humble Beginnings

In the summertime, when I was around 10 years old, I used to lay flat on my back in the front yard, stare up at the night sky with all the stars shining bright, and let my imagination run wild. I remember it like it was yesterday, that thought of, *What would life be like if you had no limits?*

My parents were Amish farmers in Ohio, so what happened when I let my imagination run wild was a long shot from my reality in those days. My parents had 10 children and there was never a dull moment growing up. I was third in line from the top. We used to wake up at 6 a.m., go out to the barn to milk the cows by hand, and feed all the animals before we headed off to school at 8 a.m.

This was not exactly my idea of fun as a kid, but I have since come to appreciate the values my parents instilled in us during those early years. We didn't have a lot, and we worked hard, but we did it together as a family. Some of my best memories are from the evening dinner table after all the day's work was done. We would debrief with stories of that day's events on the farm. I remember many nights we laughed until we cried.

My dad is one of the hardest-working men I have ever met. Farming was not very lucrative, and I can only imagine how much money it takes to raise 10 kids, so he worked a job during the day and farmed in the evenings and on weekends. At a very young age, I used to feel bad for him and think, *There has to be a better way.*

In the Amish culture, you go to school until the 8th grade then enter the workforce full-time. I worked in the construction field rough framing and roofing houses during my teenage years. During this time, I felt very lost. I had no idea what my purpose in life was. I didn't know which was worse, milking cows by hand at 6 a.m. before school or getting up at 6 a.m. to go build houses in the cold winter months in Ohio only to find myself broke, living paycheck to paycheck.

These were some of the darkest days of my life. Henry Ford said that most men live lives of quiet desperation. I was desperate for a better life, but the opportunities seemed to be nowhere in sight.

Finding Hope in Personal Development

At this point, I was introduced to a multi-level marketing company with a focus on leadership and personal development. This introduced me to people who had retired from their jobs in just a few short years. I thought I had died and gone to heaven. This was my ticket out of a job I hated and living paycheck to paycheck. I was beyond excited!

They had a list of what they called the top five books that all the successful owners in the business had read, so I bought all five books and started reading. The first two books were *The Magic of Thinking Big* and *How to Have Confidence and Power in Dealing with People*. In reading some of these amazing books in my upstairs bedroom of our 100-year-old farmhouse in Ohio, hope came alive again.

The same spirit of optimism of dreaming about a life with no limits that I had felt as a 10-year-old staring up at the night sky was alive again! I would read until the early morning hours, go to work with only a couple hours of sleep, and have more energy than ever before. I remember on one occasion being so inspired I got out scissors and cut the word "impossible" out of my dictionary.

Sadly, after working incredibly hard for two years in this business, it became apparent that I was not very good at multi-level marketing. I had spent a lot of money to grow my business and made nothing in return. So, instead of being out of my job and no longer living paycheck to paycheck, I was in more debt than when I started with no end in sight to my days at my job. I was over my head in consumer debt with collectors calling me daily. Not only had this business venture not produced the results I had hoped for, but I also fell further behind than before I started! This was a very painful realization.

Leaving Ohio

I had vacationed in Sarasota, Florida, for a couple weeks every winter during my teenage years. The year I turned 20, while in Sarasota for two weeks in February, something was different. I was crushed with feeling like a business failure, but I felt optimistic about the future and thought, *Why don't I just move to Sarasota? My business is over. My job in the cold is no fun. You only live once, and the only limitations we have are the ones between our ears (according to* The Magic of Thinking Big *book). So, why not move to Florida and work construction in a place where at least the weather is nice?*

It seemed like a very logical decision. I will never forget when I arrived back home from the two-week trip and told my family I planned on moving. It took me telling them for about two weeks before they actually believed me.

On March 20, 2006, I packed all my belongings in my car and left Ohio. I had $650 cash to my name and a below 500 hundred credit score. I understood this was a real risk. I had no connections in Sarasota beyond one uncle I had no relationship with. However, I was excited and optimistic about the challenge of finding work and establishing myself in beautiful Sarasota. The worst that could happen was I'd fail again and move back to Ohio with my parents.

Sarasota!

It took me several years of bouncing around before I found a great job in the food industry. It was very different from anything I had done career-wise up to that point. At this job of nine years, I learned relational sales and customer service.

One of the books I had read when I found personal development was Robert Kiyosaki's *Cashflow Quadrant*. After that, I was sold on the idea of getting out of the rat race. The idea of building up a portfolio of assets that produced more income on a monthly basis than my cost of living just made sense to me. While I was working hard at my job, I paid all my consumer debt and, starting from square one with a prepaid credit card, built my credit back from below 500 to 750. In the summer of 2014, after seven years of working hard and building my income and credit, I was finally ready to buy my first property.

After a couple months of searching, I found what seemed like the right property. It was a single-family residence in rough shape, but I liked it because it had a lot of potential and two livable units. The main house had two bedrooms, and the one car-garage had been converted to a one-bedroom in-law suite. My plan was to live in the small unit and rent the large unit as a seasonal rental. I made an offer and signed a contract to purchase the property.

After due diligence was over and the loan was approved, we finally closed. I will never forget the day of closing. I had worked so hard and so long to make this dream of house hacking a reality; however, on this day, all I could think about was the fact that I was signing my name to a loan of $142,000. Part of me felt like I was crazy to commit to that much debt. I worked through my fears and closed on the property nonetheless. We still own this property today and have made a positive cash flow on it every year. In retrospect, it seems laughable I was nervous about a loan of $142,000 when our business is making more than that in a good month today. This goes to show how much our perspective is shaped by our experience.

Serve Others, Steward Your Gifts and Enjoy the Dream

In 2017, I married my beautiful wife. One of my favorite proverbs says, *He who finds a wife finds a good thing and obtains favor from the Lord.* This has been my experience, to say the least.

Shortly after we got married, I quit my job, we bought a pool cleaning business, and I got my real estate license with the intention of buying more real estate. This felt incredibly uncomfortable. I knew nothing about swimming pools and near to nothing about real estate investing or sales.

I like to joke that when we got married my wife told me I better step my game up a notch as my reason for quitting a well-paying, comfortable job and going into business full-time. For anyone who knows her, it's hysterical as it just wouldn't be in her nature to do that. The truth is the opposite. Her support is the reason I had the confidence to step out and take the risk of going into business for ourselves.

Both companies grew faster than expected, and I soon realized I was a lot more passionate about selling real estate than cleaning swimming pools. Fortunately, we were able to hire an employee to run the pool cleaning business that first year so my time was freed up to sell real estate. By 2019, things were going very well with real estate so we sold the pool cleaning business to our employee.

Since selling the business, I have been in the top 1% of Realtors in sales volume in Sarasota. I never had a goal of being a top producer even though that has been the result. My business strategy is very simple: relationships over transactions. If I take care of the relationship, the transactions take care of themselves.

In 2021, my wife quit her career job in health education and came on board with my real estate business. We have since achieved financial independence and work as a husband-and-wife team, helping other people make wise financial decisions in real estate and wealth building. We wake up every morning feeling like we should kiss the ground we walk on. It is the first time in my life I truly love what I do.

We have never been more excited for the future. In many ways, it feels like we are just getting started.

Zig Ziglar is famous for saying, "You can have everything in life you want, just as long as you help enough other people get what they want." This has been my experience, we can indeed have anything in life we want if we get the focus off ourselves and genuinely serve other people.

I went from an illiterate farm boy to selling luxury waterfront properties following this simple truth with conviction. The life without limits I used to dream of as a boy has finally become my reality.

Connect with Marlin Yoder by visiting his website to schedule a meeting or to sign up for his weekly e-newsletters.

Email: marlin@robbinsresidential.com
Phone: (941) 893-7406
Website: www.marlinyoderrealtor.com

Tweetable: "You can have everything in life you want if you will just help enough other people get what they want." — Zig Ziglar

TAMMY HANE

Change Lives
Paying Inspiration Forward

Tammy Hane is a perpetual optimist, author, and multi-family real estate investor. She was formerly a farmer, the managing editor at Pasco News Publications, and an educator. Her mission: pick up others' lives with optimism and authentic encouragement. She knows giving, even something seemingly small, can make an immense impact.

A Game Changer

The afternoon study hall teacher at Woodbury Central placed a note on my desk that stated, "See Ms. Carter in her room." No, it's not what you're thinking—I wasn't in trouble. It was the second semester of my senior year, I knew Carter well, and I wasn't generally the problem-causing kind.

I signed out of study hall and headed down the old school's south stairs to Ms. Carter's room. I had taken as many classes as possible from her over the last four years, because I loved the arts—particularly English grammar, speech, and drama—and she was a uniquely engaging instructor. I didn't know what she wanted today.

Carter had papers spread out neatly in front of her on her wooden desk and a business-like look on her face. She said, "Come and look at this." I went and stood by her side and she asked, "Has anyone reviewed the results of your IQ test scores with you?"

"No," I replied. She shook her head, then started reading the details on my intelligence quotient results out loud, pointing to categories and numbers.

I was thinking, *I have no idea what these numbers mean.* The information wasn't registering with me. I shrugged my shoulders, shook my head slightly, and raised my eyebrows, letting her know I didn't get it.

She paused and stated, "This means you should be getting A's and not C's."

I nearly laughed out loud. Although I never lacked confidence, I also never considered myself a star student—I got C's. It was acceptable. I imagined myself as plain. I mean, exceedingly plain. I wasn't part of the popular, smart crowd. But I liked most everyone and they got along fine with me. I participated in many school activities and organizations—school was more of a social event for me than anything.

I grew up on a farm on the edge of a tiny, unincorporated, rural community (more like a village) in Iowa. It was a simple life, and we worked hard. Being the oldest child, I was the first to work in the fields, raise animals, shovel manure, drive tractors, and babysit the others. Most of the time, my attire was unassuming t-shirts, jeans, and boots or tennis shoes paired with my long, straight, brown hair. Even though I was happy and optimistic, I still felt ordinary, and I was genuinely fine with that.

I do not recall the actual IQ number Ms. Carter showed me that day. I just remember she showed me the results and a chart that determined my IQ was above average. *ME? Above average?*

She could tell it was not sinking in with me. So, she dug a little deeper and challenged me: "When is your next test and what class is it in?"

I took a deep breath and blew it out. "Social studies. Next week." It was one of several classes that I did not do well in and most certainly was not my favorite.

"Just humor me," Carter said. "Study like you are going to get an A on the test. Just try it out and see what happens. Then, let me know how it goes."

"Sure," I answered. But I knew her plan wouldn't work and I would just get a C again.

So, I studied. It wasn't as hard as I thought it would be. I reviewed past quizzes and made sure I knew all the answers on the study sheet. The test was shockingly easy, and I finished it quickly to my teacher's surprise and mine. And I got 100 percent.

Though I was successful on that exam, I was not convinced I was an A student. I had to try it again with my other C-grade classes. I was amazed! I studied, I tried, and I achieved A's every single time!

I WAS smart! I was jumping up and down inside and smiling more outside. My mind was blown! It was inconceivable to me that I wasn't really a C student. I only had to commit, apply myself, and have confidence that I could make the grade to create success.

A light was turned on in my head. My whole outlook on life changed. I was no longer average. I now knew I could conquer most anything. And what had it required of my English teacher? A whole ten minutes out of her day? What if she hadn't taken the time?

Out With the Old, In With the New Goals

A new challenge. I was headed off to college in a few months. I am so thankful I was naïve and had not yet developed much negative self-talk. My self-discouragements could have sounded like, *You can't afford an expensive private college* (I had picked Morningside University because it was small and closest to home), *You can't keep up the grades at that level, You couldn't possibly be an honor student, You're just a dumb, plain, kid....* Those kinds of thoughts would have held me back and dragged me under, disallowing the focus that pure confidence provided me. My positivity and newly found direction pulled me through, and I began chugging away like the little engine that could.

I established a new personal goal—to get on the Dean's List at Morningside. I set my own simple restrictions and rules. I told myself things like, *You can't go to the party unless your homework is completed.* Or, *You can't go to bed until your work is done for the next day.* I stuck to it. I paid my own way. I worked all four years for Dr. John Doohen, chairman of the Foreign Languages Department of the college—every penny of that work-study going toward my education. I had a part-time job at First Federal Savings and, at times, an additional part-time job.

Oh yes, I played also. But my work and studies came first. I made sure of it. I was on a mission. Throughout those four years, I saw a swarm of colleagues drop out and not return. Maybe it was because graduating was not their dream; maybe it was because they had no skin in the game.

By graduation day, I had been on the Dean's List numerous times, was in the Foreign Language Honor Society, and had a secondary education degree in French and English. I did it! I was feeling the impact of the life-changing encouragement from Ms. Carter. I knew I had to share the love. I wanted to do the same for others. I vowed from then on to let others know that they were smart and so very capable.

I was fortunate in the respect that my parents never degraded me or told me I was stupid. I was successful in being supremely optimistic and positively outgoing. Mom made sure of that! Others I've met have not been that fortunate.

Fast Forward

I have had many opportunities to encourage children and adults over the years. My desire to point out people's strengths coupled with teaching ways to abolish negativity and apply positivity was second nature to me, and still is. Some occasions stand out more than others.

Some years ago, a young man from Minnesota asked me to critique a manuscript he was working on. It was, without a doubt, outstanding! Although he was young, he had the vocabulary, critical thinking, and intelligent discourse of someone twice his age. I was impressed. He wasn't.

He was looking for reinforcement but did not believe he was smart or good enough. He was working full-time and going to college part-time. Nothing novel about that, right? Well, no, not until I heard his story.

This incredible individual was overcoming major adversity. He was out on his own, basically forced out. You could say he escaped. Growing up, he was barraged with degrading comments and physical abuse. He was told he was a loser, he wouldn't amount to anything, and other verbal atrocities. And he was laughed at by his parents who said he'd never make it in college. Were they wrong!

This young adult was successful in the military, had already bought and renovated his own house, and was putting himself through college, but still lacked self-worth.

I spent several hours with him that day and drew attention to the many areas where he was smart and helped him see how he was wise for his years. He brought new things to my attention and suggested a couple informative books to read. It was a great day working with someone so determined, reinforcing how much good he had inside and how he was contributing positively to society. Indeed, he was and is.

Since then, this young man has become even more successful professionally. He has stepped into a new leadership role that naturally fits his outgoing and personable demeanor. And, he is making more money than he ever anticipated at this point in his life.

Les Brown says it well, "Help others achieve their dreams and you will achieve yours."

The Best Kids

In the back of my mind, I always knew that when I had kids, they would be amazing. I couldn't wait to pass on my encouragement to the next generation: to raise them up! They would know they were smart from day one.

For me, it was easy to raise them positively. D.J. is the oldest. Anthony is a few years younger. Of everything in my life, they are of the utmost importance to me and the creations that I am most proud of. Now, I look up to them, both literally and figuratively! Am I biased? Certainly. If you are a parent, hopefully, you are biased also.

I was—and am still—genuine with them. I would tell them, "You are the best!" and praise good grades often. If they ran into snags, we would work through them, seeing the positive side and finding solutions. I made sure to follow through, follow through, follow through with whatever I said.

Don't get me wrong, I absolutely did NOT do everything right, and I made some huge blunders. But I don't live in the negative. I look for the lesson and I look forward.

D.J. was in the top of his high school class and earned a presidential scholarship for college. On graduation day, he shook hands as he received his diploma then did a one-handed cartwheel across the stage, not losing a step or his graduation cap. Amid all the "woo's" and "whoa's," many eyes turned and looked at me. I just shrugged with a huge smile, "That's my D.J.!"

When all students were through the line, they each picked up a rose and brought it to their mother or parent. D.J. presented me with my rose and gave me the biggest, longest hug he ever has. It was memorable.

Before moving to Texas, D.J. received his associate's degree in acting and music in Iowa and appeared in a number of community theater plays. He went on to graduate with a Bachelor of Science in computer information systems with a concentration in software engineering and database design from Texas A&M and secured a great job. D.J., one of the most giving individuals I know, is also passing down positivity and encouragement!

In high school, Anthony battled with a good friend and baseball teammate for the top position in his class, on his own giving up some of his favorite sports so he could concentrate on his studies. That was something to say for a sportsaholic! During Anthony's valedictorian speech, I witnessed something I had never seen before and may never see again— a long-lasting standing ovation at a high school graduation. That was an unforgettable moment.

Anthony's hard work paid off, and he ended up with some great scholarships to financially assist him through his coursework at Embry-Riddle Aeronautical University. He completed an accelerated Master of Science in engineering physics with a minor in applied mathematics and a concentration in space systems. He graduated with honors and completed a thesis, contributing to space physics research. I am so proud and grateful.

Now, I am learning from them. They each have developed incredible insight, deep wisdom, and great knowledge. They both are amazingly humble, personable, and well-rounded individuals who love learning and growing.

Would I have known to inspire them as I did if Ms. Carter hadn't talked to me that day? It is likely I would have chosen a different path. Would they even be alive? More and more, I believe that we are always right where we are supposed to be.

I have had many people say to me throughout the years, "You are so lucky to have such good kids!"

I smile and think to myself, *Luck didn't really have that much to do with it.* I had an incredibly positive upbringing from my mom, life-changing direction from Ms. Carter, and an unwavering mission to raise up others as I had been raised up.

Branching Out

Several years ago, I contacted Ms. Carter via email before she retired from teaching in Iowa. I had to let her know how she had impacted my life and the lives of many others down the line. As it had been many years, I gave her a quick summary of that day back in high school and where it eventually led me, my family, and others.

It was my turn to lift her up. She said in her reply that my timing was excellent—she had been having an extremely bad day. She said that you never know how far out those branches will grow when you take the time to elevate others.

Indeed. Inspiration and reassurance are things we can give. It costs no money and only a little of our time. Someone around you requires what we can give. It might be a simple smile.

How can we redirect negative thinking? We just need to plant that seed of confidence and help those branches continue to grow. The way I figure it, you have a brain, and you are unique and smart. I believe in you. Don't let anyone tell you anything different.

In retrospect, I was always more than just plain. And so are you.

Watch for new personal development books and positive quotes on scenic posters by Tammy Hane via Hane & Co Publishing's products on Amazon. Join her to promote encouragement and confidence in the world. Connect with Tammy on LinkedIn www.linkedin.com/in/tammy-sue-hane or email Contact@HaneAndCoPubs.com.

Tweetable: Inspiration begets motivation. Be the one who inspires. Your cost? Authentic direction, encouragement, and a little time.

DALE YOUNG

Restoring the Years the Locusts Ate

Dale Young is an executive coach specializing in teamwork, identity, and leadership. He coaches business leaders and entrepreneurs through turning their chaos into clarity to pursue their calling. Dale is also the author of The Identity Key *and a professional speaker.*

"Life is a journey;
Your dream is the compass;
Passion is the fuel."
—Dale Young, 2011

The Terrible Month

March of 2016. A double-whammy at the bottom of the worst decade of my life. The issues that had been splitting my marriage for years had finally culminated in divorce. A couple of weeks later, I was suddenly part-time at my job of 11 years. You can imagine what that did to my finances, my happiness, and my confidence. The locusts had swept through my comfortable existence and destroyed so much.

Why, then, did I feel such hope?

The Comfortable Years

I had no idea before 2012 that I was about to enter a downturn that would last a decade. Life had been reasonably good. Personally, my marriage was comfortable. We had no children, a decision that we made before marriage. We had a nice house and some friends.

Spiritually, I had committed my life to Christ in 1998 and since had been growing, serving, and learning about my faith. I was comfortable.

Professionally, I had a solid career in information technology (IT), on an upward trajectory in terms of salary, responsibility, and leadership. My new job as a director provided a stable income, a little bit of travel, management of a great team, and a level of satisfaction for me. Nothing spectacular, but comfortable.

The Calling

Many years earlier, when some coworkers were complaining about our jobs, I remember saying, "We shouldn't complain; after all, this is just a job, not a career." At that moment, I realized I wanted a career.

Years later, I had a career, but I realized now that wasn't enough. What I really wanted was a calling. A God-given, God-sized, God-inspired, God-energized purpose.

2011 gave me hope that I had found that calling. Through a series of God-incidences, I discovered Christian Life Coaching, started taking classes, and even got my first paying client. I had dreams and plans to eventually make this my full-time career. The future was bright.

The First Incident

The long downhill slide began on Sunday, May 20, 2012. I remember a light startle as I became fully awake. I was sitting on the side of the bed, fully dressed for church. The bed was made. It was as if I had sat down to do something and had one of those micro-naps. But I had no memory then, and still don't, of what was prior to that. I checked the time on my phone, said out loud, "It's time to head to church," stood up, and started calling out and looking for my wife.

Our two-story house was quiet, and I didn't find her on the first floor. I checked the garage, and her car was there, so I assumed she was upstairs and not hearing me. I sent her a text: "Where are you?"

She called me within a minute, which I thought was strange. Over the next few confusing minutes, I learned that she'd been with her family in Tennessee for the last week, she was heading to the airport later that day to return home, and I had talked with her less than 30 minutes before to confirm that I was picking her up at the airport. I had no memory of any of this, and we were both scared.

She called a neighbor to take me to the emergency room where I was admitted and observed for several hours. I was visited by my nephew Gary and Pastor Andy from church, which made me feel better. Vital signs, lots of tests, EEG... they found nothing obvious that was a cause. They labeled it TGA—transient global amnesia—and sent me home.

An incident like that shakes you to the core of your being. Fortunately, I was still part of the church, still believed that God would take care of us, and still had my passion to help people grow and live their best life.

The Descent

Later that year, my wife started talking about moving to Tennessee. Permanently. Without me. Yes, she wanted a divorce. I was shocked. Despite counseling, the gap between us widened. This led to us downsizing our house in 2013, with all the associated stress of moving and getting rid of an accumulation of things from the last 20 years.

Originally, she was not going to live in the new, smaller house, but we attempted to reconcile and continued living together. In 2014, she filed for divorce, but I continued to hope. However, our separations became longer and more frequent.

All this stress was compounded by changes in my IT job. The company I worked for had been looking for management that would take them to the next level, which meant that I had a succession of new bosses… at least six over five years. The company was changing directions, and my role was being minimized.

Friday, September 11, 2015, was the day I knew the marriage was over. I invited her on a date to see the movie *War Room*. I knew it was a Christian movie, but I didn't know that the plot involved a struggling couple who were brought back together through the power of prayer. As the movie unfolded, I was praying that this might be the turning point that would bring us back together.

After the movie, we went to a coffee shop and talked. She broke the news that she was leaving for Tennessee the next day. I was crushed and knew that the marriage was done. It took almost six months to get it finished legally, but in my mind, 9/11 was the end.

Winston Churchill said, "When you're going through hell, KEEP GOING."

The stage was set for the terrible March of 2016. The divorce was now final. My "secure" job was now part-time. Like it or not, I needed to focus on the passion that I had felt five years earlier to become a professional coach.

The Turn

Around this time, someone shared a quote with me: "You can get bitter or you can get better—and the choice is yours."

I chose to get better. I leaned into God instead of running away. I didn't understand the road He had me on, but I chose to keep walking.

I wish I could say it was an easy road. It wasn't. On my path to building a successful coaching business, there were years of losing money, struggle, and doubt.

In late 2016, I invested in a coaching program called Transformational Leadership. I received the first level of certification, which allowed me to run virtual groups using their content. I ran four or five groups and made part of my money back. This was a good program, but I felt it was too restrictive and not as powerful as individual coaching.

In late 2017, I invested in Convene. This is an excellent organization that gets Christian CEOs together in groups of up to 16 people monthly for a full day of working on their businesses. I loved the concept and the people, but I did not have enough connections and references to establish my own group. I lost money and almost a year of time.

The Breakthrough

In late 2018, a friend introduced me to WeAlign. The vision of WeAlign is to "rehumanize the world through genuine identity and belonging." They have a strengths alignment process, which uses the CliftonStrengths assessment and adds individualized coaching. I loved the vision and the process. This was the first time I had been coached through my strengths, and learning more about those strengths opened my eyes to why, up to that point, I had failed to build a profitable business.

Two things stood out to me about the process. First was the uniqueness of the assessment. You've heard how each of us has unique fingerprints. Our strength profile is just as unique. Second was my non-strengths. When I looked at my struggles in building a coaching business and looked at the things where I'm not as strong, there was a perfect correlation. I saw how this process could help others and also provide some of the missing pieces for my business.

I decided to dive into the WeAlign process, and in early 2019, I achieved WeAlign Executive Coach certification. This started turning my business around; between their process and other coaching, I started digging out of the hole.

Several business leaders who have been through this process have totally transformed their businesses to give them more freedom, income, and impact. One business owner, Sam, started her business after going through the process with me. Three years later, she now has 30 clients nationwide, 15 contractors, and is looking to take her business to the next level.

In 2020, I had been a speaker for business leaders and corporations on assessments, the CliftonStrengths in particular, for two years. Based on my experience, I published my first book, *The Identity Key*, which gives insight into the wide variety of assessments available and their relative benefits. Knowing your true identity at a deep, core level gives you the foundation for greatness; it allows you to find and pursue your calling.

One month after my book was published, the world shut down due to COVID-19. This was a setback, but as we move into a post-pandemic world, this information has become even more essential.

The Stockdale Paradox

Two decades ago, I read a book called *Good to Great* by Jim Collins. Through another God-incident, I reread *Good to Great* this year.

One of the lessons Collins shares is the Stockdale paradox, named after Admiral Jim Stockdale, who was a prisoner of war for eight years during the Vietnam War.

The Stockdale paradox is, "You must retain faith that you will prevail in the end, regardless of the difficulties, AND at the same time, you must confront the most brutal facts of your current reality, whatever they may be."

I realized that although I had forgotten the name of the Stockdale paradox, and had even forgotten the actual wording, I had *remembered* the lesson. That was exactly what I had been doing across the worst decade of my life.

Restoration

In 2021, I felt like my worst decade was finally over in a big way.

I met someone, Kayla, online. A few days later, we met in person, and through several God-incidences, we knew we were right for each other. I loved her church and her family. She had a passion for helping others in a way that was compatible with mine and yet unique to her. We were married four months later and moved into a new house. Her friendship and support have encouraged me to pursue my dreams and my coaching business. She brought her three kids and four grandkids into my life, and I'm enjoying discovering what it's like to be a parent and grandparent.

New relationship, new home in a new city, new church—new energy to pursue my dream.

Through this experience, I learned three lessons:

1. Retain faith that you will win in the end AND face the brutal facts.
2. Discover your dreams and find your passion. This will give you the direction of your calling and the power to pursue it.
3. Turn your day-to-day chaos into clarity and follow God's calling for your life, and God will restore the years that the locusts ate.

My future is now bright. I feel like God is opening the doors for me to pass on the lessons from this decade to others in the midst of their own turbulence. As I've learned more about companies and the people issues that they face, I see opportunities where these same lessons apply.

I help people get clarity on where and who they are in life at a deep core level, determine where they want to be, and create a map (or plan) on how to get there. I work with organizations in the same way. My ministry is to use my experience and strengths coaching to help individuals and organizations get out of their *chaos* into their *clarity* and pursue their *calling*.

If you would like to experience a one-hour coaching call with Dale Young at no charge, email dale@coachdale.com and mention *Next Level Your Life*. Follow Dale on LinkedIn LinkedIn.com/in/CoachDale and Facebook Facebook.com/CoachDaleYoung.

Tweetable: "Life is a journey; your dream is the compass; passion is the fuel." —Dale Young, 2011

TOM ZIGLAR

Growing Up Ziglar

Tom Ziglar is a speaker, trainer, and the CEO of Zig Ziglar Corporation, as well as the author of 10 Leadership Virtues for Disruptive Times *and* Choose to Win.

Joining the Family Business

Even with Zig Ziglar as my dad, I didn't really feel the pressure that growing up with a famous parent sometimes brings. I just don't seem to be wired that way. It was such an incredible experience having him as my father.

Dad traveled a lot, and while we were in school, he was gone up to three nights a week, 40 weeks a year. But when he was home, he would change his schedule so he could take me to school and play golf with me. For me, that was normal.

Dad was intentional and when he was with us, there weren't any distractions. He was different from most people. He wasn't afraid to say no to people, which took a lot of burden off his shoulders and allowed him to make us a priority. This is a really powerful leadership concept.

When I came into the Ziglar company, I had to work my way up. I was 30 when I became the president and CEO. It wasn't until 15 years ago that I started speaking and training. I'd never wanted to. Why would I go out there to speak when we already had the best in the world? Some of that was based on my personality, some of it was fear. I finally got talked into speaking for the first time and liked it, but it wasn't fun while I was getting ready for it. It was nerve-wracking, and my stomach would do somersaults.

I spoke several more times, and then I finally had to have a "sit down with myself in the corner" talk and ask, *What's my worry? What am I anxious about?* I realized I had burdened myself with the idea that people wanted me to be Zig Ziglar on stage. I had to step out of myself and ask, *Do people really want you to be like Zig Ziglar on stage?*

The answer was no. They wanted me to have the same principles and values but to be the best version of *myself.* When I am not myself, it comes across as fake, as wearing a mask. That understanding put the pressure in the right place, developing myself and understanding what people needed.

I realized it wasn't about me or the opportunity I had to speak. It was about every person in the room.

I decided to engage Poll Moussoulides, a speaker trainer who coaches Fortune 100 CEOs in Europe and voice coaches movie stars. I flew to Dublin, Ireland and spent two days with him. I needed somebody who knew of Zig Ziglar but wasn't in the fan club. Sometimes you run across people who are such fans that they won't tell you what you need to hear. I needed somebody to shoot straight.

Working with Poll, I realized that while I could be myself, I could not ever wing one of my speeches. The top in any profession never wing it. They have diligent intentionality about perfecting their skills. Poll's input massively influenced me and also gave me the confidence to be myself on stage.

What You Feed Your Mind Determines Your Appetite

One of my favorite quotes from my dad is, "You can change what you are and where you are by changing what goes into your mind." It's really simple. Who do you want to become? What do you have a burning desire and a passion for? Feed your mind that.

The number one lesson I learned from my dad was, control your input. Be intentional about your input. There's no action that happens without someone first thinking about it. When we intentionally choose the right input—what we read, what we listen to, and who we associate with—that changes our thinking.

Our thinking changes our beliefs. Our beliefs also change our thinking. It's a loop. In turn, your thinking changes the actions you take, and the actions you take affect your results. Your input determines your outlook, your outlook determines your output, and your output determines your outcome. Input, outlook, output, outcome. It all starts with what we choose to put into our mind.

I was in Nashville having dinner with Dan Miller, a great friend who wrote *48 Days to the Work You Love*, and his 25-year-old grandson Caleb Miller. My book *Choose to Win* is about habits. The fastest way to success is to replace a bad habit with a good habit. Caleb said, "How do you know if you have a bad habit?"

It's astonishing how awesome a question that is. Most people may feel it obvious what is or isn't a bad habit. Not necessarily. I said, "If your goal is to get lung cancer, then smoking is a great habit. Here's the problem, most people don't have clearly defined goals or a purpose, something they want to achieve in their life. To test if you have a good or a bad habit, ask yourself if what you are doing is taking you closer to or further from your goal."

Determine Your Why, Become a Self-Starter, and Make Living Your Why Automatic

Dad taught me a lot about the connection between my Why, motivation, and becoming a self-starter. Instead of making decisions for me, he would ask me, "Who do you want to become? Will doing that take you closer to your big goal, dream, or purpose? Do you still want to do that?" He was doing Ninja-Jedi mind tricks on me, and ultimately, he was teaching me how to develop a clear direction of where I wanted to go because he knew I needed to constantly be moving towards my Why and purpose to build a meaningful life.

Have you ever wondered why some people are self-starters and others seem to be stuck in a rut waiting for someone else to push them into movement?

Dad said we need to be "meaningful specifics instead of wandering generalities." Most of us fall in the middle. We are headed in sorta the right direction some of the time. What if you had a clear purpose for each area of your life AND you were making steady progress every day? Living out your WHY would be automatic!

How do we make living our Why automatic?

Self-Starter—Intrinsic Motivation
Confidence
Competence
Habit
Why

We all want to be intrinsically motivated Self-Starters. This requires Confidence to do what we know we need to do. Confidence comes from Competence. Competence is simply the result of good habits, and good habits are simply the result of doing something poorly enough times, until we learn to do it well.

Here is the tricky part. Our WHY must be clearly identified so that we keep growing through the learning phase—otherwise we give up before we make the good habit part of our life.

Implementing the right habits depends on a dream, a Why, a purpose, big enough to keep you going when the setbacks come.

My Perfect Start Routine

Every morning, I follow a routine I call The Perfect Start. The first two to three hours of the day, I have quiet time. I'm reading and getting my priorities done. I try to learn something new every day that I can share with someone else for their benefit. Somebody once asked me at an event, "What was the one thing that made Zig Ziglar who he was?" He spent two hours a day reading, listening, researching, learning something that he could internalize, simplify, and then share with someone else for their benefit. That last piece is the key—for their benefit. I encourage people who want to be like Zig to, for five minutes every day, be intentional and read or listen to something, internalize it, simplify it, then share it with someone else for their benefit. If you do that for a year, it will totally change your life.

I share The Perfect Start in my book *Choose to Win*. First, I get alone in my office with no distraction and do a process called Two Chairs (which I learned from Bob Beaudine). I have one chair for me and one for God, and we have a five-minute conversation. I ask God questions, and then I listen for four and a half minutes. *God, do you know what's going on? God, are you big enough to handle it? God, what's the plan?* It's hard being quiet, meditating, and just listening.

Then, I read or study a Bible devotional. Next, I get into whatever the major thing is. Two or three times a year, I do a gratitude practice I call 66 Days of Gratitude. For 66 days in a row, I write down three things I'm grateful for. On day one, I start with three things I'm grateful for. On day two, I read the previous day, then I add three new things to the list. By the end of the 66 days, I have almost 200 things I'm grateful for. There's a reason for 66 days. Habits take 21 days or longer to create, but 66 days is the average. Most people are naturally focused on identifying things that can hurt us, so most people are bent a little negative. I think it's just the way we're wired. We don't want to get hurt. In the old days, it was the saber-toothed tiger. These days we don't want to be taken advantage of. When you start looking for new things to be grateful for, you actually train your mind to start thinking that way. And that's a powerful way to think.

The other habit I really like is what I call The Mental Model. Brain science backs this up. If I have an important business meeting, a meeting with somebody on my team, a speech, a training, or a podcast, I write it down on my calendar. Then, that morning, I spend one minute in my mind envisioning the answers to a few questions: *Who's the audience? What's their biggest need? What are the drivers of the people there? What are they worried about? What would be a win for them?* I start playing in my mind how the event might go. If I'm going to sell something, then I think as a salesperson. *What are the objections they might have? What are they going to hear from the competition? Who are the influencers in the group who might have a say in this decision?* What I'm really doing is creating slots in my mind for when we actually have the conversation. It could go exactly the direction I want or it could veer a little bit, but it doesn't matter. Either way, I'm prepared in advance for what could happen. That makes me more productive and makes for a much better outcome in general. Allowing the subconscious to work on the situation before you get there prepares you.

Grow Yourself—Grow Your Team

A 2022 survey of 2,000 people by JobSage discovered that 28% of people quit their job in the past two years because of mental health reasons. When asked about the major contributing factors:

55% said Stress and Burnout
38% said Depression
37% said Lack of Motivation

Do you relate to any of these factors? Here is how to deal with them—focus on the solution, not the problem. The solution to stress and burnout is quality of life. If you are rocking it in your mental, spiritual, physical, family, financial, and personal lives, then stress and burnout will not cause you to quit your job.

A powerful solution to Depression is Purpose. If your work has a higher good, cause, or purpose that aligns with your personal Why and Purpose, then Depression will not be a reason you quit work. A powerful solution to Lack of Motivation is Growth. If you are growing and learning every day, then motivation automatically shows up. Think about this, if you are growing towards your purpose and living a balanced, quality life, would you quit your job?

If you lead a team of people and they know you are helping them grow towards their purpose and you are protecting their quality of life, would they quit? I think not!

What Inspires Me

I got a six-minute video from a lady whose brother had been really struggling. He had made a lot of bad life choices. He even tried to commit suicide. She said she had given him tough love. In the hospital with COVID, finally, he realized he had to make a change. And she said she would help him.

He arrived home, and when a Ziglar book showed up, he asked if he could read it. He read it three times in a week, with all the notes. Stories like that inspire me. I am grateful for every single time I am able to share a life-changing message and then see the ripples it creates.

Tom Ziglar is the CEO of the Zig Ziglar Corporation and Ziglar.com and the author of *10 Leadership Virtues for Disruptive Times* and *Choose to Win*. Order his books at www.ziglar.com. To book speaking engagements, please email tom@ziglar.com.

Tweetable: Our WHY must be clearly identified so that we keep growing through the learning phase —otherwise we give up before we make the good habit part of our life.

WENDY GRIFFIS

From Unemployed to Designing a Lifestyle of Influence and Income

Wendy Griffis is an industry leader and Realtor® in the top 20 agents in Jacksonville, FL. She wrote the book Recognize the Difference *to educate consumers that there are different types of real estate agents. She has been seen in* Florida Realtor *and* Buffini & Company Magazine. *She is passionate about sharing her experience in personal and financial growth.*

The Painful Truth

"Your position has been eliminated."

Those words rang in my ears long after the phone call ended.

I should have seen the writing on the wall. My manager, and his manager, had been laid off over the course of the previous few weeks. When I received a call from someone I had never met, apparently their manager, I sat stunned, thinking, What did I do wrong? What could I have done differently?

The feelings of inadequacy and helplessness were palatable. It is normal to feel a deep sense of rejection when you lose a job. Eventually, when the company filed for bankruptcy and shut the doors, I felt lucky I wasn't one of the employees escorted out with a look of shock and no last paycheck. But, at the time, my dismissal felt deeply personal. This was going to be the LAST time I would allow Corporate America to control my destiny.

Can You Make Money in That Real Estate Thing?

I've always been an achiever. In college, I held leadership positions in clubs and graduated magna cum laude with a degree in statistics and a minor in business administration.

I believed in go to school, get good grades, get a good job, and climb the ladder to success... until I got knocked around a bit in various jobs. No matter how hard I worked, the salary remained the same. In the companies I worked for, I felt like I was just a number. But, I had hope for what we could achieve, so I kept striving.

My husband and I were young and excited about our future. We decided it was time to settle down—well—to buy a house, which felt like the next grown-up step.

I LOVED my real estate agent, though I know I drove her crazy. I had questions about everything and spreadsheets analyzing options. I wanted to understand the process clearly. She took the time to explain and guide me through it all. So, in January 2000, after the world did not end with Y2K, but tech companies were collapsing, and after my position had been eliminated, I thought I would try my hand at that real estate thing. I called my agent, and she told me how to get my license. By February 2000, I hit the ground running.

Except... it was not what I expected.

You Own a Business

I never liked the idea of "being in sales." And I certainly did not understand how working for commissions meant you could be helping people and not get paid, until I didn't get paid for a month... for two months… and more. Even though I worked very hard to serve my clients, it certainly wasn't easy.

Eventually, I did start making sales. By my second year, I had built my confidence and knowledge and quickly became what our industry calls "a top producer," someone whose sales volume is typically in the top 5-10% of all agents in the area. As a young agent, I leaned on my knowledge of the technical parts of contracts, negotiation, and transaction management. But I did not understand that there is WAY more to being a real estate agent. *I later realized it's possible to make money selling real estate, but to have a career that compounds over time, you have to treat it like a business.*

I never owned a business, and I didn't think of the sales I was making as a long-term career. That is, until I was introduced to my business mentor Brian Buffini. By introduced, I mean I sat in a Buffini & Company conference called Turning Point Retreat where I heard him speak. New ideas started flowing, and I caught a vision of what life COULD be: *a life where you built a legacy business, pouring yourself into your clients in such a way that they would become lifetime supporters and advocates.* And I took action—immediately. I've found there are people who jump right in and trust the system. And then there are those who put one toe in or watch from the outside to see if it could work. In my naivety, I just believed. And I'm glad I did. But there are things they don't tell you at the seminar that took many years to understand.

The Great Recession (Depression) of 2008

The world would like to call what happened a great recession. To me, it was a depression, in more ways than one. First and foremost, it lasted eight years for me and my family. It started in 2006 when I started seeing a decline in my ability to help my clients sell their homes.

Why isn't this home selling? What is going on? How many of these price adjustments will we need to make before we've got a buyer? What is a short sale? How do I help a client do one? What do you mean I just worked a year on the transaction and now it's foreclosed and I get no compensation?

Unless you were an agent during this time, it is hard to fathom just how difficult these circumstances were. I was struggling to help my clients while I was living the experience first-hand in technicolor as my husband lost his job, we lost our house and all our assets, and my income dropped to 10% of what it had been.

The breaking point came when my good friend told me, "Wendy, you should talk to someone." At the time, I did not understand how depressed I was. I remember finding a counselor and making an appointment. The lady said, "So, why are you here?"

I said, "Well, my friend said I should talk to someone, so, well, I'm only here because of that."

She said, "So, tell me what is going on?" Then, my composure broke. And I began to sob.

The counselor gave me some perspective. I had my identity tied to my real estate success. So when I was struggling, I blamed myself. But she explained that I am not the real estate industry, and what happens there is out of my control. It was the industry that I put my hopes and dreams into that was the issue, not myself.

I understood now—I was doing my very best to guide people, people who placed their trust in me, through the process of buying or selling a home—and that I cannot control the world around me. I can only control my reaction to it. But, even with this understanding, I wanted to quit.

The Lunch That Almost Ended My Career

I had lunch with an agent at my office who I trusted. I told her that with my husband not having found a new job yet and the volatility of the real estate income, I couldn't afford to live. She graciously offered to help if I wanted to pass my business along to her, but she encouraged me to keep trying.

I also reached out to all my friends who still had "real jobs" and tried to get interviews for a job. I quickly learned that once you've been a real estate agent for 10+ years, Corporate America feels like you have no skills anymore. So, I was effectively unemployable. And therefore, *there was NO TURNING BACK*. Life and business continued on, and I determined that I would figure it out. Luckily, as the market started to improve in 2012, so did my circumstances.

Hope Is a Powerful Aphrodisiac

I was invited to be an ambassador for Brian Buffini's Peak Producers training course. My first thought was *Why me?* And my second thought was *Well, let's check it out.*

I contacted a couple of agents at my office and said, "Would you watch this with me?" And we did. The Peak Producers course was inspiring, and I learned SO MUCH. I took it over and over and over—*I'm not exaggerating, like two or three times a year since*—because I wanted to share it with others, and I got so much out of doing so. Why? Because it gave me HOPE. Hope for a better future by providing systems and ideas that I could implement to help my mindset and business grow.

I learned that when I had no hope, I did little to change my circumstances. I felt like a victim. But when I had hope, my actions and attitude changed. And when my actions and attitude changed, my results changed.

Neil Pasricha, author of *The Book of Awesome*, says, historically, we have thought about finding happiness wrong. We think, *Work hard, have success, be happy.* But it's actually, *Be happy, work hard, have success.* With hope, I became happier! It also helped that the market started to improve, but the key lesson is that I did not give up. I kept doing the things to grow my business, even without seeing the immediate results. And they eventually came.

Your Income Will Grow as Fast as Your Personal Growth

Who really wants to change? Not me! I like myself just the way I am… except… I wanted more, but I wasn't sure how.

As far as the real estate industry goes, there are awards for production every month, and every year. *Sidenote: There is WAY more to a career in real estate than production numbers. There is also lifestyle, net income, and a holistic view of life.* I would get the awards, and I felt good about my growth and how my business was developing.

It was fun to turn clients into friends and friends into clients. I felt honored when a past client would refer me to a friend or use me again. But, I would sit at the award ceremonies and think, *How can I get THERE? That NEXT LEVEL?* I was disappointed that I couldn't break past my ceiling... until several events occurred that shifted everything.

The first was connection and collaboration with others in the industry and Buffini community who were farther down the path than I was. I cannot emphasize enough the power of being a part of a community of givers. Just being around them at events was intoxicating, especially when their influence would challenge me to push out of my comfort zone. In particular, it was routine to discuss what books we were reading. Except, I wasn't reading any books. This first lesson taught me that to get ahead, I had to change my mindset on reading. So, I made a commitment to read a book a month. Confession: at first, I didn't really "read," I listened to audiobooks. But it got me on the path. My first book blew my mind: *The Power of Ambition* by Jim Rohn.

Now, I routinely read a couple books a month, and I have learned that once your mind is expanded, it cannot go back.

In addition to reading, I found immersing myself in retreats, conferences, and seminars compounded the growth. My sense of self, my vision for what was possible, and my empathy for others grew. And, as a side benefit, my income skyrocketed. My opportunities increased. And then, something magical happened.

I Could See Building a Company Around That

Our industry is constantly "recruiting" agents from one brokerage to another. It's one thing I find challenging to wrap my head around—this dance of promises made, carrots dangled, and the counting of the dollars. I am an extremely loyal person, so though I will rarely say no to a meeting, it takes A LOT to make me switch directions.

During a very interesting recruiting meeting, I had a conversation about the positive experience I've had synergizing with agents in our community and our responsibility to help each other grow and be better. I communicated how much we should champion the givers in our industry. I knew how we all felt about impacting others, one client at a time, and how I personally felt about impacting my peers, one agent at a time. What I have found is that it's HARD to be the "positive guy"—the one who people think is a little weird—when I talk about personal growth and positive peer pressure being instrumental in my success. But those on the journey with me have learned we are all better together. And in that meeting, I was so excited to find a real estate brokerage who not only agreed but also wanted to build a company where together we ALL can create a LIFE BY DESIGN.

We began with an idea that turned into a company of like-minded, forward-thinking agents. Agents who understand that when you GIVE to your clients, to your co-workers, and to your community, success is inevitable. But, defining what success looks like to EACH person is what matters. Yes, there are production numbers to count. But, the system we follow talks about Buffini's Five Circles in Life: spiritual, family, business, financial, and personal. We set goals in ALL areas. We brainstorm, collaborate, synergize, and participate in each other's lives. We are designing the lives we want to live.

Studies have shown that work production is measurably increased and life satisfaction is greater when people have friendships in their industry. For a long time, I did not have these deeper friendships. I was the agent who could "do it on my own." The irony is, my sales and income skyrocketed as soon as I began to share my experiences with others, and in helping them, I have greatly helped myself.

I have two favorite Zig Ziglar quotes. The first is short and sweet: "You can have everything you want if you help enough people get what they want." The other is longer but just as impactful: "There is no better way to stay inspired than spending time with inspiring people. There is a healthy sort of peer pressure that keeps us pushing forward, a symbiotic effect that causes us to become more in the group than we could ever become by ourselves."

These ideas guide my philosophy of building a life by design. Life can be done alone, but if you help others get what they want and don't try to do it alone, your results will compound and you can stay inspired, even during difficult times.

Influence and Income

I have felt the pain of wanting to grow and not knowing how, so now I feel compelled to help those who want to take their business and life to the next level. We all have persevered through challenges, and my obstacles have truly fueled my passion to help others.

I feel deeply grateful for the success I've had and the lessons I get to share with others. I understand clearly the power of never growing weary of doing good. We need to learn and grow, surround ourselves with like-minded people, and design the life we've always dreamed of.

Wendy Griffis believes in bringing an authentic voice to the real estate industry. Influenced by personal growth industry leaders and Buffini's "It's a Good Life" message, she is passionate about paying success forward. Learn more about how she positively impacts others and if you qualify to be a part of her synergy group on www.wendygriffis.com.

Tweetable: Reading, immersing myself in a positive, growth-minded community, seminars, and training gave me hope. When I had hope, my actions and attitude changed. And when my actions and attitude changed, my results changed.

JEREMY MELANCON

You Don't Have to Be the Best to Saddle Up Anyway

Jeremy Melancon is a custom home consultant and real estate professional. After traveling the US riding saddle broncs and competing in over 120 rodeos each year, he designed a life of financial freedom which allowed him to build the home life he wants with his family.

The Only Way to Get Good

When I was 17, I went to see some of my friends compete in the Texas High School Finals Rodeo. They were bronc riders, and while I had grown up around horses, I had never really paid attention to saddle bronc riding.

After watching it one time, I wanted to be a bronc rider.

According to Wikipedia, saddle bronc riding is a rodeo event that involves riding a bucking horse that attempts to throw off the rider. Originally based on the necessary horse breaking skills of a working cowboy, the event is now a highly stylized competition that utilizes horses bred for strength, agility, and bucking ability. It is recognized by the main rodeo organizations, such as the Professional Rodeo Cowboys Association (PRCA).

I couldn't wait to get on my first bronc. I had been on horses that bucked before and was starting colts for extra money in high school. When you were starting to train a young horse, I was the guy that would start riding it for the first 30 days. So I had been bucked off plenty, but bronc riding wasn't a controlled environment. There are no starter horses that stop when you are falling off. The only way to get good at riding broncs is to be really bad at many, many attempts.

Bronc riding is scored by two judges, each giving up to 25 points for how difficult the horse was to ride and 25 points for how well the cowboy rode the horse and maintained control for the full eight-second ride. One hundred points is a "perfect ride."

Cowboys who can spur in rhythm with the horse—pull their feet back up to the saddle seat and then kick them forward up above the horse's shoulder, all before the horse hits the ground—score the most points. The only problem is, once you nod your head, the bronc leaves the chute faster than anything you've ever done.

When you start off, you really want to spur, and people are giving you great uplifting advice, but you still can't seem to get your feet moving. As soon as you nod, the world blurs and the ground jumps up and slaps you in the face. Then, they'd say, "Stick it out, and after enough tries, things will just click."

My coaches turned out to be right. I got pretty good at riding broncs. I owe my college degree to a rodeo scholarship. In college, I had a successful trip to the College National Finals Rodeo, where our team at Sam Houston State University brought home the first men's championship title for our school since 1968.

After college, I joined the Professional Rodeo Cowboys Association (PRCA) and qualified for rodeos including Houston, Cheyenne Frontier Days, Salinas, Pendleton, and other historic rodeos across the US. If you follow the sport, I have probably been to your hometown rodeo.

Rodeo to Real Estate

I always say that rodeo breeds entrepreneurs. Imagine going on a job interview and telling your potential employer, "I can't work Thursdays, Fridays, or weekends and will need two or three months off during the summer to travel the country rodeoing." Not too many would take your phone calls I would think. Since I wasn't one of the guys winning every weekend, I would do anything to earn extra income to keep up with travel expenses.

Rodeoing involves a lot of driving. You travel with a four man buddy group so you can split expenses and windshield time. When it was your turn to drive the night shift, you were normally on your own with a passed out passenger who was supposed to be keeping you up but knew they had to get their rest for their own turn. I was really interested in real estate, but it was tough to find guides on the subject that were easily consumed while driving thousands of miles. I found *The Real Estate Guys Podcast* one night while driving, and it kind of became what I was known for. The guys would wake up come daybreak, throw something toward me at the front, and say "Come on, the real estate dudes again?" just to give me a hard time.

When I wasn't traveling to rodeos, I spent most of my time scouting single-family homes that needed repairs most people didn't want to do.

The plan was to remodel them into rentals or flips. Like bronc riding, this was something I wanted to know more about and be good at, but I didn't know any more about remodeling a home than I did about spurring that first horse.

My wife and traveling partners helped fix up the first investment property I bought, but the second one showed me I was in over my head. Back then, YouTube wasn't the robust educational network that it is today.

Another rodeo family we knew introduced me to a great contractor named Tony. Tony laughed when I told him that I wanted a hard bid before he started remodeling. He said, "I'll give you a bid, but you're not going to like it." He explained all the unknowns that we could possibly find and wisely told me that if I wanted to learn what I said I wanted to learn, my best option was to come alongside him as a helper and learn as we fixed it up. I was still going to college, so I would come help him between classes. This would also save me money since we wouldn't have to hire someone else. Tony told me that when I ran out of money, he would go to another project. When I won another rodeo, I'd call him back and we would get it finished.

We did get it finished and then we started remodeling homes all over Huntsville, Texas. Tony and I would work on projects of all different shapes and sizes and with unique problems. Tony's experience and patience were gifts. He would let me make mistakes and go along with my wild ideas, then help me get them across the finish line when I got stuck. With an amazing mix of experience and patience, Tony was the definition of a mentor, and with so much one-on-one time, he helped me collapse the timeframe between what I wanted to build and the skills I would need to do it. One ugly house after another, my wife and I slowly grew our real estate portfolio of small rentals that we had brought back to life with Tony.

Leveling Up and Building the Dream

Rodeoing slowed down as my wife and I started a family and our other interests and passions grew to demand more of our dedication and time. My wife and I decided to lean into our experience gained through college rodeoing and the skills that I had been working on with Tony and trade in our portfolio to start a multi-family project where you could live under the same roof as your horse. We would design and build the property for college rodeo members so they could have their horse and an area to practice nearby.

This property really turned into a passion project. The homes I had remodeled and kept as rentals at this point all had a few acres with them so that I could offer my friends and college rodeo teammates a place to live and keep their horses. These types of properties showed me a great opportunity in our area. We went to work building this dream, and today we have an elite community where college rodeo athletes live and train alongside their animals. With 42 units, 78 horse stalls, two arenas, horse pastures, and a gym, our community is a perfect place for equestrian lovers of all kinds.

As Tony and I started building, others drove up and asked if we could build for them. I went to Tony and told him someone asked me to build their house! He had gotten a similar phone call, so we decided to partner together on both projects and split whatever we made instead of hiring each other and keeping it all separate. I sanded down an old real estate sign I had, put peel and stick letters on it, and stuck it out by the road.

The calls were slow at first and most of our calls were from referrals or word of mouth. At first, we weren't just home builders. We would build your shop, add a garage, fence your pasture, anything to stay busy and keep steady work in front of the guys we had helping us. However, as time went on and we built our reputation, we started getting more requests than we could handle. So we dropped some of the services that we used to stay busy until we narrowed our services down to our unique way to serve. And, helping clients navigate building a custom home became what we were known for in our community.

Today, we own and operate Turnkey Custom Homes. My mom helps with the accounting and my dad came on to help train me in sales. A bronc riding buddy helped get us through that first new construction build. My best friend from middle school also manages projects with us and even my brother works with us every once in a while. Together, we get to go out each day and help people navigate the crazy world of building a custom home. In his kindergarten graduation program this year, my little boy said that he wanted to work for Turnkey Custom Homes when he grew up, and I couldn't be more proud.

A Rodeo Entrepreneur Mindset

I wouldn't trade this journey for anything. There are still things that keep me up at night. I have found that it helps knowing that I am not the only one that thinks this way—that there is no line you cross where all your concerns magically float away. I am terrified of losing people's money. I am scared to think of laying off friends and family. I am scared to imagine not finishing someone's home.

I've been bucked off plenty in business. Like how learning to move my feet finally just clicked in bronc riding, in business, you have to get bucked off and keep getting back on and nodding your head before things click.

These lessons clicked for me after I heard them over and over again and then put in the time—

Celebrate the journey. From my experience, when you start a business, you are just doing something that interests you. You study and learn technical skills so that you can get deeper into a world you want to know more about. Then, you continue until you reach a level where someone notices what you have been working on and asks to hire you. This is validation that your work is important. I believe this is time to celebrate a victory. Celebrating helps me to remember that what I am trying to accomplish isn't a finish line or a box to check but an endless study to improve on. When I learn something new, I also realize that before that time I didn't know it. The last client didn't get the benefit of me knowing what I just learned. If I am not careful, this can make me focus on what other experts may know and start to think that maybe I am not ready to help my clients. But instead, it helps me to remember that even when I was just starting, someone believed I could help them at my current level and getting better only helps me to serve better.

Don't hide from fear. Sometimes, laying in bed, I think about the what ifs. This can help me in a sense because I think through the "what if" situation to the worst scenario. Then I end up hypothetically working through the situation and find out that it may not be that scary after all. This also gives me an opportunity to think through the threats and weaknesses I may be concerned about. Most of the time I come away with a very positive frame of mind.

You don't have to be the best. You may attend a seminar that has helped people learn a skill that they then used to grow a business larger than you even thought possible. But, that doesn't mean you have to reach the same height to effectively use the skills you learn at that seminar. No matter where you are in your business, what you learn and practice can help the people right in front of you. I feel better when I appreciate where I am than

I do when I'm constantly working on the next step. It seems like each time I focus on learning for the sake of being better instead of for the sake of growth, the growth shows up. Relationships are the most important things in our life for our peace. Focusing on how you can help someone makes you the best you can be for them. And when you become that, they have every reason to return the favor.

I love being a business owner and getting to spend time with people that we have built relationships with in the endless pursuit of solutions. Just like in saddle bronc riding, different things click at different times. I wasn't the best bronc rider, and I don't want to try and measure what it means to be the best entrepreneur, but at least I'm "movin' my feet," and I will keep doing that as long as I can help others.

Building a large project can be intimidating. Jeremy Melancon has disrupted the world of custom home construction by helping others understand and work through their home-building goals. To be prepared when you start building, reach out to Jeremy@BuiltByTurnkey.com or visit www.BuiltByTurnkey.com.

Tweetable: Starting a business is doing something that interests you until someone asks to hire you. This is validation and should be celebrated. There is no finish line in business but an endless study to improve on.

DR. GURPREET SINGH PADDA

Thinking in Spectrums
How Crisis Sharpens an Unfocused Mind

Dr. Gurpreet Singh Padda is a successful pain medicine physician who also has achievements in hospitality, real estate, computer science, and crisis investing. With his intellectual curiosity combined with his ADHD superpower, Dr. Padda creates novel solutions to big problems.

Chaos at the Edge

I was born in a turbulent period in Punjab, India, less than a three-minute rocket launch from the border edge of Pakistan, just 17 years after the violence of The Partition killed and displaced millions of Indians and Pakistanis. India was in its adolescence, experimenting with communism and not quite certain if it would survive into adulthood.

My grandfather had been the elected governor of Lahore, which was now under the control of Pakistan. My family had been politically-active freedom fighters, helping India gain her independence from the British. But at this time, after the Brits had looted trillions from the country as they departed, the country was facing economic collapse and starvation and sectarian and political violence was a seething undercurrent to the intermittent Indo-Pakistani Wars literally in our farm fields.

There had been *fatwas* issued to execute the members of my family, especially any of my grandfather's male heirs that might someday have political aspirations. I, unfortunately, was a male heir. I spent much of my early childhood playing with my rifle-toting bodyguards and my ever-present dog that spoke only German (a trained Belgian Malinois I realized as an adult). When I did manage to escape my guards to play with other kids and sneak a piece of candy or other food, I would be quickly discovered and given an emetic because I might have been fed a poison.

Due to my extraordinarily poor attention span and hyper-inquisitive nature, it was decided that I should be relocated to a distant boarding school where no one would know who I was, thereby reducing the risk of poisoning. I didn't have any parental supervision at school, so the teachers didn't have anyone to report my inattention to schoolwork to. As long as

I wasn't disruptive to the other children, I had tremendous independence, and my intellectual curiosity was allowed to bounce between different concepts and ideas I found interesting.

Coming to America and Capitalism

My father was studying physics and was recruited to a position in the United States when I was seven. When I was nine, my mother and I joined him in the US where she pursued her studies in mathematics. I hadn't had direct parental supervision during boarding school, and now I was entering the American school system in the urban core of St. Louis, Missouri. These schools required children to focus and sit, but thank God, I could pretend not to speak or understand English well. This was also before the days of chemical brain restraints, so I was not prescribed any amphetamines to control my inattentive behavior.

America was utterly amazing to me. You could do anything here. You could go get ice cream and no one immediately forced you to throw it up. The dogs here weren't guard dogs, and they played with you even if the adults were nearby. It was a different world; communal strife, starvation, and the sounds of air raid sirens were unheard of. You could do the things you wanted to do and buy things without asking for permission from a government official. Even then, I realized that we had left the communism of India for American capitalism.

As my English continued to improve, I wanted some of the cool toys I would see on the television. I had ADHD, and as part of that, I hyperfocused when I found something interesting I wanted. I would do other kids' homework for money and, as I got older, I started building businesses.

Starting to Focus, But Not Too Much

Even then, I realized I had an affliction that kept me from being at the very top of my class. I totally knew the academic material and had learned way more than what I needed to for school. I could test really well when I wanted to but was easily distracted, to the point where I would sometimes earn an F.

I didn't concentrate well, and my mother did everything she could so I wouldn't take apart every electronic device in the house. I still remember her admonishing me to complete my tasks, even if I was doing 15 or 20 little projects. Sometimes when I would take things apart and reassemble them, I would make sure they worked as intended, but I was left with three or four extra parts which I would have to hide. That's when I realized what a minimum viable product was. Sometimes things worked just as well with a lot fewer parts. Most importantly, I could let my interests wander far afield, as long as I paid attention to closing all my loops by finishing the tasks I started.

Expanding Capitalism and Leverage

When I ran out of things to "fix" at home, I started offering my services to other people. I started off fixing small appliances and lawn mowers. Then I ended up doing landscaping and, eventually, interior rehabbing. At 15, I started hiring other people to help me. I couldn't yet drive, so I would visit the jobsite first thing in the morning, have a crew member drop me off at high school, and later have them pick me up. During lunch, I would check in from the school cafeteria payphone. I learned to manage other people and leverage their professional skills.

For some odd reason, the more balls I had in the air, the more focused I became. My grades suddenly shot up, I started getting honors in every class, and I was making a lot of money for a teenager.

The Beginning of Passive Investing and Creating a Syndication

When I got into medical school, I knew that I couldn't actively do rehabs and study. I had to figure out something I could do to make money that didn't require my direct participation. I started buying things I could flip, like real estate.

Later, while in surgical residency in Cook County, Chicago, I started buying apartment buildings on the west side of Chicago, rehabbing them, and flipping them. That's where my real estate projects really started to take off.

At the same time, other people began to express interest in investing with me. Investors allowed me to do all the super cool stuff: finding projects, determining how to turn them around, fixing the buildings, and then selling for a profit.

I couldn't believe that other people just wanted to watch their bank accounts steadily grow while they let me have all the fun with all of these complex moving parts.

I Love Medicine, But...

I didn't always want to be a doctor. I knew I loved science because I liked asking a question, creating a number of possible solutions, and then discerning the least complex answer. To me, elegant simplicity was a critical element for all solutions. I initially wanted to go into computer science, because I could create solutions in the form of elegant code, but I also loved biology with all of its complexities and never-ending surprises. I was 17 when I started medical school, the youngest person in my six-year program. I graduated when I was 22.

Initially, I went into surgery, but I got bored. It was too mechanically repetitive. I was fascinated by neurochemistry and the concept of consciousness. I transferred to anesthesia and eventually specialized in pediatric anesthesia. Looking at an EKG screen for slight and subtle waveform changes, all while monitoring and adjusting ventilation, blood pressure, and anesthetics on an infant undergoing liver or brain surgery, knowing that my decision and response time had to be faster than the six seconds it took for a rhythm to pass by on the screen or my patient may not survive, seemed to keep me constantly alert and focused on the complexity at hand. I found that my hyperfocus was hyper-useful in caring for my one patient at a time.

Rediscovering Leverage to Solve More Problems

After nearly 10 years, I wanted to pull back from that narrow focus and solve bigger and more global problems. I was good at what I was doing in pediatric anesthesia, but I wanted to help in a bigger, broader way. I wanted to create change that could affect a lot of people. I had completed an MBA in international finance as I was transitioning away from pediatric anesthesia, and I started to look at collateral fields I had expertise in that would allow me to manage and help thousands of patients at a time.

There was an ongoing epidemic of pain, and my neurobiology background and fine-point three-dimensional skills paired well with interventional pain medicine. Observing and studying my patients, I concluded that there was also an epidemic of addiction and an epidemic of obesity, all in the same group of patients. There had to be an elegant solution that explained this apparent complexity. This problem was devouring nearly two-thirds of the US healthcare budget, a $1.7 trillion problem to solve.

Eventually, it became clear to me that this was an issue of metabolic inflammation resulting from processed food consumption (a combination of vegetable oil and refined sugars) and a lack of physical activity. The human body has stores of a carbohydrate called glycogen in its liver and muscles. These stores have to be depleted daily. If the glycogen carbohydrate stores are not burned for calories, even a small amount of carbohydrates consumed as food are stored as fat. The vegetable oils and refined sugars in processed foods lead to tremendous insulin resistance, and the resulting fat accumulation causes inflammation. Interestingly, the historic recorded rise in cases of inflammation from these processed foods is mirrored by rising rates of ADHD.

Natural Crisis Investing and Contrarian Thinking

In high school, I was the only brown kid with a turban in a nearly all-white school. I didn't fit in, probably because I was also a little goofy, always inquisitive, and always trying to figure stuff out. There was no one in my school that looked like me or who had shared experiences we could bond over. The social isolation "allowed" me to focus inward, and to observe other people, akin to how Jane Goodall must have felt observing chimps in the wild.

That ability to focus and observe benefits me both as a physician and as an investor. I look at how things are playing out, create a hypothesis for what I think is going to happen, and then I test my hypothesis.

Growing up in a world of crisis, I learned to observe subtle clues. My very life depended on it. As an adult, I am attracted to crisis situations, because a crisis contains both a threat and an opportunity.

My investment style is contrarian. I'm always scanning the horizon, asking myself what's lurking and what's on the other side. Scanning the horizon is akin to scanning the incoming EKG data combined with all of the other vital signs and medical observations, but now the patient is an economic puzzle.

The Value of Urgency and Fear

Having ADHD with an inward focus but with all sensors on hyperalert, I learned to create mental models for task completion. The primitive limbic system accepts the interpretation of threat and reward projected by the neocortex. I find this means that if I gamify specific tasks by creating micro-rewards for full task completion and micro-punishments for task failure, I achieve far better outcomes and I better align my dopaminergic drive with my goals.

One example might be creating project-specific checklists for an acquisition broken down by phase. As I check off the elements, the boxes turn green. I don't tell many people about the project which prevents me from having ego involvement and might cause me to have dopamine release just from discussing the positive ramifications. I have a contra-checklist that I create as well for items not successfully completed, and I pair that with self-imposed physical exercise (I hate burpees). Once the project is fully completed, I usually will reward myself with a celebration dinner with my immediate family and friends.

How I Approach Real Estate Investing

I look at each project I am involved in through multiple lenses to find solutions that are profitable, elegant, and aesthetically beautiful. I look at not just the project, but also the environment it's in, the emerging trends in the local path of progress, the community demographics, and the drivers of health and wealth in that community.

Between my business partner and I, we have approximately $24 million in residential and commercial real estate assets. We manage the rehabs directly and do all of our own design work. We don't like to build simple boxes just to build boxes. We want to situate our projects to be in harmony with the pre-existing environment. If there's a mature tree, we want to take advantage of that and build around the tree and use landscaping to showcase it rather than take it down. We like to bring the outdoor and indoor spaces together, so we do a lot of patios, and try to maximize the connection to the environment and create a feeling of spaciousness and harmony.

We have specialized in deep value-add projects, often converting derelict urban assets back to functional use. We work in neighborhoods well before gentrification occurs, because that's where the most interesting problems and crisis opportunities are. These projects uniquely benefit from a simultaneous hyperkinetic and hyperfocused approach. This approach creates unparalleled returns for our investors who can rest assured that someone is looking at that six-second EKG screen.

Contact Gurpreet Singh Padda, founder of RedPillKapital, with decades of real-life experience in crises investing at info@redpillkapital.com.

Check out his content on his personal LinkedIn or www.redpillkapital.com.

Tweetable: Growing up in a world of crisis, I learned to observe subtle clues. My very life depended on it. As an adult, I am attracted to crisis situations, because a crisis contains both a threat and an opportunity.

BECKY BOUHSINE

The Power Within
Addict to Entrepreneur

Becky Bouhsine spent 12 years living in addiction before she discovered personal development which became the breakthrough to shifting her thinking and the anchor to her recovery. Becky is the founder of Iconic Elite, raising awareness to impact lives through social media and coaching.

The Outsider

At the age of 14, I saw myself as the outsider looking in on a world that had no place for me. In my eyes, I was that girl no one liked.

I was bullied at school. With the beginning of social media, it was constant. The school system added pressure, placing me in every class known as "the bottom set." This began deep rooted self-limiting beliefs that would soon explode.

I was the youngest of my brother and me. We grew up within a dysfunctional family. My mum and dad's relationship had its moments of toxicity fueled by Dad's alcohol consumption. No one was aware of the helplessness I felt. I didn't have the tools to express myself emotionally. I just knew what I was feeling was more than sadness.

Through my 14-year-old eyes, I didn't belong. Sobbing on the floor of my bedroom, the pit of my stomach aching from the dark and emptiness inside, I pleaded with God to let me die.

Goodbye Mum

Boxes of medication surrounded me on the floor. I wrote my final letter to my mum. I apologized and let her know that she hadn't failed as a mother, but I was no longer able to hang on. I climbed into bed, believing this was my last night and I would finally rest in peace.

I was awoken by my mum's voice in panic and her shaking me. I was disoriented and numb. At the hospital, the noise was piercing and the light was blinding. I was in pain, physically from the medication I had taken and emotionally from the realization that I was still alive. I was desperate to no longer feel the painful, dark void within.

I was diagnosed with depression and placed under the care of Child and Adolescent Mental Health Services, where I would begin the process of counseling with the added help of antidepressants.

Life After School

At age 16, I left school after completing my GCSE exams. I felt no sense of achievement however, leaving a school where I had never felt accepted was nothing but a relief. I began to train as a beauty therapist at a local college. The idea of making clients feel good about themselves appealed to me.

At age 17, the dynamics at home had changed. Mum was still healing from my suicide attempt, which made her overprotective. I saw it as an attempt to control my life, and our breakdown in communication became explosive.

I began to rebel, telling lies constantly to my mum about what I was up to. I was drawn to older, bad boy types. I purchased a fake ID and booked my first tattoo. Tattoos became both a way to express myself and my body armor, protecting me from the outside world.

The void within me was only getting deeper and darker. I didn't care if I lived or died, and my behavior became riskier: hanging out with an older crowd, going to nightclubs underage, and having my first experience with drugs.

I felt like I had been reborn when I first indulged in ecstasy. My alter ego had arrived, but it was more than that. Not knowing I was about to unlock Pandora's box, I saw this drug as the key to how I could survive life.

The Spiral Down

Drugs became my escape from reality, my way to disconnect from any uncomfortable emotion or responsibility. Drugs were my coping mechanism.

And they became a coping mechanism I desperately depended on when my mum was diagnosed with a brain tumor. For the first time, I felt truly alone in this world.

By the time my mum returned from six weeks of treatment in the UK, my drug-taking had become reckless. I weighed under seven stone (less than 98 US pounds). With that amount of weight loss, my friends branded me with the nickname Amy Winehouse.

When I turned 18, Child and Adolescent Mental Health Services discharged me because I was no longer in the age bracket. Not long after, I experienced my first accidental drug overdose.

As a consequence of my actions, I was referred to the local Alcohol and Drug Services where I was encouraged to discuss my use of drugs. Was this a deterrent from using drugs? No, in fact, my drug of choice was about to change.

Life on My Terms

At age 19, my relationship with my mum had broken down further. I decided to leave home and begin living life on my terms.

Well, life on my terms didn't live up to my expectations. My boyfriend at the time found himself in prison for drug importation. My party lifestyle began to disintegrate as I isolated myself from the world. I began to self-sabotage further in the form of self-harm. This was another way of releasing my pain, but it was also a punishment for being me. I hated who I was.

I started experimenting with prescription medications. I no longer chased the high. Instead, I chased numbness. It wasn't long after that I had my first taste of heroin.

I was naive and careless, playing Russian roulette with my life, which accelerated my life into a world completely unknown to me.

The Intervention

At age 20, my appetite for heroin had grown. A total of four overdoses now I had miraculously survived. I was powerless and totally unaware of how my actions were affecting those around me.

On the bank holiday of May 2010, I ended up in prison. I had been sentenced to two years after a series of altercations that involved drugs and alcohol. This was the only intervention that saved me from ending up in an early grave. Prison gave me the time to reflect and gain clarity.

Prison was the first place that I felt a sense of real happiness and, ironically, freedom. There were no judgments. I had more tears of laughter than tears of sadness. With my time being used productively, whilst engaging with the services that were there to help, I was finally able to deal with the anger that lived inside of me.

During my time in prison, my niece was born. Due to good behavior, I was granted a home visit. In that moment of picking her up and looking into her eyes, I felt a strong wave of unconditional love, something I had never experienced before.

The emotions were so strong that I made a promise to her that I would hold onto life. I didn't want her to live the life I had led so far. I wanted to be there so that I could be that person she could turn to in her darkest hour of need. I could be for her that person I never had.

Acknowledging the Addict

The first four years after prison were still a roller coaster ride. But I no longer lived in denial and had accepted that I was an addict.

At age 23, I attended a local rehab facility. It was not my decision, nor was I ready to stop using. During my three month stay, I was able to peel back layers until I felt bare. I was beginning to like who I was. I was no longer a slave to heroin. Rehab somehow altered the way I saw drugs. I was able to see the other side. I was also able to let go of the guilt I had buried from the past. It changed the way I used drugs.

Two weeks after leaving the bubble of rehab, I relapsed. I was 24, and this was the only world and identity I knew.

By 25, I had gained my first job since my release from prison. This was the first time anyone had taken a chance on me. Within five years of working for the company, I became a competent, qualified legal secretary with meaningful and loyal friendships. On the outside, I was seen as a professional, but on the inside lay the secret drug addict.

Approaching age 30, I began to question everything. I had a good job, but I had no feeling of fulfillment. *Was there more to life? Was I meant to work until it was time to retire, live life struggling on a pension, making the life I had left even smaller, to only then die?* Surely, everything I had been through, and coming close to death several times, meant I was here for more.

The Fork in the Road

That year, ten years after being sentenced to prison, I was back in court. I had lost my job and was facing data protection charges due to an emotional error in judgment I made to help a friend not end up back in prison.

Without me realizing it, everything I had endured gave me resilience. I needed this resilience as I was facing a fork in the road. I had two options and a decision to make which would impact the rest of my future.

Do I let this moment define me and fall back into a world of drugs and chaos? Or do I learn from my mistakes, take this moment to be a new start, and fall forward into a world of possibilities?

I decided to fall forward. I was determined not to become a product of my environment.

I knew I would need to make changes within myself if I wanted to live a different life. My biggest decision was to stop using.

To help ease the transition, the Alcohol and Drug Service referred me to a doctor who placed me on a maintenance prescription drug which reduces the symptoms of withdrawal. That began the long, gradual process of tapering off over time with the supervision of the doctor. This decision also meant changing my environment and the people I surrounded myself with.

I had finally come to a place where I was tired of chasing something that was destroying me. I'd had enough of living without purpose. I had always had a desire to serve others but didn't know how or if this was even possible. Now, something inside of me was ready for more, ready to be challenged, so I could achieve a fulfilling life that mattered.

The Anchor

I knew the difficulty of finding a new job with another criminal charge added to my record, but I felt this new, burning desire for life. Whatever was about to enter my life was about to be huge because I was now determined to be the navigator of my destination.

I learned that sometimes we have to lose something big, like my career as a legal secretary, to gain something bigger. When I was approached by a global company featured in Forbes for its digital educational products and services, I was excited. Through that company, I met a community of people all looking for more out of life, all aspiring to be something, but more than that, all looking to impact the lives of others through education, personal development, and mindset.

When I attended my first company convention, I realized that these individuals' previous lives were tougher than anything I had experienced, yet they were on stage having reached a high level of success, impacting lives globally, and earning multiple sources of income. This was an inspiration.

Society had conditioned me to think that to be successful you had to have achieved at a high level in school. No one had taught me the value of finding a life skill like trading the Foreign Exchange.

This was my new, healthy obsession. I made personal development a daily ritual. I incorporated my own morning routine with the help of my mentor which consisted of meditation, reading and writing my goals, affirmations, journaling, visualization, and prayer. My morning routine and personal development became my anchor to my recovery and staying clean.

I was dedicated to being coachable and willing, which is how I came across the late Mr. Bob Proctor. I learned that, as individuals, we are the highest form of creation with the power to create our own reality. What we think we become. What we visualize we materialize.

Finding Purpose

Over time, I developed a personal mission. Personal development was so powerful in my life, and I know for so many it is entirely lacking. The idea of people in pain when this solution exists, didn't sit right with me. My passion became re-educating society about the power of personal development and our ability to shift and reprogram our mindsets to create the lives we desire.

I started sharing this message on social media daily, especially on Instagram where Iconic Elite was born—a brand built on authenticity, transparency, and equality—where I began creating content and sharing the tools and methods that helped me, all focused around living a purposeful life to show others how I went from surviving to thriving, to lead by example so that they can too. I also enjoy being on podcasts where I can share my story and spread hope to those in search of making a change in their lives.

Then, I began a mentorship program so I could show members of my team the same strategy I used to help me gain my $10k funded Foreign Exchange account. Once they understand the basics, my desire is that they continue to learn and become their own experts.

Today, at age 32, I no longer live with the deep void within me. The burning desire to impact and serve others, and in doing so living a purposeful life, was the key for me to no longer feel empty. This naturally transitioned into launching my new business Iconic Elite Coaching as a mindshift and recovery coach providing one to one online coaching for women globally.

Throughout this journey, my mum continues to be my biggest cheerleader. I am grateful for the life I have lived and the lessons I have learned and continue to learn so I can share my story and be the voice for those who have not yet found theirs. I truly believe that sometimes we have to endure our own pain to be able to lead others out of theirs.

To stay connected with Becky Bouhsine, visit Becky's Instagram @iconicbexofficial. To subscribe to her tribe, go to www.iconicelite-coachbex.com. For further information regarding personal development workshops, one-to-one coaching, or having her as a podcast guest, email: iconic_elite@hotmail.com.

Tweetable: I made the decision to fall forward. I was determined to not become a product of my environment. I knew I would need to make changes within myself if I wanted to live a different life.

BASKAL KORKIS

Playing Bigger
Optimizing Full-Service Real Estate

Baskal Korkis offers complete financial and real estate services, in advising, tax strategy, bookkeeping, mortgage, insurance, investing and more, to high net worth investors. Born in Syria, Baskal now lives with his family of five in Tampa, Florida. He runs his companies full-time, invests, and manages an educational Instagram with nearly 170k followers.

Investing from a Young Age

I was born in Syria. My father, a tank mechanic in the military, left for the US when I was born to build a better life for our family. Three years later, he brought my mom, my older sister, and me to live in New Jersey.

We lived in a rough neighborhood. I often got into fights and didn't do well in school. Starting at age 8, I worked at a barbershop sweeping up hair. When I was 11, my dad got hurt at work, and we moved to Florida for his health and the warm weather. In a new environment, I changed the way I saw things. I applied myself. I worked small jobs and, in school, I realized I was really good at math. The more I worked, the more I grew.

When I was 14, a conversation with my uncle inspired me to invest in real estate. From 14 to 19, I spent my time learning finance, accounting, credit, rentals, and construction from several mentors. I saved money, and by the time I was 19, I was able to buy my first duplex. By the time I was 23, I owned 23 units.

Fifteen years later, I owned and managed about $13 million in commercial and multifamily real estate and I had built multiple full-service companies for accounting, insurance, mortgages, construction, advising, and anything else a high net worth investor might need.

I started posting about my work online and on social media about 10 years ago. I wanted to show people what is possible and how I got to this successful point in my life. I showed my businesses behind the scenes and how I made my investing decisions. People started to notice and wanted to invest with me. I started working with select people, and I was able to help many people in the real estate game grow and learn.

My Mission to Share the Knowledge

In 2019, my now business partner came to me about taking her on as an investor. I said no for about six months. Eventually, in a very nice way, she wore me down.

She had a lot of ideas. She thought that together we could do more deals and strategically position properties for their highest and best use. She seemed like a good person to partner with, and I could tell we were going to do something good. After that, she started bringing her friends and family to invest with us.

Part of me resisted this shift. I was very comfortable, making really good money, and didn't feel the need to grow or bring on partners. But I started thinking about back when I was 20 years old and buying a seven-unit property. I was stretching hard, trying to buy a property that on paper I could never do. I was praying for it. That made me think. I was no longer really stretching myself. I was not really pursuing and trying to be great. I was just settling for good.

Right now, most people are losing their money to inflation. They're losing their money to taxes. When I was in my early 20s and renting out apartments in low-income areas, I would see people 65 years old, collecting social security, and living in a $400 studio because their money had disappeared.

Many who come to us for help have been paying a crazy amount of tax. I think, *Why?* I have not paid more than a thousand dollars in income tax, legally, in any one year, ever. There are all these rules in place to help save you money on taxes, but you have to know about them and know how to use them.

I realized that I'm very good at what I do. I'm more profitable than my competitors. I was given a skill that could help a lot of people. I've been doing this since I was 14, so I have the knowledge and the experience. That skill, that success, is a responsibility. I didn't want to see people not achieving their dreams and living in fear or having a painful retirement. I decided, as long as I was working with the right people who were positive, good people to work with, I would help them in addition to what I was building for myself.

I Had to Grow to Help More

I started thinking, *What could I do to allow me to help more people faster?*

At the time, we were raising a large fund and then buying multiple properties to deliver great returns to the investors. We were buying about $9 million worth of properties in a quarter. That was good, but many more people were coming to me. We just weren't helping enough people by operating this way.

A $3 million raise took a long time, then it took a long time to acquire all the properties we needed. But what if I only needed to buy one building, not nine? Increasing the scale of the buildings would shorten the timelines and allow us to work with more investors and help more people.

Scaling up was challenging. A lot of it was psychological though. I needed to level up my mindset and change my belief system. Part of it was overcoming my self-doubts and all the ANTS (automatic negative thoughts). It seemed overwhelming to think about a $9 million deal. I was thinking things like, *It's too big. Why me? How could I?*

But I needed to do this because there were people who needed my help. I had faith in God. I knew that I had the skills to do it and God would help me through it. I just started going for it. Once I started getting into the weeds, I started realizing that those negative thoughts were not accurate and I was able to make it happen.

The Next Level, A $9 Million Property

I took all the skills I learned up to that point doing multiple million-dollar deals and I started looking at larger properties.

I found this $9 million property—an 11-acre industrial park near a new medical school. Brand new offices and apartments were going up right across the street. It was an awesome opportunity.

I thought, *Man, but it's a lot of money.*

Then I thought, *But in 10 or 20 years, I'm going to say—just like I've said in the past—I could have bought that. It is a great deal. Why should my investors and I miss out?*

The next question was, *Okay, interest rates are super high. How am I going to make this deal happen? We have to put 50% of the money down.... Alright, well, is that the end of the world? It's a great property. I know everybody's used to putting down 25-30%, but maybe 50% is the new norm.*

That's when I got creative. I came to the conclusion that if anybody was going to do this deal, and for it to financially make sense in the current market, it would have to look a little different.

I spoke with the owner, and we agreed on a way to structure the deal that not only made the sale possible but also decreased the initial amount we had to put down and made the profitability so much better. Then, I went and presented the opportunity to investors and found a group that liked the plan. Six months later, everybody started structuring their deals the way I structured this one.

I could not help a lot of people and make a major impact by being small. Now, we've expanded the capacity of our team. We're able to bring in great professionals to help us provide a good product to people. That was one of the biggest goals. As a result, I'm able to accept more investors instead of turning people away.

The people coming to me now are investment managers that have their own investment groups. I'm still working with some individuals, but the managers have tens of millions of dollars and hundreds, if not thousands, of people underneath them. I help them with my knowledge of taxes, investing, and strategy—with the goal of providing wealth preservation for generations. This is how I can help not one person at a time, but hundreds, potentially thousands, of people at a time.

The benefit of me being 37 is I plan to be like Warren Buffet and invest into my 90s. I'll be able to set things up and manage the fund long-term. Still, it's shocking to see myself here, talking about doing deals of this size. This opportunity came as my mindset was evolving. It was great timing and a great way to level up.

Risk and Reward

Scaling up really was inevitable because I recognized that I would lose more by staying small than the risk of going big and maybe making a mistake. I lost more by passing on opportunities than I would have if I actually took the opportunity and made a mistake along the way.

Every two to five years, I look back on the previous years and ask myself, *If I was going to do anything different, what would I have done?* Even after going through the '08 crash, every time, the answer is: *I wish I went bigger. I wish I went harder. I wish I pushed more.*

I've never done something and thought, *Man, I really wish I didn't do that.* No. If I do it and it goes bad, I think, *Man, I did that and it really, really hurt. It sucked going through it, but I got through it.* I got through it and I learned something.

Today, most people are not investing. After 2008, the market went up, and coming up on 2020, people started to decide they would wait for another crash and then buy. When a crash comes, prices will go down —but the fact is—interest rates will go up. Interest rates and pricing usually aren't both low at the same time. There is no great reward where there is no risk.

Financial advisors are all being taught by the same group of people that are basically only teaching advisors how to make them profits by selling their products. That means your financial advisor would never know it's a good idea to invest in real estate, a business, oil and gas, or gold. They don't know because they're not taught.

If you go to a real estate agent for investment advice, they're not going to tell you to invest in gold or stocks and bonds. They only know real estate. You have to be careful who you're getting your advice from because they're going to be biased based on how they were educated.

That's why I share so much on Instagram and YouTube. Everything I share is free. At this point, I've only ever offered one educational product, which I priced super low. I often go to The Real Estate Guys events to learn and teach there as well. We do a lot of that, and when investors come, we do tours and Zoom meetings. During that entire process, I'm educating. I don't ask anyone to invest with me. I educate people, share what I'm doing, and explain why I'm doing it. Then, if a potential client thinks I'm right and agrees with my investment philosophy, they're welcome to join us.

My long-term goal is to help others understand the financial freedom I've created for myself. I want to teach people how to get control of their finances and how, at the same time, you can work for yourself instead of working for the bank. Don't live in fear. Pursue your dreams and with the right strategy, achieve your dreams.

Reach out to Baskal Korkis about full-service financial and real estate services for high net worth investors anywhere in the United States. To learn more, follow Baskal on Instagram @BaskalKorkis.
Email: taxsmartinvestor@korcf.com
YouTube: @BaskalKorkis
Website: korcapitalfund.com

Tweetable: Every two to five years, I look back and ask myself, If I was going to do anything different, what would I have done? Every time, the answer is: I wish I went bigger. I wish I went harder. I wish I pushed more.

PASTOR DONALD RUCKER

When God Whispers

Pastor Donald Rucker is the Founder of Christian Development Center. With 40 years of leadership in ministry, he has transformed many lives by teaching people of their unique purpose, inherent potential, and the power they possess to make a difference in humanity.

Following the Whisper

I sat on a bus on my way to Las Vegas, a city I didn't know and had never visited. I grew up in Mississippi, The Sip, as we call it today, and Vegas was only a city I saw on television. But there I was, on my way to Vegas to marry someone I didn't know because I heard a voice tell me to marry her.

The voice in my head said He had a purpose for the marriage. Man, millions of thoughts raced through my head. *What are you doing? Are you crazy? What will your family think when you tell them you heard a Voice in your head tell you to marry her? Will you be the laughingstock of your family?*

Our marriage, our ministry, and the mission work we do are all results of God whispering His desired plans and purposes to us. That's right, God whispered to my wife Ethel and me 39 years ago to marry each other because He wanted to demonstrate to others how He could take two broken and dysfunctional individuals and make them whole through the process and principle of Oneness.

I Am Loved

The first whisper occurred in Altadena, California. I came to California at the invitation of my sister, Dot Cooper, who promised I would find better opportunities. While establishing my life in California and making plans for my future, my sister, who I lived with at the time, was constantly nagging me to attend her church. My sister was a church girl, and she was determined to get this heathen to know her God. After much nagging, she wore me down and I agreed to attend her church, only to get her to leave me alone.

On my first visit to her church, I heard something very intriguing. The man standing behind the podium was screaming! Over time, I came to understand it was his style of preaching. But, in the moment of his screaming and preaching, I heard him say God loved me! Now, there were probably 50 to 60 people in attendance that Sunday, but he seemed to be speaking directly to me.

The intriguing part of this for me was, why would God love me? I had struggled for many years wondering if my mom loved me. *If my mom didn't love me, why would God? After all, didn't He know about my ungodly deeds? Or how I cursed her out in a fit of rage?* Well, that got my attention and propelled me down a journey of discovery. It was on this journey where the God whisper became a way of life.

While attending my sister's church one Sunday (Yes, she not only wore me down but won me over to her church. We call it membership.), I saw in my peripheral view this woman who I had seen before. But this time, I saw her in a different light. As I watched her, I heard the God whisper. He said, "This is your wife!"

What? Wife? That wasn't in my plan! I didn't join this church to get married! But I couldn't deny this whisper. After all, I'd heard it before. I remembered the first whisper: *I love you!*

We Built Our Ministry

After I married Ethel, we began building our family. We had three children, Daniel, David, and Erikka, when the next whisper occurred.

We were attending a church in Pomona, California. During this service, I heard the whisper, *Your ministry is to be called Christian Development Center.* I must admit, I wasn't thinking about a ministry or starting a church. I was struggling to grow this relationship with the God whispers and trying to live according to His principle with Ethel and the kids. I have come to understand that the Whisperer was leading us into a business, a business of empowering, educating, and equipping people with the knowledge of their unique purpose and the necessity of sharing their unique contributions with humanity.

Ethel and I launched Christian Development Center in March of 2000 from the comforts of our family room with three reluctant people, our children, who like us, didn't have a clue about starting a business or running a ministry. We were following the whispers which had become a regular occurrence in our lives. The instructions in this occurrence were to open our home and start a Bible study. The whisper promised He would draw people to our home like He drew the animals to Noah's ship.

Without any marketing tactics, people came to our home seeking the Bible study. The Bible study grew and grew! It forced us to seek out other accommodations for the people coming.

We found the Brethren Campus in Upland, California. They had a small space attached to their gym auditorium for lease. The lease was affordable, and we signed our first leasing agreement for the office space. Man, the joy and excitement we experienced were simply amazing! Our faith and confidence in the God whispers grew. We were amazed to watch how following the whispers had moved us from the comfort of our family room to our first office space for our new ministry and business!

Serving Every Way We Can

From that small office, the ministry has moved up level by level for 22 years, simply following God's whispers. Currently, we are housed in a 10,000 square-foot building with a fenced-in playground for our children's ministry, a full-size kitchen, office spaces, a multipurpose room, and ample parking for members and guests.

Our current location came from a whisper to move from the Upland Brethren Campus to Montclair, California. Now, we didn't know where in Montclair we were moving to. We were only told by the whisper it was time to move. So, we hired a real estate agent and began the search. After two years, we found the building advertised in a local paper called the *PennySaver*. To our amazement, the building had been advertised for over six months with no inquiries. After contacting the lawyer and agreeing to terms, we signed our second lease agreement.

Once established in our new home, the ministry and business continued their growth and expansion. Through community fairs and open house events, we gained knowledge of the needs of the community. Our desire and commitment to be an effective service provider was the initiation of our outreach campaign.

We developed several new outreach programs tailored to the community. Our monthly food and clothing distribution feeds and clothes 400-450 families. The Joshua Project prepares and equips youth and young adults ages 12-25 with financial literacy. We also offer parenting classes, and our

NRooted Love workshops, where we offer married couples, singles, and families tools for healthier and more productive relationships.

Over time, we realized the importance of partnerships. Our partners, both nationally and internationally, have branded the ministry and its outreach efforts. Our partner Samuel Lawrence in Nigeria, through our monthly financial support, helps orphans, widows, and children in his region. In Kenya, we help sustain and provide food and clothing to an orphanage. Our partners nationally are the City of Montclair, Metro Honda/Acura Montclair, Target of Montclair, Dunkin' Donuts in Upland, Montclair Hospital, Community Action Partnership of San Bernardino, Catholic Charities, Kyle Wilson, Veterans Resource Program in Richmond, CA, and finally, the membership of Christian Development Center. Our partner Rhonda Harris, founder and CEO of Veterans Resource Program, recently acquired land to build 200 brand new units in the Oakland area for homeless veterans. There's an African proverb that says, "It takes a village to raise a child." Well, we believe the concept applies to ministry and business. All of this is a direct result of following the God whispers.

Determination and the Unseen Future

Our future is bright because the God whispers are our guide. As we look to the future, there are a few goals we would like to accomplish, including safe haven homes for women and children. With domestic violence on the rise, it will be critical to have a place for restoration, recovery, and reflection for this population in our community. We also envision an apartment complex where we can offer truly affordable housing to those on fixed and low monthly incomes. Finally, we plan to develop our NRooted Love workshops further with a curriculum that can be taught in Zoom presentations and small meetup groups across the globe.

It's been an amazing adventure learning to follow the God whispers in our lives. Many lessons and life experiences have sprung from it, not to mention the challenges and adversity. One thing stands out to us in following God's whispers: every whisper required determination to press into the unseen future, an unseen future which held the possibilities, potential, provision, and power to change not only our lives but also the lives of others.

Donald Rucker can be tracked via social media and at www.christiandevelopmentcenter.org. To learn more about your purpose, potential, and power, email him at pastorrucker@gmail.com.

Tweetable: Fulfillment in life comes not through money and materialism but through discovering your created purpose!

SHANNON ROBNETT

Searching for Greatness

Developer, builder, syndicator, blockchain enthusiast, and philanthropist Shannon Robnett owns multiple businesses, providing vertically integrated investments to Main Street. Shannon, his wife Jessie, and their seven children travel the world looking for real assets, cash flow, and freedom.

Hungry

I don't know where it started, but the desire to learn more has always been with me.

As I have walked life's road, this desire has served me well, but it always lacked something. Not a catalyst but an environment—somewhere to grow—somewhere that causes pursuits to take on an exponential growth cycle of their own.

As a second-generation builder and developer, independence, tenacity, and figure-it-outness were ingrained in me from an early age. Higher learning, however, was not really pedaled in our home, so when I had the opportunity to pursue it, the cost analysis just didn't add up for me.

We were taught to work hard, have integrity, and figure it out on our own. We solved problems independently using our backs and brains. And this worked fairly well, but it never led to building blocks that built on others' building blocks. Don't get me wrong, my parents were very successful in the figuring-it-out department and turned their life story into the all-American dream. But, it was all adlibs in a silo with no real outside influence or collaboration. They tax-planned on their own instead of using paid consultants, found all their own loans instead of using a broker, and avoided lawyers at all costs. They found a successful groove and worked it into early retirement at 50. They were debt-free and living on mailbox money.

I followed this model for the first part of my adult life, but I knew there had to be more. I just hadn't quite found it yet. And that was exactly what led me to the brink in 2008. As a builder, I was working for others as my main source of income and developing small projects on the side. When the banks stopped lending in 2008, 80% of my work went away and I was left scrambling.

I was a lone wolf out to conquer the world, but as we all know, 2008 was the year of world-crushing events that devastated the hopes and dreams of millions worldwide. The old model was broken. Without real mentors to challenge me to think about new solutions, I floundered. This was made worse by a series of health problems that robbed me of my basic mobility.

Searching for Greatness

But my learning didn't stop when my cash flow did. Honestly, I just had more time to learn new things.

I went out of my way to think, but I wasn't finding myself growing rich, like the title of the famous book says. I spent time getting more information, but I was really struggling to find a place in the post-2008 wreckage to apply the information and get back out of the valley.

After trying more than a few different strategies, it all started to come together. In 2016, I met a future partner regarding a development, and he had the opposite problem I had. He had money but was unfamiliar with the development process. So, a beautiful partnership was born. And $64 million dollars later, I was off and running again.

We put together a beautiful project, way past the limits of what I was an expert in. I was working double-time. I was being stretched and growing just to keep up. I was plugged in with no one, and I was frustrated with my inability to find a sounding board in the industry. I was doing it, but I was alone and feeling lost and out of my depth. I knew I couldn't sustain this.

I was missing the OOMPH, the rocket fuel, the next level mojo!

My hunger for knowledge just continued to grow. The more I knew, the more information I needed. I was listening to podcasts and reading books, but was still looking for "it."

I started my own podcast as a way to get exciting people who were doing great things to talk to me. I began to build friendships with other successful people, and along the way, I began to associate with others that were like-minded.

I was able to see where we were able to create some synergies. We bounced ideas off each other and things started to accelerate. But it seemed that for every step forward there were two side steps, and a step back, and then, we would reevaluate what went wrong, improve our process, and try again. I felt like I was working without a road map and without a safety net.

I noticed my circle beginning to expand. The minds in the circle were getting bigger. The lives they lived were starting to look like the life I wanted to have. I could see how this was headed in the right direction. I also began to see how those who didn't align with growth began to fall away and come around less often. Maybe Darwin was right!

A Tribe to Call Mine

I raised money for a deal in Boise, Idaho. We knocked it out of the park and were soon underway on another $80 million deal. Things were going well, right?

They looked that way, but I remember thinking, "I just wish I had people who had walked in my shoes that would be open and honest about what this journey was supposed to look like." I was yearning for this community, especially in light of the fact that history repeats itself and those that do not learn are bound to repeat it. I desperately didn't want to repeat 2008.

I continued to plow ahead and work to aggregate the circle of influence I desired. I also started to look inside. Maybe it was me. Maybe I was the obstacle. Did I need to be fixed? I still had those close to me who doubted me, and I began to doubt myself.

I was still trying to run as a lone wolf. My habits were proving really hard to change. Then I heard someone say, "In order to really succeed, you have to help others solve the problem they have, and even more than that, you have to be relatable."

That sounded like a whole lot of vulnerability to me, and I was not about that at all. In fact, vulnerability was really the last thing I wanted in my life. I mean, after all, what would people think if they saw that I didn't have it all together and often got it wrong? What would that do to my credibility? This bothered me like a festering sliver.

I started listening to other people who were saying the same thing, and I truly valued them and their opinion. I thought I would try an experiment and begin to really work on helping others solve problems, being relatable, and answering those questions.

The truth was the vulnerability was not that bad, and the act of trying to meet the needs of others was a challenge I loved. I tried a few other things that expanded my trusted circle and increased my clarity on who I really was. I grew to know on a deeper level not only who Shannon the business person was but also who just-Shannon was, what he thought, and what he was dealing with on a daily basis. I believe this awareness began to attract a few more high-profile players, the big ballers, who had achieved a level that I and others I knew were looking to learn from.

I began to reach out to networks of other entrepreneurs. I also began to attend more conferences, to intentionally interact with more people who were where I wanted to be. As an introvert, this was probably the most uncomfortable thing I have ever done, and it was truly a test of how bad I wanted to move to the next level.

Early on in my career, I only attended a few conferences and I would attend with a very different attitude. I would sit in the back or roam the hallways and call that attending. I wouldn't intentionally meet anyone or really speak to others. Now, I pay extra to sit up front. I purchase the VIP package, meet the speakers, network with other attendees, and really engage. I finally began to look at the speakers as people, just like me, who had figured out how to tell their story, with all the bumps and bruises along the way that left their marks on their investment thesis and changed their implementation strategy. Now, I find myself often in the company of people like Ken McElroy, Brandon Turner, Robert Kiyosaki, Robert Helms, Mark Moss, Jason Hartman, Russell Gray, Kyle Wilson, and George Gammon to name a few.

I began to find a rather large and scattered group of people, all looking for something like I was: an environment that had all sorts of information to go with many different areas of expertise. A smorgasbord of knowledge from all walks of life, different business models, and varied motivations but one desired result. A tribe coming together as a sounding board, simply to be useful to each other. The collection of information wasn't really the genius. That was in the people themselves and in gathering with the desire to share. I had a desire to grow and absorb it all. As I pushed into the center of this growing group, I found myself being mentored in sales by Russ Gray, taught tax strategies by Tom Wheelwright, and sharing my ideas with others who were also raising millions of dollars a month.

I found myself traveling simply to engage people, more often than ever. I was looking for my tribe in the self-help sector, the wellness space, and the financial and tax worlds, by way of old-fashioned networking. I traveled from Boise to Miami to have lunch with Dr. Chris Martensen of Peak Prosperity, and man, was it worth it! I naturally tapped into the real estate space, and each time I made contact with people, I found that they were, like me, on the journey to live better, more connected lives. I began to build strong relationships with fellow entrepreneurs and learn by watching and interacting.

But, at the end of the day, I realized the true journey was always going to be inside me. You see, every time I found myself more connected with my goal of finding more invigorated and actioned knowledge, I watched another handful of people walk away discouraged and lacking connection. I began to realize that while it took energy from me to connect with others and give, the relationships I formed and nurtured always gave back more. And, it wasn't until I committed to giving of myself at all costs that I really began to see results. A mental commitment to give first, to immerse myself, truly unlocked the conversations that became connections and then building blocks. Putting myself out there first finally produced the results I was looking for.

Giving First

Knowledge is a lot like beauty; it truly is in the eye of the beholder, and if neglected, it will soon fade. When I really looked at ways I could be of value to others and contribute to their journey, I found my place. Time and time again, I left an interaction with another person feeling better because of it.

In reflection, I saw my growth, and in that, the next rung of the ladder came into view. Constantly looking to get more information about how to level up so I could give away more information and level up others continued to bring me the growth I desired and allowed me to help others on their journey.

They say a journey of a thousand miles starts with a single step. I would say that the journey starts with a single conversation. It is never truer as it applies to the inner journey that must take place to bring about massive growth. It's also necessary to participate 100% in this life. Remember, it's the only one you get.

These were truly the people that I desired to surround myself with, and doing so was the start of something truly life-changing. The relationships I needed, that fed me, pushed me, and truly aligned with the results I was looking for took a majority of my time, and as a result, I began to see relationships that did not match what I was looking for remove themselves from my life.

Soon, not only did I know I had found my tribe but I also began to see that what I was in search of—freedom to be me with an empowered backup band—was the same thing these people were looking for. I was hanging out with nine-figure people who were actually happy and more interested in honest, uplifting conversations than flashing status or discussing divisive topics.

We found ourselves looking for reasons and opportunities to connect on things we did agree on rather than focus on what we disagreed on, ultimately strengthening bonds rather than feeding division. My tribe was definitely starting to feel like home. The Rolodex I had always looked for, of empowered individuals who would answer my call and give me their time and more importantly their hard-earned wisdom, was starting to truly come together.

Finally, Results

The shocking thing was what this began to do for my business. I found more harmony with my employees, and less stress in my life. Fun began to be a regular thing for me, and our projects seemed to work better.

As I began to see the truth in the phrase *You are the sum of your five friends*, I also realized I would rather have four quarters than one hundred pennies. I asked myself these same questions you should ask yourself to start your journey of real growth.

Do you want more in your life? Look at who the people are around you, not just in business but also in life. Are they genuine? Do they truly care about you and others? Are they open-minded and accepting? Do they like to be part of a bigger conversation and actually learn from the opinions of others? Even if they don't agree with the point of view, are they respectful? Do they contribute to the journey of others?

If the answers are yes, congratulations, you have a tribe. If you cannot answer yes, then you have some hard choices to make if you truly want to level up. Growth has a cost, and in these choices, you learn what you are willing to pay for your true success.

Check out Shannon Robnett's podcast *Robnett's Real Estate Rundown* or go to his YouTube Channel: Shannon Robnett, LinkedIn: Shannon Robnett, or Instagram: ShannonRayRobnett. Learn more about what he has going on at Shannonrobnett.com. For more information on Shannon's investment deals, contact him: Shannon@ShannonRobnett.com.

Tweetable: The difference between those that have everything they want in life and those that don't is usually the result of an unseen journey the majority will never undertake.

ANGELA STREET

The Ultimate Blessing in Disguise

Angela Street is a motivated leader and teacher. As a successful entrepreneur, she has helped many hardworking, middle-class consumers become debt free and retire. She is passionate about teaching others how to create residual income, financial independence, and generational wealth, using the vehicle of a licensed financial service franchise.

The Day That Would Give Us a Brand New Life

December 20, 2015, was one of the most devastating days of my life. I still remember sitting on the steps in our kitchen and showing my husband the text message as my heart sank and fear, along with a whirlwind of other emotions, came over me. I will never forget the words my husband said. "Angela, now is where we will TRULY exercise our faith."

My Love of Dance Started Young!

When I was four years old, my mom put me in dance class. I immediately fell in love. At age 12, thanks to my bonus mom Jan, the owner of the studio asked me to be an assistant teacher. I was thrilled and I loved that even more!

At 17 years old, due to my commitment and creativity in choreography, I was awarded a position as head teacher and a class of my own. When they saw my choreography, people would ask me, "How do you know what to do?" My answer was that I couldn't really explain it. The song told me what to do. When the dancers performed my choreography, it felt RIGHT, good, and pure. I would get goosebumps and cry many tears as the movement and unity of the dancers created THAT feeling—the story the piece was meant to convey. And the biggest most FULL feeling was when others watching the piece had those same feelings! The accomplishment and pride I felt was overwhelming.

At age 27, after two years of begging the owner of the studio to start a competitive dance team, she finally agreed! I was eager for the opportunity to coach, compete, and win! I was so excited that my career as a coach and choreographer was going to the next level. And I couldn't believe that I was so much in love with my JOB. I knew I was very fortunate, as many people do NOT love what they do.

We learned a lot the first few years. We got better and started winning! We traveled all over the United States competing, and the time spent with the 60-80 families was priceless. We were truly a family. My daughter was a competitive dancer as well, which allowed us to be together all the time! Life was great!

Divine Timing

I dreamed of owning the dance studio, and then the opportunity came. After months of planning and going over paperwork with lawyers and the studio owner, we were finally ready to purchase the studio at the start of 2013.

You know those moments something so profound happens that you remember where you were and what you were doing? I had one of those moments in February of 2013.

I was doing dishes when my son came over for a surprise visit. I greeted him with a dish in my hand and then went back to the sink to finish washing. That's when he said, "Hey Mom, you're going to be a grandma."

Immediately, I loved that child like I cannot explain. With all of the excitement you can imagine, I gave my son the biggest hug ever. I was overwhelmed with a love that made my heart more full than I have ever felt.

Sometimes God prompts us to do things even though they may not totally make sense. The next day, I made one of the toughest decisions of my life. I decided not to purchase the studio.

I was very emotional and crying while I told the studio owner that I could not go through with the studio purchase. It wasn't easy to explain, but I knew that my calling was to be a grandma and I would not be able to dedicate the time the studio needed. So, life went back to running the competitive dance team while we anticipated the arrival of my granddaughter.

The birth of my first grandchild on October 9, 2013, changed my life in a way I will never be able to explain. Grandparents, particularly grandmothers, probably DO know what I mean. Living paycheck to paycheck and living for the weekend, life was amazing. And I truly mean that. Even though our financial life was hanging on a string, we loved life. And, we had another grandchild, a little boy, by December 2015.

We had countless sleepovers with Kathleen and Eli. We did everything together! We had many trips to story hour at the library, the park, the lake house—you name it, we did it together.

Divine Line Up

In the summer of 2015, a friend was very persistent in calling me and asking to set up a time for my husband and I to listen to, basically, her sales spiel.

Then, tragically, my husband's good friend was in a terrible car accident. He was in a coma for two weeks and then he passed away. He had children, and that woke my husband up. Kevin said to me, "Angela, we must get private life insurance."

This was a turning point, and little did we know, our ENTIRE financial future would soon be going in a very different direction.

Our friend had been calling us for months, asking if she could show us what she was learning about so that if we, or someone we knew, could benefit from what she did, we would feel comfortable referring them. We had rescheduled three or four times due to different things, mostly procrastinating because we felt "all set" with the life insurance through Kevin's employer. When we learned, to our dismay, that life insurance through work would not pay out if you were not on active payroll, we decided it was time to take that meeting.

I gave our friend a call, and she sent her business partner to help us out. He drove an hour and a half to our house. That alone was impressive customer service to us. The information he explained was so clear and made so much sense, I wondered why this hadn't been explained by anyone else this way in the past. We purchased life insurance through him.

We also wanted to make sure our retirement was well-planned and to get out of debt. We were pleasantly surprised that this company could help us with that as well!

We wrapped up, and the agent was walking out of the door, when Kevin said to him, "Hey John, what did you do? Play college ball?"

The agent said "No, bro, why do you ask?"

Kevin said, "Well, you've got that big ring on. It looks like a national championship ring." Kevin is a HUGE University of Michigan fan and had seen a ring like that on a player from a town near our hometown.

John said, "Nope, when you make six figures with our company, they give you this ring. There is a business opportunity with us. Do you want to hear about it?"

Kevin looked at John over his glasses and said, "You make six figures?"

John proceeded to explain that to do the work he did, we would first need to take a class through the state of Michigan. Then he would train us on how to use the financial licenses. Out of pocket for a background check and study tools, this was $124.

Kevin had to think about it. But I was in! I couldn't stop thinking about the class, not necessarily because I wanted to start a business, but because our adult children each had a child, and my mom-heart kicked in. I wanted to take the class so we could be better educated in the areas of finance we were NOT taught in school.

I Am So Thankful We Did It Together!

By the end of the next day, I enrolled in the class, and then Kevin said, "You know what, sign me up. I want to make sure the life insurance we have works just like we think it does." I was so excited that we were going to take the class together!

It was an hour and thirty minute drive to the training. I remember being there and saying to Kevin, "I feel like we are at church." Even though there was not a religious word spoken, I felt a spirit. And everything we were learning made so much sense to me. It was good, just right, and exciting, all at the same time.

We found out the next scheduled class was the very next day. I said to Kevin, "I am calling a co-worker. If I can get coverage for my Saturday dance classes, we are driving back for this class tomorrow."

After two long days of information that I wished we'd had years ago, we were tired and our brains were extended to the max after years of being out of school. But, I will never forget the excitement and empowerment Kevin expressed ALL the way home! He was so excited about the knowledge and the possibilities and that we could make some income part-time to put towards paying off our debt and building our retirement.

But, we still had to pass the test! We scheduled it for two weeks out, on Thanksgiving weekend 2015, also the day of the Michigan vs. Michigan State game, which is a national holiday according to Kevin!

We drove two hours to take the test. We both went in at the same time, but I came out first. I had no idea how I did. As I waited for the results, my heart was pounding. That 30 seconds seemed to take hours. I was so excited when I found out I passed! I went out to wait for Kevin. I kept praying and saying, "Ok, Kevin, you've got this." Nearly 30 minutes went by, and I saw him walking out with his head down. I was so bummed for him. But then… he couldn't contain himself. He started running, put his arms up, and was screaming, "I passed!" We stopped for lunch and watched the BIG game to celebrate our win!

After that day, we went back to our normal lives and jobs, not having a clue that the biggest change in our lives was almost upon us. It was business as normal until December 20, 2015, when I received a text message that would change our lives forever.

The Message

The last line of that text said, "I am sure you will find a better opportunity elsewhere." I couldn't believe that I was being fired via text message after a 27-year dance instructor career.

The next thing I remember was three days later, sobbing on the stairs, not knowing who I was or what to do next. Kevin said, "This is the first time we will be depending on our work ethic and our faith. Call John and see what we need to do to be successful with the license."

I was afraid, but I was also excited by the possibilities. I called John, and one of his first questions was, "Are you coachable?"

I immediately said, "Yes, I am!"

We proceeded to get underway with training and a plan. Much of what we did was foreign to me, but there were also many things I already understood. Building a financial agency was very similar to building the dance team. They both required great leadership, skill with people, problem solving, and teamwork. God had been grooming me for the last 27 years to be ready for this next step in my career and my life.

Our biggest challenge was that, for a little while, even the people we loved and cared about the most would not give us the time of day to hear what we were doing so that they could better refer us. But that led to growth in our character and work ethic. We were going to do whatever it took to be successful and help people, if only to prove to ourselves that we could do it. We persisted, and once we were able to explain what we offer, success started to snowball.

Just a short two and a half years after I lost my lifelong career at the dance studio, we were able to retire Kevin from UPS at age 44. There we were: business owners in the largest industry in the world.

Only God

One day, I was chatting with a new life insurance agent I was training.

During our conversation, I asked what her son's middle name was. I am not even sure why I asked, but the reply was, "Charles."

I am also not sure why I asked the next question: "How did you come by that name?" She said her son was named after an amazing guy who had been a mentor to her husband. His name was Charlie.

My eyes filled with tears and I got chills. I asked what the mentor's last name was, and in fact, yes, this was my husband's friend who had passed away while in a coma.

I proceeded to tell her the story of why we do what we do and how losing Charlie had started us down the path. Emotions were running high. She said, "Charlie is always talking to us, and that is simply amazing."

Six-Figure Beginning

We now have achieved the income milestone and earned the ring that intrigued us to the idea of starting this business and changing our lives. But nothing compares to the many opportunities we have had to touch people's lives and do God's work. What we have is a ministry to touch and change people's lives. Even with the heartache, I would not change the events of the past six years for anything. God is good, and we continue to ask him to lead us to the people that we can help. This is just the beginning. There is so much more we can do by continuing to share what we have learned.

We still live in the same town as the individual that sent me that devastating text. When I see them, in my heart I say, *Thank you, thank you, thank you. Thank you for allowing God to work through you.* I believe He knew I would NOT willfully make the decision to take this path, so He did it for me. And I thank the messenger from the bottom of my heart.

It is so interesting how if one thing were different, the entire trajectory of your life could have been different.

Sometimes our darkest times turn into the most amazing, fun, full-of-life experiences—experiences that you would never have lived—unless you said yes and figured it out as you went! Let go and let God!

Angela Street is looking for those who would love to open, operate, and override a franchise in the financial industry. Run your office virtually or in person! The options are endless and flexible. Please contact her at 989-397-3390 or angelastreet1970@gmail.com. primerica.com/astreet

Tweetable: Sometimes the worst things that happen in our lives lead to our new true purpose.

JAY JOHNSON

Code 3 American
A Sniper's Final Shot to Save America

*Jay Johnson is a veteran and long-time law enforcement professional. Jay is an investor, syndicator, and general contractor who has overseen the development of multiple design-build projects. His unique public service experience, passion for business, and love of country resulted in the Code 3 American movement to **enrich humanity and save America through financial independence**.*

The Explosive Years

I have the heart of a patriot, and I believe our flag is a sacred symbol of freedom. Immense sacrifice is sewn into every fiber of our flag, and though the fibers could be unraveled and repurposed, the sacrifice cannot be repaid.

I was 19 years old and had already served one of four years in the United States Air Force when September 11, 2001, exploded into our lives. I was serving overseas, assigned to an airbase in England. I remember the day well, especially how an instant seriousness settled in the air like fog. Everyone knew someone would pay, and if tradition continued, our fighter wing would be among the first to mail the payment. My job was to assemble and maintain the munitions our airpower soon began delivering in Afghanistan.

From England, I deployed to Turkey for Operation Northern Watch prior to the second Iraq War. The mission was to enforce a long-standing no-fly zone above the 36th parallel in Iraq. Later, a permanent change of station relocated me to a base in Texas to support high-speed bombers and airlift operations. From there, I deployed to Uzbekistan and Diego Garcia as a part of the Global War on Terror campaign.

I excelled in military culture. Service before self and sharing a common mission fueled me. The flag made me proud, and the most impactful song I ever heard was Lee Greenwood performing "Proud to Be an American" as I sat on the back of a Humvee in Uzbekistan. Yet, I also wanted to be back home and close to family again. Choosing to leave the military was one of the tougher decisions I ever made.

College and the Entrepreneur

After the military, I began college to pursue a career of service in law enforcement. I barely had my military uniform stored when I arrived for college orientation. They handed me a bright-colored lei, slapped a nametag on me, and ushered me to play silly games with people three months out of high school. I guess it was supposed to build a sense of camaraderie, but all I felt that day was tremendous doubt, fearing I'd made a huge mistake. I stayed because I "needed" a degree. Spoiler: The GI Bill made college profitable. Otherwise, that degree would never have paid for itself.

While in college, I started a construction company doing small jobs. I had enough money to buy a few tools, and my first purchase was a set of screwdrivers for $19.99 so I could adjust some doors. That job made $33.17 before expenses and swallowed about six hours of my life. I needed bigger jobs, and more than a few times I agreed to complete a project I wasn't certain how to do. I worked for tools and equipment, acquiring a bit more each time I completed a job, and the projects continued increasing in size.

Detective, SWAT, Leadership and Raw Lessons

While finishing college, I put on a uniform again. I fell in love with my new police career and quickly excelled. It was fun and a return to the camaraderie I missed from the military. Once again, I was standing for something bigger than myself and working as a team in pursuit of a common mission.

Law enforcement was like a bunch of mini-careers. I've operated as a patrol officer, detective, SWAT operator, SWAT assistant team leader, sniper, firearms instructor, tactics instructor, patrol corporal, school resource officer corporal, and patrol team sergeant. I experienced ups and downs and have seen some terrible things. I investigated my share of death in all forms from natural to homicides and suicides. I witnessed many hard lessons that death in raw form teaches, lessons never expressed in a funeral home's sterile environment.

As a team, we saved lives, and I particularly remember helping save a child. I saw that boy a year or two later and felt joy as he walked and joked with his friends as teenagers do. He had no idea who I was.

As a detective, I honed the skill of interview and interrogation which ensured some terrible people will never rape or abuse young children again.

The downside was conversing with the devil himself and learning things I wish I could but never will forget.

I discovered leading teams through dynamic situations and making instant life-or-death decisions tests one's fortitude and demands a steady hand. My most impactful leadership lessons were forged from poor decisions.

Integrity, Attitude and Loyalty

I met my wife while attending the law enforcement academy, and soon, we had a daughter. This was the moment that really began to shift my thinking. At first, I was scared to death, but I promised my daughter I would never let her down and never abandon her, no matter what. To raise my family, I wanted a nicer house than I could afford to buy. Though my construction business had increased in scale, I had never built an entire house. I figured since other people had, I could too. With this, we got started. I didn't have much money, I lacked experience, and I still have no idea why the bank gave me a loan.

After building our home, I continued operating and expanding the construction business. Looking back, I have learned attitude and relationships, not money or education, are what hold us back or propel us forward. With integrity and discipline, money can be sourced from others. Solely on a handshake, I have received five and six-figure loans multiple times.

Life of Freedom Encounters Fierce Resistance

Prior to having children, I arrogantly believed I could solve everything by working harder and longer hours. Once my eldest daughter was born, I realized I couldn't find enough time in the day. This worsened every year, and I began to dwell on the eroding time I had left with her before she grew up. I discovered this was one of the few things that depressed me.

Our second daughter blessed us, and I realized I had multiplied my internal conflict. I would live those young years again with a new buddy, but this too would pass quickly. Since having our first daughter, eight years of managing our companies, a full-time job, and crazy hours left me with less energy for my youngest. This produced guilt. Constantly, I battled the fact the girls would get older and likely end up in different locations. Enjoying time with my kids, future grandchildren, and family could not be negotiable forever. I started becoming laser-focused on engineering a life of freedom.

But I faced two plaguing problems. First, I was extremely busy. Second, it seemed I was consistently making better money, yet it was becoming harder to get ahead. But why?

A Life-Changing Phone Call

Minor surgery to my dominant hand delivered a temporary solution to my "busy" problem. During my few weeks of recovery at home, my buddy called and told me he read a book which reminded him of me: *Rich Dad Poor Dad* by Robert Kiyosaki. Suddenly having some time, I agreed to listen to it.

The book was life-changing. I then read *Cash Flow Quadrant* and was hooked. I quickly became an avid reader and began gorging myself on everything I could find to better understand how to develop a life of freedom. I became a student of the financial system, taxes, Wall Street, and real assets.

I dramatically reduced my exposure to mainstream news, eliminated political talk radio from my auditory diet, and focused heavily on personal development. I began making significant yet strategic investments in myself by traveling and building real relationships with like-minded people, attending conferences, and joining mentorship programs. I soon discovered the fierce resistance I and so many others were facing.

This yielded great personal friendships with wildly abundant-minded people. I was blessed to develop personal friendships with several of the same mentors and experts I began following at the onset of my journey. Before long, I found myself enjoying vacations with Robert Helms and his family. I've enjoyed many meals with people I look up to like Ken McElroy, George Gammon, Victor Menasce, and many others. I even found myself visiting with Robert Kiyosaki at a birthday celebration for mutual friends.

Own Your Story (and Listen to Your Wife)

I am proud of my life of service, but as I put myself out there, I discovered I avoided revealing my life in law enforcement and found myself steering conversations toward my experience as an entrepreneur and home builder. Essentially, I was deleting my life of service from the narrative.

I started believing that, as a police officer, I had invested years climbing a mountain, only to get to the top and realize I had climbed the wrong mountain. I was building in a new direction. My wife insisted I incorporate my whole story, but I was slow to listen.

One evening, I found myself at a high-end investment conference. Over dinner, I said something that captured Wagner Nolasco's attention. Wagner is a large developer in Florida who has developed well over $750 million in real estate. I learned Wagner had a life overflowing with volunteer service. He even put himself through a law enforcement academy to accomplish his dream of becoming a police officer. In our conversation, Wagner extracted my story and found it sad I tried to hide it. In short, my wife and Wagner insisted I embrace my story in everything I was doing. Soon, I started to shift. Wagner and I became friends and discovered a shared desire to help first responders build wealth.

One Last Mission

SWAT teams often make a suspect's environment uncomfortable and then achieve compliance by offering access to a more comfortable environment that SWAT also controls. This tactic has been implemented by many for centuries, which is why economic sanctions are often the first tools utilized during global conflict. In history, oppressive governments often formed by controlling much of a society's wealth and resources. Today, political agendas are being advanced by tethering them to spending and bailout packages that are crucial to keeping Wall Street bounce houses inflated and Americans employed. One simple example is a government agency requiring hospitals receiving federal funding to require vaccines for staff which placed many in uncomfortable positions. I'm not pro or anti-vaccine. I am pro-America where we employ legislative processes to establish law, not workarounds exploiting Americans' economic vulnerabilities. Will this happen again? If so, for what?

Americans routinely surrender their hard-earned money to the Wall Street casinos where the insiders risk the least and benefit the most. Expensive fees and puny tax benefits result in marginal inflation-adjusted returns, and most people don't realize that because real financial education is not taught in school. Relying on social programs, pensions, stocks, 401Ks, and even what were once considered safe jobs, have come to have one thing in common: they are all heavily subject to policy decisions of elected people seeking power and control for their own self-interests. History tells us one thing for certain: when societies surrender control of wealth to the few, good things do not happen.

Economic achievement is being criticized, and the middle class is being crushed. In the coming years, I believe automation will continue replacing workers, and dependency on government social programs will accelerate at exponential rates. To pay for it, governments will continue creating and spending money and this will steal more purchasing power from hard-working savers unless they own real assets that benefit from this process. Steadily, more Americans will reach retirement age poorer and more reliant on social programs that a minority control.

Police work routinely injected me deep into people's lives and revealed life behind the curtain. I met many who could use a hand, but I also observed many more engineering lives of hand-outs enabled by a system that kills the will to try. This sounds harsh, but I believe it is true and that this rapidly developing dependency on expanding social programs will prove dangerous for our country.

The result is widely developing vulnerabilities where future people in power can force the compliance of the masses. It's our patriotic duty to create and preserve more wealthy individuals to prevent this from happening.

Even if I am wrong and more of us simply increase our personal wealth, is there much downside? If I'm correct, the old saying will prove true, "He who has the gold makes the rules." During tactical training, I often said, "You have to see what you are looking at," and "Predictable is preventable." Code 3 Americans do see and are maneuvering toward a position of advantage.

In emergency services, a Code 3 response is an emergency response to a rapidly changing situation. Our situation is rapidly changing, and more Americans need to implement a Code 3 response to acquire real, necessary, and decentralized assets. I have always stood for something bigger than myself and as is said on a SWAT team, "If you see a void, fill it."

My journey evolved into the Code 3 American Community which is a collaborative environment for anyone who has or who wants to build real wealth. The community provides educational content and recurring online investor meetups for free. The wealth divide is growing and many promise solutions in exchange for power. Sound familiar? It is in the best interest of those with wealth to share their wisdom with others. The community provides that environment. We also established Code 3 Assets, LLC to provide tax-advantaged real asset investment opportunities for those meeting legal requirements.

Patriots gifted us the United States of America and the best way of life the world has ever known. Our children deserve it, and patriots of the past demand a return on their investment. Politicians claim checking a box next to their name will solve the problem, but Code 3 Americans know the answer is real financial education coupled with Main Street investing back into Main Street.

The mountain I climbed provided the raw vantage point required to see the field. Age eventually forces everyone from a uniform, but I still have a lot of fight left in me.

I'm a Code 3 American with one more mission: It's time to enrich humanity and save America through financial independence.

Discover opportunity and make a difference by joining a network of others on the same mission. To learn about the Code 3 American Community, email community@code3assets.com.

To receive three free reports detailing lessons Jay Johnson learned from his SWAT experience about life, business, and investing, email swat@code3assets.com.

Tweetable: Predictable is preventable, but you must first see what you are looking at.

TC CUMMINGS

Lessons From a Navy SEAL

TC Cummings, former Navy SEAL, is a high-energy, visionary coach and trainer. He is passionately committed to delivering exceptional services for executives, individuals, and corporate teams. TC uses his Navy SEAL experience and his Noble Warrior Training philosophies to elevate performance through professional development of teamwork, communication, leadership, and engagement.

Childhood and Early Emancipation

I was born in the Midwest. My father got a job with Eastman Kodak and moved the family to Rochester, New York. At the time, Rochester boasted the highest percentage of PhDs per capita. It was a very white-collar city.

Like many others, I had a challenging childhood, and my family broke apart. My mother moved us to Buffalo, New York, during the collapse of Bethlehem Steel. We're talking extreme blue-collar. Mom was doing all she could just to take care of herself, so I did my best to care for my kid brother. When I was 14, Dad invited me to come live with him and his new wife. Remarkably, I said yes on the condition that he send me to the toughest school! The all-male, Jesuit Catholic college prep school that kids were dragged into kicking and screaming. I still remember Dad shaking his head in disbelief.

Success leaves clues. At the age of 12, I'd learned that on the opposite side of adversity is benefit. Like any mathematical equation, the greater the adversity, the greater the benefit. I had survived the adversities prior, but I couldn't get the best out of myself on my own. I proactively sought a demanding environment of adversity.

Two years later, life got more interesting. My stepmother and I reached an impasse, and my home became an unsafe place from which I was legally emancipated. I chose to continue going to school and worked to pay for food, heat, rent, and all. Coming home from work six or seven nights a week between 1:00 a.m. and 3:00 a.m. and being in Homeroom by 7:40 a.m. allowed about four hours of sleep. Summer breaks were harder as I took on three jobs a day to make ends meet. I had the stress of moving 12 times in 24 months—including one month I spent homeless in Rochester, New York, living in my '70s rust bucket of a car (a gift from my dad). I would sneak into school before anybody showed up so I could use the showers, then sneak out of the locker room before anybody saw me. I like to think the faculty knew but just turned a caring blind eye.

There were two times during those two years that I nearly hung it up. I was just so tired. One time, while living on Lake Ontario, I couldn't take any more. I was going to just swim out into Lake Ontario as far as I could. That way there would be no mess. I figured nobody would miss me. I didn't want to make any noise. I just wanted to rest.

I was on my way out the door when the phone rang. I'm never there at that hour but I picked up the phone. It was my best friend, Probir. With understanding reverence, he simply said, "Hey, TC. We haven't heard from you in a long time. I just wanted to see how you are doing."

When I got off the phone, I fell to the floor and balled my eyes out. It was love. Somebody expressed love to me at the right moment.

Navy SEAL Training

I was going to be a psychologist. I was lined up for an appointment to the United States Naval Academy, Annapolis, one of the toughest schools to get into. My psychology teacher could not believe my life story. He couldn't conceive of how much stress I was under. My life story didn't compute with his textbooks! To be true to myself, I needed to first learn about human dynamics before becoming book smart. Reality over intellect.

That's when, in 1986, I sought the greatest adversity I could find, and I was directed to the previously secret US Navy SEAL Teams.

To join the SEALs, you had to be enlisted or an officer of the US Navy, and you had to qualify not only in your age but also psychologically and in your physical and intellectual capabilities. I was highly qualified, and I had to wrestle with my recruiter, who kept trying to get me to go into the nuclear submarine program to fill his quota. As demanding as that branch of the Navy is, I wanted the human experience only found in Basic Underwater Demolition/SEAL training (BUD/S).

About a third of the people who try out for the SEALs qualify. Then only half of them actually get and accept orders. Some commands don't want their best characters to leave, others have second thoughts. It's a serious commitment. It's better to have second thoughts earlier than later.

In my BUD/S class, we began with 153 men. Eighteen of us became Navy SEALs. BUD/S is the world's most demanding military training, lasting six and a half months. There's a lot of pressure, but at the end, you have respect because you've shown your capabilities. Graduation is followed by six to nine months of advanced training before earning your Trident as a SEAL.

Day in and day out, BUD/S is a grind. You start most days on the beach, in the surf zone or on the grinder by 5:00 a.m. You may have a calisthenic workout for 90 minutes. I remember being on our backs with our hands under our tailbones and our feet six inches off the ground. The instructor, Ralph Cherry, who became a good friend of mine, said, "Feet off the deck until… (looked around at the predawn sky) the sun comes up." Easily 45 minutes of abdominal exercises. And, when (not if) you fell out, you earned extra attention, which may look like an instructor with a water hose on your face.

After the exercises, we might have a six-mile conditioning run in the soft sand on the beach. If you didn't keep up, you got singled out. You might be run down to the water in your full uniform, so you'd get heavy with water and sand when you began doing exercises like mountain climbers. *It pays to be a winner!*

The instructor leading the run would eventually circle back so that you'd get a chance to catch up. That's a great point in life from BUD/S. Always give people a path back to honor. When you're extremely exhausted, you have to dig deeper inside yourself: *Do I want more of that special treatment, or right now, do I want to make myself go through the pain to keep up with my class?*

At the conclusion of that run, we'd jog one mile to the chow hall for breakfast. Jogging a mile back, we'd have eight miles under our belts by 8:00 a.m. At about 8:15 a.m., we had class. In the warm, calm classroom, the temptation to drift off is strong. Somebody would fall asleep, and immediately, an instructor would help you learn to not let yourself fall asleep. Incentives were provided like the inflatable boat full of ice water outside of the classroom for you and a swim buddy, who didn't do anything, to immerse yourselves in. Back in the classroom, you were shivering with cold, but awake.

By lunch, we'd have more physical exercise. Maybe we'd run a mile to the swimming pool, strip down, tie our hands behind our backs, tie our feet at the ankles, and enter the water. Everyone swimming like this generated so much tumultuous water that you inevitably inhale water. This is all to prepare for worst-case scenarios. Even with as much as we train, real life is going to be a little different. *Murphy's Law is reliable!* After that, we'd go for lunch.

In just this half-day of the 27-week BUD/S, we see opportunities to quit. The truth is, BUD/S Instructors are often SEAL Operators who are working this job to spend more time with their families. At the end of three years, they return to a SEAL Team where they will deploy. The last thing they want is somebody unqualified on their team. SEALs embrace the axiom that *the team is only as strong as its weakest link. And there's always going to be a weakest link.* The question is, is that weak link strong enough to get me home?

Communication Is Your Responsibility

The SEALs are a brotherhood with tremendous love for one another. (Though we don't always like each other!) Trust is paramount on a team. To trust, you have to be an effective communicator. Part of my Noble Warrior approach, which leads to Outrageous Authenticity, includes taking one hundred percent ownership of how you are being heard.

How often do you get on a Zoom call and the other party is not listening? Well, you can't make them listen. Still, it's your job to take ownership of how you're being heard. I believe if I say something to somebody and they only get a portion of it, I've failed.

In the SEALs, one of the tools we relied on I call *Confirm and Verify*. If I tell Joey, "The rain in Spain falls mainly on the plane," and Joey says, "Got it," do I know what Joey heard? It's my responsibility to own what they hear from me. Using the above tool, I ask Joey, "What did you hear from me?" *I am responsible.*

Personal ownership disturbs a lot of people. In the SEAL Teams, we make sure that we know what they heard is what we needed them to hear. Demonstrably, I make sure that I know you heard what I needed you to hear. In this environment, you can also always trust that I heard you. It doesn't mean you like me, but you can always trust me. With that trust, you can learn to respect me, and you can feel respected, *because you know I'm respect worthy*. That is one element for engendering intimate teamwork relationships.

Authenticity and Ownership

I've traveled a lot. That's what SEALs do. But also as a Corpsman, I was always traveling to take care of others or to expand my education. In 1991, when I came home from seven months in the Persian Gulf, they said, "Welcome home, Doc. We heard you saved the platoon!"

I scrunched up my nose. There were no hand grenades thrown that I smacked away with my hockey stick. It turned out, my Lead Petty Officer, who I had sent back a week earlier for an elective surgery, had told everybody that I had saved the morale of the platoon.

We had a situation where my platoon had very suboptimal leadership. We did the best we could with what we had, but we didn't have a political say in anything. Once the Persian Gulf War was concluded, we were tasked to stand by in the area. After about a week and a half of boredom, our senior leadership canceled morning musters. It was sort of like a snow day! Initially, it felt wonderful, but intellectually, I knew that *the devil finds work for idle hands*.

Not being in charge, I made an announcement: "Tomorrow morning before breakfast, I'm going to lead a workout on the deck of the ship at 6:00 a.m., if anybody wants to join me." Eighty percent of my platoon joined me, and they all thanked me. It was camaraderie and working together, and they said that we should repeat daily.

In the late mornings, I held advanced first aid training. Again, 80 percent of the team, including my future leaders, showed up. Being a certified armorer with the Department of Justice, I alternated daily classes of medical or weapons care. Afternoons, we would weight train and share book readings.

This inspired others. Soon, a teammate asked if he could lead the workouts. That's the dream! Someone else to carry the torch while you then focus on building the next thing. Another guy came and offered to do a class on dive calculations. Another on radio communications.

Where morale had been sinking quickly, I, a mid-level leader, demonstrated ownership of my team by contributing my authentic self, with no attachment, to be of service. That inspired the other mid-level leaders to also contribute. When everybody has ownership, they also have pride, and when you have pride, the last thing you're going to do is just lay around. And when there's ownership, when somebody is sick, someone else with ownership is going to jump in and take over. It was an unbelievable compliment from my peers.

Noble Warrior Training

I approach all people, as **multidimensional, holistic, and dynamic beings often embroiled in messy relationships (sometimes with ourselves)**. I developed the two-pronged paradigm of Noble Warrior Training 20 years ago. One is that *where you see yourself relative to the law of cause and effect determines power*. Your mindset is not what you want to think, it's where your heart is really truly coming from. It's your consciousness. Are you at Cause or are you in Effect?

The second thing is that we're all ultimately facing the same enemy. Everybody has the same "worst enemy." I believe there are two sides of ego, a constructive and a destructive side. On the constructive side, you're contributing to relationships. Ego becomes destructive when it separates from synergy. When it becomes about you, to the detriment or neglect of others. The power of the whole is greater than the sum of the parts. And that's exactly what the SEAL Teams live. We are completely synergistic, which is how we are able to do outrageous things with so few assets and so little resources. "The difficult done immediately, the impossible done by appointment only!"

My purpose in life is to participate in leading a global shift of consciousness from effect to cause. And this leads to not just authentic, but *outrageous authenticity*—where just so little bothers you, where your joy is inspiring, where in your silence you stand out, and where the people who have ears to hear it will hear it.

To receive a daily email from TC Cummings that's been going for 22 years with a hand-chosen quote to inspire you to maintain or to reclaim the driver's seat of your life, email info@TCCummings.com. Follow TC on LinkedIn and visit TCCummings.com.

Tweetable: The power of the whole is greater than the sum of the parts. That's exactly what the SEAL teams live. We are completely synergistic, which is how we are able to do outrageous things.

GABRIEL CRAFT

Value, Success and Multifamily Real Estate Investing

Gabriel Craft is a passive investing evangelist dedicated to helping high-achievers retire earlier. Gabriel coaches in real asset investing and provides low-risk, high-return opportunities to help investors build real wealth, win back time, and secure their financial future for themselves and their families.

My One Ticket

At 17 years old, I was making a huge decision to leave my home in Santa Cruz, California, and travel to Washington, DC for college. Five schools had denied my admission, but one offered me admission and a full academic scholarship.

After track practice one day, I rode my bike to my favorite place in town, West Cliff Lighthouse. I remember sitting on the edge of a cliff overlooking the Pacific Ocean and fighting a strange feeling in my belly that something bad was about to happen to me. The waves below were pacifying my anxiety, but I really did not want to leave home.

I was doing it out of duty. I was doing it because I thought it was my ticket to a better life. Staring out across the ocean, I accepted that this next move would be an adventure and not necessarily one I'd enjoy.

Reality Struck

In my first semester on the East Coast, I was crippled by insecurity. That winter, there was a pretty sizable snowstorm. In my California-thin jacket, I walked to the corner store in deep thought about how alone I was.

I was extremely depressed, in part due to my apparent inability to make friends. My nature is that of a "super-extrovert," and this lack of a social network pushed me deeper into a bad place such that I did not make the grades required to keep my scholarship. With that, I had experienced the most significant failure of my life.

In the spring of 2001, I got on a plane back to California with no idea whether I would come back to school. I was only certain that I was a loser and not meant to be a global success and multi-millionaire as I had, perhaps naively, planned.

Burgers and Fries

For a while, I had no resolve. I was a cook at an amusement park that summer while others were off at corporate internships. I could feel myself drifting away from that life of bountiful success and recognition I'd imagined college would provide. Yet, cooking for six to eight hours a day is a great way to force deep introspection. The aromas and freshness of a kitchen—even in a fast food diner—opened up my senses. Then, while my brain was partially focused on easy tasks like flipping burgers or lifting baskets of fries, I got a ton of time to think.

Early on, I was pretty sure I would not go back to face the circumstances that had resulted in such a catastrophic loss of momentum. But as I continued to cook, surrounded by the merriment of an amusement park, I kept flashing back to moments when I had been happy.

In high school, I tutored my college-aged sister, Amber. Brilliant in her own right, she lacked a gift for mathematics. When I was in grade school, I was a bit of a math whiz. Algebra had always been my favorite subject, and helping my big sister who was my biggest hero was an enchanting opportunity. After a few short weeks, Amber figured out solving for unknown variables and quadratic equations and breezed to an A- in her final exam. She gave me full credit. I was so proud of myself that I decided to help my friends who were also struggling with math. I built a small but successful after-school math tutoring program which would become a centerpiece in my college applications and, ultimately, my scholarship.

In July of 2001, in the back of Whiting's Foods Burgers and Fries, I had an epiphany. I found myself alone in the walk-in freezer with tears in my eyes. I had decided to face my fear. I would return to school. But I had given up on the millionaire aspect of my dreams. Instead, I would double down on what I was good at, helping people. I would be a math teacher and help people overcome their fear of math.

I was going to have to take out tens of thousands in student loans, but I had a purpose bigger than myself. I still felt miserable about so many things that had happened the year before, but deep down, I realized that I was in the middle of an adventure not the end of one. I was ready to grow.

Success Means Service

I got a part-time job and stacked my classes on Tuesdays and Thursdays so I would never be absent. I passed every course with flying colors and even managed to make a few East Coast friends. And more than that, I had made a huge leap forward as a person. I had developed grit.

With some hard work and a four-year college degree under my belt, I became a self-sustaining human being in my mid-20s. I got a job as a math teacher in South Central Los Angeles and helped young people learn problem-solving and analytical thinking.

Most kids fear math until they are good at it. Helping people overcome that fear was something I enjoyed. In the process, I got to withstand the daily pressures of teaching middle schoolers. I describe the job as one part mentor, one part stage actor. "When all else fails, make them laugh," was my motto. While they came into my classroom to learn pre-algebra, they often got more than a fair share of "I've got to show you a future where you too can work your way out of poverty."

Turning Point

Teaching felt great. But, I distinctly remember a conversation with my girlfriend—who would eventually become my wife. I was burnt out and certain we would have to wait a couple of decades before we could have kids because we barely made enough money to support ourselves. The look on her face was heartbreaking. She would not say it directly, but having children and the safety of enough income regularly passing through our bank account was a fundamental part of her vision in life.

I absolutely still wanted to work to improve the lives of others, but it was time to do something different. I started to have a different relationship with money. I started to realize that a life of service isn't necessarily counter to a life of building capital. With more money, I would have the opportunity to have a greater impact. I just didn't know how to do that yet. So, I did what made sense to me and enrolled in business school.

Business school was a great opportunity to step back for a couple of years and really think about what I wanted to do. I went down a couple of different paths. My education in teaching took me toward consulting. It was a really fun job in high demand and a great way to learn how great businesses are structured.

A class on corporate social responsibility changed my whole outlook on business. I came to see that when you are in business, you are creating a ton of value for society. You can have a big impact while also solving a business problem. That impact then multiplies when you give away some of your profits in philanthropy. It's not that greed is good, but greed is not as evil as I thought it to be when I found it in my heart to become a teacher. It was a game-changer for me to understand that if you can make money, you're creating value. That change in perspective made me comfortable sticking with my new consulting career for a lot longer. I understood that it would not be wasted time. It wasn't just about the money. I had the opportunity to provide a service that brings people value.

I also took a class on real estate with Peter Allen at the University of Michigan—which has a strong history of owner/operators in commercial real estate, including Stephen M. Ross who built skyscrapers in Manhattan and all over the country and Sam Zell (who I got to interview while there), one of the largest operators of multifamily real estate in the country and the creator of REITs. In the class, we learned how to analyze real case studies —value-add properties in Detroit. That course planted a seed. The avenue of commercial real estate made a lot of sense. I didn't have the means to get there yet, but I knew that soon I would start to pursue it.

I got motivated, and as soon as I graduated, my plan was by day (and some nights) I'd do consulting, then, where I could, I'd also begin investing in real estate, at first in single-family homes.

Ever since I was young, my big brother, Mike, had a lot of influence on my path in life. First off, he can dunk a basketball with two hands, hard! Watching that made me fall in love with basketball. Mike also graduated business school (a little before me, "but not as good a school" as I liked to remind him in jest as often as I can). And most critically, he got me in the habit of listening to BiggerPockets podcasts daily and we'd talk a lot about when we would make "our first move" into real estate.

Eventually, he decided to make a move. He bought a value-add duplex in Toledo, Ohio, from an investor on BiggerPockets.com and continued to buy single-family homes, duplexes, and triplexes.

Then, to get me to take action, he made me re-read *Rich Dad Poor Dad*, which was a game-changing novel about wealth and a huge component of my journey. And I purchased my first property in 2016. Starting with single-family projects in a state we didn't live in taught my brother and me the value of having great partnerships and how real estate really can be a team game. You need to have a great team in place if you're going to turn this into a business, even if you're local. We also got to practice direct marketing and wholesaling.

Stepping Up to Multifamily

In 2017, my brother and I partnered on our first multifamily, a six-unit apartment complex. That was the start of my foray into multifamily. We bought another one later that year. And we screwed up! We didn't do anything right as I later learned. We just bought it, with no due diligence. We made money, but not as much as on our single-family properties and with way more headache. I realized we were not managing this right and we needed some scale to go bigger faster.

At one point, we had 24 units in Toledo. As we built our portfolio there, I realized where I was living in Dallas was a booming market, and I started doing the same things locally. Over time, we transitioned out of Toledo.

Serendipitously, by going to Meetups in the DFW area, I ran into this little pocket of local, brilliant investors led by a mentor in the space, Brad Sumrok. I felt at home and jumped headfirst into that community. That's when I started doing deals as a passive investor. I was making as much money doing that as I was flipping houses, but I didn't have to do any work! That was awesome. I wanted to go even bigger, even faster and become the person who actually created those kinds of deals.

I transitioned into a cushier tech job at Salesforce in 2018, one of the greatest companies in employee satisfaction, which is one of the reasons I work there to this day. My financial life unfolded like human behavioral scientist Andrew Jebb found in his research on wealth. When I started teaching and making $70k a year, I was independent and the money made a big difference. Going from $70k to $120k made a really big difference too. We were able to afford a bigger house and nicer stuff. We were still living check to check, but we felt good. After $120k a year, in my opinion, not much changes if you stay an employee. If you just spend the money and you're not getting your money to work for you, your life isn't going to feel any better. In fact, it starts to feel empty.

That's where time becomes the problem. You're giving up your time to make your salary. That was underscored during COVID for me. I realized I didn't have to leave home at 5 a.m. and come back at 7 p.m. I could spend more time with my kids. In 2020, I shifted and really started focusing on my single-family and multifamily business. Today, I'm still an employee but I have a lot more time flexibility and am putting my business first. I'm in a weird place where if they told me tomorrow I was being let go, I wouldn't experience fear and panic.

I talk to my brother every day. I would not have taken action if it weren't for his example. Now, I'm blessed to be in the position I'm in. He also taught me the importance of focusing on one thing until you're successful. And I'm going to stay focused on real estate and multifamily until I've reached my goals.

I am in the middle of that journey. Since 2021, I've been sponsoring deals and putting them together. It's been fun. I'm creating an army of people who see that there are way more opportunities out there to make money than the stock market or bonds. Real estate as a vehicle for creating wealth is way different, especially in times like we've had recently. It's a way for your Average Jane or Joe to build financial freedom. If someone wants to leave a legacy, real estate has got to be the best path forward.

To learn more about Gabriel Craft's massively easy path to financial freedom through value-add real estate investing, text "MEET" to (831) 428-2341.

Tweetable: Nothing in my financial life has been more rewarding than investing in value-add real estate. The first deal is scary. The second deal will make you an investor for life.

JENNIFER KUNRATH

Wild Horses

Jenn Kunrath is a published author and voiceover professional. She has recorded for clients including Microsoft, Amazon, and ZooTampa. Her focus is on writing books with strong morals and messages. This includes a children's book to teach kids to be aware of the world around them as well as a list of fairy tale rewrites that cast strong and capable heroines.

Luck of the Draw

It was a lottery—horses assigned to trainers at random. I gazed through the pipe panel fencing at a little brown mare that would be mine to tame, mine to train, mine to hopefully ride. For the moment though, she was a wild mustang and had never been so much as touched by a person. So, we had some work to do.

With plastic bags on sticks, the horse was urged through a series of chutes into the back of a trailer. I was fortunate to have a couple sponsoring me with a space to keep the mustang as I trained. They were also doing the transport and drove her back to the farm, with me following behind in my compact car. I watched as the mustang tried to jump out of the gap between the back door and the top of the trailer, my heart lurching each time she did.

We managed to get back without incident, parked the trailer next to the pen we had put up for training, and let the horse loose inside. That was day one of my 100-day challenge, a competition the Bureau of Land Management (BLM) dubbed the Extreme Mustang Makeover.

A Daunting Prospect

Most people don't realize that there are more than 50,000 mustangs currently in government holding. As a protected species, they must be cared for. Due to limitations of federal lands though, not all of them can stay wild.

The average herd of wild horses doubles in population every four years. This exponential growth is unchecked, given they have no real natural predators. Once in a while, a mountain lion or a bolt of lightning will manage to take a horse down. Overall though, these horses thrive. Because of this, periodic roundups are coordinated. This is to make sure that the wild horses on federal lands are not in excess of what can be sustained. After sorting and gathering, selected mustangs go into pens.

Not many people would know where to start when training a wild horse. The prospect is daunting. Many of the horses stand in those pens for years, unadopted. This costs taxpayers multiple millions of dollars every year and isn't the best option for the horses either. In response to this issue, a competition was brainstormed, a showcase of how trainable and versatile these horses can be. Trainers have one hundred days to take a horse from, as they say, "wild to mild."

Just getting my mustang to the farm had taken a whole day and I was well aware the clock was ticking.

Gaining Momentum

At the end of day five, I still couldn't touch her. She flickered away, her skin shuddering every time I tried. I was convinced I had bitten off more than I could chew.

In the past, I had retrained thoroughbreds off the track, and though they came with their own set of issues, all those horses were familiar with being handled, saddled, and ridden.

Starting from zero was something I was no longer confident I was equipped to do. Mired in the depths of my self-doubt and certain I had found something at which to fail, I confided in a friend. After a pep talk and the reminder that I had no choice but to persist, I went back in that pen, armed with a newly resolved sense of determination and handfuls of alfalfa hay. That night, my efforts were rewarded by the first few touches on her shoulder.

For that first week, I had been calling the horse by her number, *2045*. She was a plain bay mare with no markings except for one small dot of white on her forehead that was usually hidden by the hair in front of it. After getting to know her a little better, I finally found a name that fit. I called her *Lark*, and by day eight, I was sitting on her back. After that, we made progress fast.

Being Consistent

Training Lark involved a lot of hard work. Every evening, I would drive up to the farm at 5 p.m., trading an office in an open cubicle where I wrote code across my three monitors for a dirt arena and light that grew more golden as the sun set. Weekdays, I was there for at least four hours every evening, often past when it got dark. There were days I was so tired when I got home that I would make myself a slice of bread and butter and mindlessly put the knife in the fridge while the butter stayed on my kitchen counter. Weekends, I stayed in the guest bedroom of the farmhouse so Lark and I could work in the morning, take a break for lunch, and then resume for the rest of the evening.

My hard work paid off.

In a few short weeks, Lark went from the horse I could barely touch to the horse I rode through a Fourth of July parade. Close to the end of our one hundred days, I could even stand on the saddle and hula hoop. She was ready for the competition where we would show just how far she had come in a short time. One thing I was not sure I was ready for though was the decision I had to make—would I adopt her myself or let her be auctioned off into a new home?

The Showcase

My family came to the final event, support I hadn't thought to expect given I am the only one who rides and also the only one in my family without allergies. They had seen Lark in those early days when she was still a wild thing wheeling in her stall. My dad almost made the decision for me, wanting to buy Lark as a surprise because he was so overcome by the change and trust we showed in our performance.

I'm glad he didn't. A big part of the reason I wanted to do this training challenge is that it is important for these horses to become ambassadors. If Lark had stayed with me, her exposure would have been limited. I was already convinced that with time and training mustangs can be great horses. Lark needed to go somewhere where she could prove this to someone else.

A lady with a cute farm in Newberg, Oregon, became Lark's adopted owner. Together, they do endurance rides of 50 to 100 miles. What I am most proud of are pictures she sent me with her three-year-old daughter leading Lark out to pasture. In those frozen moments, Lark's good nature and confidence shine through.

A Ripple Effect

So much good came out of this singular experience. So much good that would have been missed if five days in I had believed myself incapable. Lark's adopter went on to sponsor two more horses. One was trained by an exchange student from Rome who had a moment of self-doubt similar to mine which I was able to coach her through. I visited the student and her family a couple years later. That was yet another amazing experience for me both in terms of the welcome and the culture I enjoyed during my time in Italy.

More fundamentally, the lessons I learned by facing my doubts proactively in that moment of challenge have translated to other areas of my life. I've built a six-figure career in a male-dominated field, working as a solution engineer in the tech industry. I have the confidence to carry myself well in my role. I've grown a life that I can be grateful for and proud of, owning multiple properties and maintaining finances both balanced and intelligently leveraged.

I indulge in dreaming big but also put in the hard work to back up those aspirations. I've built a freelance career that I love in professional voiceover, have multiple side streams of income, and still take the time to write every day because that is a passion of mine. To date, I've completed six full-length novels. Every story I write, I weave in variations of the morals that have guided me through life.

My intention is to encourage those who read my stories to be brave and to realize they are capable and only as limited as they let themselves be. That is my message in this story, something I hope will spread beyond the binding of this book. You are as great as your aspirations. Never be afraid to challenge yourself and remember to dream big.

To connect with Jenn Kunrath about voiceover, copywriting, or other writing services, email jennkunrath@gmail.com. Current projects and updates are listed on Jenn's website: www.jennkunrath.com. Her books can be found on Amazon in Kindle and paperback format.

Tweetable: You are as great as your aspirations. Never be afraid to challenge yourself and remember to dream big.

CHRIS CHICKERING

The Unexpected Gift

Chris Chickering is a psychotherapist, bestselling author, speaker, trainer, recording artist, and CEO of Chris Chickering, Inc. He helps people build upon their inner strengths, break through barriers, and fulfill their untapped potential and provides solution-focused therapy and coaching, trainings, workshops, and keynotes.

"Everything negative—pressure, challenges—is all an opportunity for me to rise."
– Kobe Bryant

An Unexpected Detour

It was 11:00 Friday night, and I couldn't have been happier. In 12 hours, I was flying to meet my father and little brother in Las Vegas for the NBA summer league, an annual tradition we cherished. Since I had finished packing and my flight didn't leave till noon the next day, I decided to jump in my car and go listen to some live music for a while.

Four blocks from my house, flashing blue lights and the squawk of a police transponder. I was getting pulled over. "License and registration, please," the police officer said while standing outside my driver's side window.

"Sure," I said, handing them over. "What did I do wrong, officer?"

"Sir, you were going 40 in a 25," he responded.

"Oh, I live four blocks from here and guess I was a little too excited when I…" I said, trailing off as he returned to the squad car. After what felt like an eternity, he finally returned.

"Sir, will you step out of the car please?" he said.

"Sure," I replied while opening the door.

"Sir, will you turn around please?"

"Wait a minute!" I said, shocked, "Am I being arrested?!"

"Sir, you have an outstanding bench warrant for your arrest in Bernalillo County."

"Well… what did I do wrong?!" I pleaded.

"Sir, I have no idea. All I know is you have an outstanding bench warrant for your arrest in Bernalillo County for $120. So, unless you can pay that right now, we need to take you to jail."

"No problem," I said. "Here's my credit card. You can put it on there. I have cash too."

"Sir, it doesn't work like that," he said.

"Like what?" I replied.

"Sir, we don't take cash or credit cards, *only* money orders."

"Ok," I thought, racking my brain. "Well… is there any way we could drive to the nearest money order place? If we did that… then I could *easily* give you a money order." I said, keeping a smile on my face.

"Sir, that's not an option. Will you turn around please, sir?" he said while closing the distance between us.

"Well, what's going to happen to my car?" I asked, feeling the cuffs tightening around my wrists.

Getting Processed

Located 14 miles south of Santa Fe on Highway 14, the Santa Fe County Adult Correctional Facility appeared out of the darkness as an impenetrable fortress, complete with 30-foot high walls crowned with snarls of barbed wire and enough spotlights for an arena concert.

Stepping through the outermost door, I found myself in a narrow hallway where I was escorted into a small cell. Entering, I noticed a man in his mid-40s sitting quietly.

"What are you here for?" I asked.

"DUI," he replied, "you?"

"I have no idea," I said, "For some reason, I owe Bernalillo County $120."

"I hear you…" he said, nodding into the distance.

Then something came into view. It was a half-eaten ham and cheese sandwich which had apparently been thrown, or perhaps smashed, into the wall so hard that, almost like a magic trick, it hung there, somehow clinging to the wall.

I noticed my cellmate looking at me looking at the sandwich, at which point, I blurted out the first thing that came to mind, "Pardon me, would you have any Grey Poupon?"

Truth be told, this was the first and only time I'd been to jail, and as such, I had no idea what to expect. By this time, it had to have been close to one o'clock in the morning.

According to what I learned in the squad car, all I needed to do was get a bail bondsman or friend to drop off a $120 money order at the jail for me. The instant that happened, I was free. And, to make that happen (no later than 9:00 a.m., so I could make my noon flight to Vegas), I *had* to use a phone.

"Hello!" I yelled through the bars. "Is there anyone there?"

A distant "Yes," echoed in response.

"Sorry to bother you," I said, "but I was told I'd have a chance to call someone, and I was wondering when...."

"We'll get to you when we get to you."

Around 30 minutes later, a correctional officer opened the cell door and escorted me down a hallway to a small room with a stethoscope and blood pressure cuff lying on a card table. Another correctional officer took my vitals and asked, "Are you concerned for your safety?"

"Not yet," I replied, as we both let out a small chuckle.

I was then led to a counter where another officer handed me an orange jumpsuit, boxers, and slides.

"I want you to go into that bathroom, take off all your clothes, and put them in this plastic bag," she said. "Then, I want you to put these on," she continued, gesturing to the orange jumpsuit on the counter, "And let me tell you, if you come out of that bathroom with one shred of your own clothes on, I am going to be *pissed*."

There's no other way to put it. Looking into the bathroom mirror and seeing myself in that orange jumpsuit for the first time sent cold shivers down my spine. I took a deep breath, and then heard a voice within say, *This experience is a gift, because it's giving you an opportunity to practice staying positive in the face of difficulty. This experience is also a game. To win the game, all you need to do is stay positive and not allow negative thoughts to enter your mind.*

Emerging from the bathroom with a new purpose and attitude, I handed the bag filled with my old clothes to the corrections officer. She zip-tied it shut and tossed it in a thick plastic box, which she then padlocked closed before sliding it down the hall and out of view.

Too Bad You Didn't Get Pulled Over for a DUI

It was now 2:38 a.m. The wall-mounted phone was in a cramped, closet-sized booth with a small wooden bench. To the right was a long list of bail bondsman's phone numbers. I entered, closed the door, and started calling.

First number… no answer. Second number… no answer… till finally, two-thirds of the way down the list, I heard a "yeah" come through the receiver.

"Hi, my name is Chris, and I'm at the Santa Fe County Jail, and I need someone, hopefully you, to come down here as soon as possible with a $120 money order so I can get released."

"It's too bad you didn't get pulled over for a DUI," the bail bondsman replied.

"Excuse me?" I said.

"Because then, your bond would be $3,000. See, we are paid a 10% commission on the value of your bond, and no one is going to go down there for $12."

"I'll pay you extra," I pleaded. "Whatever it takes. I just really, *really* need to get out of here tonight, and…."

"It doesn't work like that," he said. "I'd love to help, but I can't, sorry. *No one will.*"

With that, I made the dreaded decision to start calling friends. After a long string of voicemail messages, I called my friend DJ. "Hello?" the groggy, high-pitched voice said. At that moment, I realized I had just woken up DJ's wife, Barb.

"Hi, Barb? It's Chris… Chris Chickering," I stammered.

"Oh, hi, Chris…" she said.

"Barb, I am SO sorry for calling this late. Can I talk to DJ?"

"DJ is in Atlanta visiting his parents, Chris," she replied.

"Barb, I was pulled over a few hours ago and I am in the Santa Fe County Jail wearing an orange jumpsuit, because… I owe Bernalillo County $120…. And the reason I'm calling is… I need to give them a $120 dollar money order to get out of here… and I was wondering if… there was any way you could get up, drive to the AllSup's on Cerrillos and Baca, get a $120 money order, and bring it here for me?"

Silence.

"Chris, what time is it?" she said.

"It's 3:02," I replied.

"Chris, I can't make it right now, but I will be there by 6:30 with that money order."

"Thank you, Barb! Thank you! You have NO IDEA how much I appreciate this," I said practically with tears in my eyes.

"I am happy because I'm grateful. I choose to be grateful. That gratitude allows me to be happy."
– Will Arnett

The Great Revelation

Noticing I'd exited the booth, a guard took me to a room filled with a pile of thin foam mattresses and blankets, and said, "One of each."

From there, I entered a 10- by 20-foot room with beige cinder block walls, a sitting bench around the perimeter, and a combination stainless-steel toilet / drinking fountain perched in the corner. I tiptoed between the six inmates who lay sleeping on the floor, laid my mattress down, and went to sleep.

Sometime later, I woke up, looked at the cinder block walls, and thought, *You really don't have problems. The problems that you think are problems, aren't*, and fell back asleep.

I was awakened by the sound of the cell door opening. A guard stood outside with a large cart filled with food trays. I grabbed one and sat down.

Powdered eggs, a small pile of Cheerios, and the nastiest muffin you've ever seen. Every single bit of food on the tray was the exact same shade of beige as the tray, and everything on the tray was also the exact same color as the walls!

I ate a few bites of the powdered eggs, looked at the wall in front of me, and heard a voice inside say, *You really don't have problems. You live in a world where the food you eat has solid nutritional value. You have the privilege of eating food that has color. Like blueberries... And... in the world you live in, you actually have the privilege of being able to see color—to see green, orange, red, and blue. Those colors, those beautiful colors... don't exist in here.*

And at that moment, I felt immense gratitude for my life.

Shortly thereafter, the cell door swung open. My name was being called. Barb had come through.

In no time, I was back in my clothes, cell phone and wallet in hand. A large guard escorted me across a large fenced-in outdoor courtyard to a gate which led to the parking lot. As he unlocked it, I turned to him and said, "Last night was the greatest gift of my life."

"I'm happy to hear that," he replied with a smile.

*"Sometimes the hurdles aren't really hurdles at all.
They're welcome challenges, tests."*
— Paul Walker

Sprint to the Airport

After retrieving my car from the impound lot, I was thrilled to make it home by 8:50 a.m. That was more than enough time to shower, drop off my dog at the kennel, and make my flight to Vegas, or so I thought.

Pulling out of the kennel parking lot and onto I-25 South towards the airport, it was hard to recall a time I'd ever felt better. Strangely, temporarily having everything taken from me made me realize how amazing my life was. I cracked the window, set the cruise control, and cranked up the stereo, grinning from ear to ear.

Then I noticed a faint glow on the dash: "Engine Overheating, Slow Down." A few moments later, white smoke began billowing from under the hood. I pulled the car to the side of the road, jumped out, and kicked the ground, cursing my predicament.

I'm embarrassed to report that this rant continued for quite some time, till finally, I thought, *Wait a minute. You can be grateful for your life when you are stuck in a jail cell. Can you be grateful for your life standing in 100-degree heat, stranded on the side of the highway with a broken-down car?*

Yes, I can.

I looked at the beautiful clear blue sky and the light-gray tones of the mushroom-like clouds and was once again filled with gratitude… remembering that those colors, those beautiful colors, were not available to me, such a short time ago.

Conclusion

There's an old saying, it's not what happens to you in this world that counts, what counts is what you do with what happens to you. And circumstances that appear to be "bad" or "horrible" on the surface can instantly transform themselves into amazing gifts-of-gratitude the moment you realize these circumstances are in fact opportunities for you to learn, grow, and evolve. Such was the case with my unexpected visit to the Santa Fe County jail.

Oh! And, in case you are wondering, the $120 was for a parking ticket I'd forgotten to pay ten years prior. And yes, I finally made it to Vegas to meet my dad and little brother, and yes, we had an amazing time!

Chris Chickering is a psychotherapist, bestselling author, speaker, trainer, and recording artist. He helps people build upon their inner strengths, break through barriers, and fulfill their untapped potential, as well as providing trainings, workshops, and keynotes. Reach him at: www.SolutionFocusedSecrets.com/gift, 505-670-0712, Chris@ChrisChickering.com

Tweetable: This experience is a gift, because it's giving you an opportunity to practice staying positive in the face of difficulty. This experience is also a game. To win the game, all you need to do is stay positive and not allow negative thoughts to enter your mind.

KYLE WILSON

Lessons From Mentors Jim Rohn, Brian Tracy, Zig Ziglar and More

Kyle Wilson is an entrepreneur, business and marketing strategist, publisher, seminar promoter, and speaker. He is the founder of KyleWilson.com, Jim Rohn International, and LessonsFromExperts.com. Kyle hosts the Success Habits *podcast and the* Kyle Wilson Inner Circle Mastermind *and has published dozens of #1 bestselling books.*

Plant a Tree

At the age of 26, living in Vernon, Texas, I made the decision to sell my modest house and move to Dallas. I didn't have a job lined up. I didn't have anything lined up. But, a friend shared with me a quote by Martin Luther. In response to the question, "If you were going to die today, what would you do?" Martin Luther said, "Even if I knew that tomorrow the world would end, I would still plant a tree today."

That hit me hard.

So, I went and bought a peach tree, and I planted it in the front yard of the house I was selling. And that did something for me. I guess, at the time, I had almost a fatalistic outlook. I thought our world was in some turbulent times. This was during the Cold War, and the news was always bad. And, at times I thought, *What's the use?*

Planting that tree helped ground me and helped lead me to a more long-term mindset.

Getting into the Seminar Business

I moved to Dallas, and after several serendipitous events, I got a job working for a seminar company. That opportunity launched me into a new world that eventually led me to starting my own company and putting on large seminars all across the country.

One of the speakers I would hire for my events was the iconic Jim Rohn.

Eventually, I made Jim Rohn an offer. I would have exclusive rights to book him to speak and we would create products together. Within the first 12 months, I took Jim from 20 speaking dates a year at $4,000 each to over 110 dates a year at $10,000 each (and eventually $25,000 per talk).

I went to work creating a product line including launching a viral quote booklet that went on to sell over six million copies.

My focus was to build the product line and a customer list using what I call The Wheel. Within two years of launching and building Jim Rohn International, business was booming, and I had grown a team of 20 people. I found that Jim was the gateway to personal development for so many people.

With my focus on list and customer building, I decided to also launch Your Success Store where I could market other speakers' products and book them to speak at the companies where I was booking Jim. The speakers included Brian Tracy, Les Brown, Mark Victor Hansen, Bob Burg, Jeffrey Gitomer, and many more.

Working with my mentor, friend, and business partner, Jim Rohn for 18 years (he passed away in 2009) as well as Brian Tracy, Mark Victor Hansen, Les Brown, Darren Hardy, and many more going on 30 years now has been one of my life's greatest honors.

It has also been the catalyst for much of the success I've had.

I want to share some of the lessons I've learned from these legends and mentors that have helped me next level my life!

1. The Major Key to Your Better Future Is You

Jim Rohn said the major key to your better future is you. Not the government, the economy, your boss, or your negative friends or family!

At the time, I was a victim of the outside world. And when I heard Jim say that, I really caught the pass. I figured out that, truly, the major key to my better future was me and that I was the one who held the key. Wow!

The fact is, the biggest influences in our life are the things we control.

What's my attitude? What's my work ethic? What books am I reading? What am I choosing to listen to? What am I choosing to watch? Who am I spending time with? Am I attending seminars and doing things that can really make a difference?

All of these things, including my health, my finances, my attitude, my work ethic, and who I spend time with, I get to control.

2. Success Is Predictable

Jim Rohn said that success is predictable.

It's like a garden. If you plant a tomato seed in the right soil at the right time, and you water it and take good care of it, odds are in your favor that after a period of time, you're going to have a harvest.

When I first heard this, I tended to be a short-term thinker. I wanted immediate, quick success. I didn't realize that there is a blueprint to success you can follow and that it will take time to get results.

If you do the right things, in the right order, over time, good things will usually happen.

Some things have a longer gestation period than others. If you want a vineyard, you are not going to plant a grape seed and, in a year, have wine. It's going to take four or five years. Everything has a gestation period. But once you figure out what that is and what the principles are, if you follow those, the odds of success are dramatically in your favor.

Instead of going for the short-term fix, instead of going for the too good to be true, I learned to follow principles that are guaranteed to work over a period of time.

3. Be a Student not a Follower

Jim Rohn said, be a student, not a follower. He said to make sure that whatever you decide is the product of your own conclusion.

He said to take advice, but not orders. Make sure everything you do is the product of your own conclusion.

This gave me permission to take it all in and find what was valuable and applied to me and leave the rest.

There isn't a cookie cutter. Get the principle that applies to you and personalize it to your unique gifts, skillset, and calling.

4. Bring Value to the Marketplace

Jim Rohn said, if you want to be successful, learn to bring value to the marketplace. He didn't say, learn to be a good networker. He said, learn to bring value. And then he said, if you want to be wealthy, learn to be valuable to valuable people.

I really caught that pass. And I realized for me to become wealthy, I had to be valuable. This dramatically changed my life.

I became good at putting on events that connected talent with the marketplace. That made me valuable to both sides. I now build platforms to do this including podcasts, groups, books, and more, connecting talent with an audience where both sides win.

In everything I do, I want to always answer first, "How will this provide value?"

5. Getting the Plane off the Ground

I met Brian Tracy in 1991 and promoted him in my events (we still work closely together today).

In 1992, I went to Brian's house in San Diego, and we were talking and masterminding.

He said, "Kyle, listen, you don't have kids yet. You are ambitious. I've got a piece of advice for you. I really encourage you to, for a couple of years, just go pay the price. Success often is like an airplane you're trying to get off the ground. In the beginning, it's hard. You start at zero and have to overcome inertia, and then you're only going 20 miles per hour. Then you're going down the runway at 40, and then 60, and then 80. It's still not enough to get the plane off the ground, but the amount of fuel you burn is tremendous. Once you're off the ground and at 30,000 feet, the plane uses less fuel, and it's going 300 miles per hour."

He said, "You want to get the plane off the ground so you can benefit from that momentum. Otherwise, you're always starting over. I've been doing this a long time, and I have to tell you, most people are like that plane going down the runway at 80 miles an hour yet never taking off. They're always starting over, often never willing to pay that initial price. I encourage you to pay the price to get the plane off the ground. Don't do it at the expense of your health or your family. But do it at the expense of TV or activities that really aren't going to matter 20 years from now."

What great advice from Brian! I took it and poured it on for the next few years, and that changed my life forever!

6. Prime Time Is Big Time

I got another incredible piece of advice from Denis Waitley. I had the good fortune of being Denis' agent (in addition to Jim Rohn, Ron White, and others) up until I sold my companies in 2007. Denis is still a great friend today.

Denis told me early on, "Kyle, I've written 18 number one bestselling books, and I wrote them all at night because in my day job I was traveling around the country as a paid speaker. And that's hard work. You're traveling, preparing, shaking hands, and signing books. So, the 18 books I wrote over a period of 20 years, I wrote at night, during what is called prime time by network TV. The majority of people use that time to watch other people on TV living their lives. But for me, prime time was about building my second stream of income."

What great advice from Denis.

Remember, be a student not a follower. Prime time for you may be focused time with your family (especially if you have young kids). You get to decide what is most important for you and yours.

7. Never Do a Good Deal with a Bad Guy

One of the all-time, best pieces of advice I've ever received came from the great Zig Ziglar. Zig said, "Never do a good deal with a bad guy." It's pretty simple. And easier said than done sometimes.

This advice and insight from Zig has saved me heartache, time, and money!

Don't let the promise of some irresistible deal or fear of loss allow you to fall into the trap of working with someone who you will almost always eventually regret.

Always ask yourself whether the deal is win/win/win. If not, then the odds are it won't end well.

8. Stretching the Rubber Band

I had the honor of co-authoring *Chicken Soup for the Entrepreneur's Soul* with Jack Canfield and Mark Victor Hansen. Back in 1995, Mark made the comment to me that they were going to sell 100 million books.

I thought, *Okay, Mark is this big thinker and is saying outrageous stuff.* I said, "Mark, come on. If you sell 10 million books, you'll be the biggest author in this space."

Well, guess what? They went on to sell over 500 million books!

When I look back now, I think of the several years I spent with Mark traveling the country and doing events. We were really close, and Mark and his big thinking had a great influence on me.

I'd get a phone call from Mark, and he would have Paul Williams, the multi-Grammy-winning music composer on the line. Or I'd arrive in Los Angeles, Mark would pick me up, and we would go to Jay Abraham's house for dinner.

Mark was always taking me into bigger worlds and greatly expanded my thinking. I call it stretching the rubber band. Mark stretched the rubber band of my ability to see things bigger than I could have ever seen myself.

Mark and I are still really good friends today, and he has been on my podcast, been a part of two of my books, and has spoken at my Inner Circle Mastermind.

Plant Your Tree

My mentor, Jim Rohn, said, "The time's going to pass: the next six months, the next year, the next two years, five years, and 10 years. The question is, will you have gotten started?"

The fact is everyone starts at zero. Every one of the people you are learning from, at one time, started at zero. Jim Rohn, Darren Hardy, Brian Tracy, and Steve Jobs all started at zero.

There will always be those ahead of you in what you want to accomplish. That's the truth. But you can't get better until you get started.

If you're not very good and if you're at the beginning, that's okay. That's been the path for everyone.

The key is getting started.

They say the best time to plant a tree was 20 years ago, but the second-best time is today.

To learn more about Kyle's Inner Circle Mastermind, #1 Bestseller Book Program, and Marketing VIP Coaching go to KyleWilson.com or email info@kylewilson.com.

To receive over a dozen interviews by Kyle with Darren Hardy, Les Brown, Brian Tracy, and more, email access@kylewilson.com with interviews in the subject. Follow Kyle on IG @kylewilsonjimrohn.

Tweetable: The fact is everyone starts at zero. There will always be those ahead of you in what you are wanting to accomplish. That's the truth. But you can't get better until you get started.

BOOK EDITOR AND WRITING COACH

Takara Sights is the editor of *Next Level Your Life*. She has been publishing inspirational and motivational books with Kyle Wilson since 2015. Takara is all about developing clear and impactful language that connects readers with age-old wisdom from new voices, and she revels in working one-on-one with authors as they develop and share their stories. She currently lives with her wonderful partner and fantastic dog in Los Angeles, California.

BOOK PUBLISHER

Kyle Wilson is the founder of Jim Rohn International and KyleWilson.com. Kyle has filled huge seminar rooms, launched and published multiple personal development publications, and produced/published over 100+ hours of programs. Kyle has published and sold over 1,000,000 books including titles by Jim Rohn and Denis Waitley as well

as his own books including *Success Habits of Super Achievers* with Brian Tracy, Les Brown, Darren Hardy, Denis Waitley, Mark Victor Hansen, *Persistence, Pivots and Game Changers*, and *Bringing Value, Solving Problems and Leaving a Legacy*. Kyle is the host of the *Success Habits of Super Achievers* podcast and the Kyle Wilson Inner Circle Mastermind.

ADDITIONAL RESOURCES

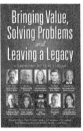
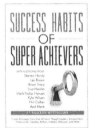
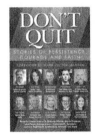

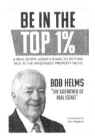

Order in Quantity and SAVE
Mix and Match
Order online KyleWilson.com/books

Printed in Great Britain
by Amazon

19949598R00159